Towards an Ecology of World Languages

Towards an Ecology of World Languages

Louis-Jean Calvet

Translated by Andrew Brown

polity

Ouvrage publié avec le concours du ministère français chargé de la culture – Centre national du livre.
Published with the assistance of the French Ministry of Culture – National Centre for the Book.

Polity Press
65 Bridge Street
Cambridge CB2 1UR, UK

Polity Press
350 Main Street
Malden, MA 02148, USA

ISBN-10: 0-7456-2955-5
ISBN-13: 978-07456-2955-1
ISBN-10: 0-7456-2956-3 (pb)
ISBN-13: 978-07456-2956-8

A catalogue record for this book is available from the British Library.

Typeset in 10.5 on 12.5pt Sabon
by Servis Filmsetting Ltd, Longsight, Manchester
Printed and bound in Great Britain by TJ International Ltd, Padstow, Cornwall

For further information on Polity, visit our website: www.polity.co.uk

Contents

Acknowledgements

I would like to thank my colleagues Robert Chaudenson, Pierre Larcher and Catherine Miller (Aix-en-Provence), Patrice Brasseur (Avignon), Ahmed Boukous (Rabat), Caroline Juillard and Anne-Marie Houdebine (Paris) for reading and commenting on my work and making useful suggestions, and Salikoko Mufwene (Chicago) for reading and discussing my work with me: these are themes that we are both passionately interested in. Lia Varela (Buenos Aires) read my work and gave me information on the Spanish of Buenos Aires and other help without which I would not have found certain essential documents concerning the language of Christopher Columbus.

I would also like to thank the different universities which invited me to teach (the Cantonese University of Foreign Languages in China; Tulane University, New Orleans, Louisiana; the Senghor University in Alexandria, Egypt; the University of Buenos Aires in Argentina; the University of Niamey in Niger; the University of Brazzaville in the Congo; the Universities of La Coruña and Vigo in Spain; the University of Louisville, Kentucky; Chuo University in Tokyo; the Universities of Rabat and Casablanca in Morocco; the Universities of Alger and Tlemcen in Algeria; the Ecole Normale Supérieure of Libreville in Gabon, and the Direction Nationale de l'Alphabétisation Fonctionnelle et de la Linguistique Appliquée (DNAFLA) in Bamako, Mali, etc.). Thanks to these invitations I was able to gain access to documentary sources that are difficult to find in France, and to explore different areas of fieldwork that provided me with much new material.

The author and publishers are also grateful to the following for permission to reprint copyright material:

Elsevier, for the diagram on p. 115 reproduced from Didier Goyvaerts, 'Kibalele: form and function of a secret language in Bukavu (Zaire)', in *Journal of Pragmatics*, vol. 25, no. 1 (1996), p. 140;

Oxford University Press for the illustrations of street signs on p. 36 from Bernard Spolsky and Robert Cooper, *The Languages of Jerusalem* (Oxford: Oxford University Press, 1991), pp. 6, 7 and 94.

Every effort has been made to trace the copyright holders, but if any have been inadvertently overlooked, the publishers will be pleased to make the necessary arrangements at the first opportunity.

INTRODUCTION

Practices and Representations

We have only an approximate knowledge of the number of languages spoken across the world, and the number of countries, of which we of course have an exact list, is for its part subject to variation due to conflict (ex-Yugoslavia and ex-Czechoslovakia, for instance, have broken up into different political entities). Let us assume, to simplify our calculations, that there are 5,000 languages on the world's surface, and 200 states: that would give us an average of twenty-five languages per country. Of course, averages are only averages, and we know countries in which more than 200 languages are spoken (Congo, the Democratic Republic of Congo, Cameroon, India and so on) and others that are close to monolingualism, without ever completely reaching it (Iceland, Rwanda, etc.). But these figures show us that the most widespread situation is indeed that of multilingualism – that there are no, or practically no, monolingual countries.

However, not all the languages that coexist in this largely multilingual world have exactly the same functions, fulfil the same roles, or cover the same extent. Certain are spoken only by small groups, a few families, a village or a tribe. Others, much less numerous, are spoken (more or less well) by hundreds of millions of speakers. At the same time, they are not used for exactly the same things, do not communicate the same meanings, and do not govern the same social relations.

Furthermore, these languages fall into different types: they can be classed from a genetic point of view into language families (Indo-European, Semitic, Bantu, etc.), from a functional point of view (pidgins, creoles, vehicular languages,[1] major world languages, etc.), from a formal point of view (isolating, inflected, agglutinative languages, etc.), and from an institutional point of view (regional, national and official languages, working languages in international organizations, etc.). That is why it is extremely difficult to present an overall picture of the linguistic situation across the world. Linguistic maps, which can be very precise, give us only a limited range of information – the geographical zone in which a language is spoken, or the overlap between different linguistic zones. Other maps, which we might call politico-linguistic, highlight instead the states in which these languages are used or enjoy an official function, while linguistic atlases mainly give information about dialect variations, usually within the boundaries of a particular country (a linguistic atlas of France, Switzerland or Italy) or region (a linguistic atlas of Corsica, of Normandy, etc.). But linguistic frontiers rarely correspond to state borders; in particular, the relations between languages, the way their functions include or complement one another, are not taken into account in these maps.

Besides, how can the relative importance of languages be measured? Certain ill-defined adjectives are sometimes used to give an idea: *minority* languages, so-called *minor languages*, *less-spoken* languages, *vehicular languages*, *majority languages*, *major world languages* and so on. But these classifications are far from being unambiguous and have more to do with ideology or power relations than with science. Thus the term 'international' most often describes languages that are used as working languages by international bodies (the UN, the Organization of African Unity, UNESCO, etc.), ignoring those which are international *de facto* if not *de jure*, such as Swahili, Bambara and Malay (all spoken in several countries) or those which have been excluded from international organizations for political reasons, such as German and Japanese, the languages of the defeated nations in the Second World War. And in the list of the most widely spoken languages (Chinese, English, Arabic, Spanish, Portuguese, French: in fact the six working languages of the UN and UNESCO), people tend to ignore Hindi, Malay and Bengali, which are nonetheless highly placed in the charts.

What is more, we intuitively place great value on certain languages – the same value which impels parents to ensure that their children are taught English, German or Chinese at school. On what criteria are these choices based? And by what criteria does a country choose to teach certain languages rather than others in its educational system – when, for example, Spain decided in 1996 to make it compulsory to teach English at primary school, or when Nigeria made the same decision for French? We have a strong sense, without being able to theorize it, that this value is in some respects a market value; it means that languages are a capital, and the possession of certain of them endows us with surplus value while others enjoy no prestige whatever on the market. And it becomes immediately obvious that the notions of 'value' or 'prestige' have to do as much with representations as with realities, but that these representations foster and reinforce the realities. It is because we attribute a 'market value' to English that the vast majority of pupils take it as their first language at school and thereby increase its 'value'.

When individuals acquire some consumer product, for instance a car, they are guided in their choice by a certain number of more or less objective factors:

1 The analysis they make of their real or imaginary needs: for instance, they think they need a fast car or an estate car, a diesel engine or a petrol engine, etc.
2 Their tastes, determined by fashion, advertising, advice from friends or neighbours ('I'm really pleased with my car, its petrol consumption is almost zero').
3 Their ideology, which may lead them to reject a certain make or boycott a certain country of manufacture ('buy French', 'buy American').

So they make their choice, and this (the purchase of a certain model, a certain make) plays a (clearly limited) role in car sales statistics: *it is in this sense that representations determine practices and have an influence on realities.* Our relation with languages is to some extent comparable with this process. If we except the language that we inherit from our parents or from the society in which we are brought up ('mother' tongue or 'first language'), one that in general we do not choose, we then face a series of choices: what languages would we like to see taught in schools? What languages are we going to learn in multilingual situations? Which languages will be used in our social lives, etc?

From a certain point of view, we acquire languages in the same way that we acquire objects, basing our choice on a certain idea of their usefulness, and on the benefits we hope to reap from possessing them: here too our representations determine our practices. However, an object is a personal property that we can keep in reserve, use, give away, destroy or resell, and that loses value as it is used. Language, on the other hand, is a collective property over which the individual has neither any real rights nor any real powers and which actually gains in value the more it is used. To put it simply, the more a car is driven around, the more it loses in value (a second-hand car is less expensive than a brand-new one and, unless it becomes a collector's item, will end up sooner or later in the scrapyard), whereas, over a certain period of time, the more a language is used the more value it will gain. And this value is one of the factors that determine choice: people will rather choose to learn a language that is widely spoken across the world than the language of a small Amazonian Indian tribe, and they will favour a language that they think they will be able to use on the labour market, a language that will be a plus on their CV. They thereby increase the 'value' of the chosen language; here again, representations have an influence on realities.

This means that, even if to the linguist's eye all languages are equal (the most widely spoken languages and those that are in the process of disappearing, those languages in which hundreds of thousands of books have been written and those that have not been transcribed), the world's languages are in fact fundamentally unequal. To be sure, absolutely any dialect form of a little-spoken language of the Amazon basin or Africa deserves to be analysed just as much as English, Chinese or French and, so long as one undertakes the necessary labour of coining new words, everything can be said, written or taught in absolutely any language. But the fact remains that a discourse which would represent English and Breton, or French and Bobo, as socially equivalent would be both unrealistic and ideological: all languages do not have the same value, and their inequality is at the heart of the way they are organized across the world. To maintain the contrary would be an act of blindness or a sort of demagogy, granting the same importance to a mosquito as to an elephant, to a human being as to a butterfly: there are 'elephant languages' and 'mosquito languages' which it is difficult to consider on the same level, except of course from the point of view of the science which describes them. This comes down to saying that 'elephant languages' and 'mosquito languages' are all languages, a remark that borders on tautology.

It would thus be idealistic to believe that these 5,000 or so languages have the same weight, the same market value, the same uses, and the same future as each other: there is what we might call a 'stock exchange of languages', with constant developments, fluctuations in value and so on, as in stocks and shares. This idea is only distantly related to the concept of 'linguistic market' proposed by Pierre Bourdieu, which implies that there is, within a given space (usually a nation), a 'legitimate' language by which are measured other forms, social or regional dialects. I am talking about a global phenomenon which is not linked to national spaces and which may be subject to more rapid fluctuations than those experienced by 'national' languages and the linguistic markets in which they register.

These languages were initially considered from two different points of view: either in isolation or genetically. In the first case, this resulted in grammars: Sanskrit was described by Panini in the fourth century, Latin by Probus, Spanish by Nebrija, French by the seventeenth-century Port-Royal grammarians, Arabic by Sibawayhi in the seventh century and so on. These descriptions were affected by power relations and by the times in which they were written, even if these earliest grammarians were not always aware of the fact: nobody wrote the grammar of a minority language that had little prestige; rather, it was the dominant languages that were described, those associated with political or religious power. In the second case, phonetic laws were postulated, languages were grouped into families, an attempt was made to reconstruct vanished languages and so on. And these two directions lay behind the linguistics that dominated the twentieth century, from Saussure to Chomsky. The European and American versions of structuralism had in common the fact that they both produced an abstraction ('langue' or language in one case, competence in the other) which made it impossible to understand the phenomena of communication. In the one case this communication was confused with codes and in the other with machines for producing sentences. These more or less effective *modellings*, necessary to a certain stage of the development of the science of linguistics, should be put in their proper place: they are *limiting views*, which select from their object of study only those factors which suit the analysts or are grist to the mill of their theories and make their task easier.

For communication cannot be reduced to a code or a model for sentence production. The codes, which are necessary but not sufficient to communication, are the constantly evolving product of a need to communicate, a quest for communication and an awareness of this communication. Furthermore, individuals may understand each other perfectly well by using codes which on analysis can be considered to be different: all speakers of the same language do not have the same grammar, and one sometimes finds 'interlectal' situations in which individuals communicate by using forms which a linguist would classify as different languages (this is the case, for instance, in certain relations between a creole and the language from which it springs). Conversely, communication may function perfectly well between speakers using forms which they consider as different languages but which the linguist classifies as variants of the same language: this is, for example, the case of 'Serb' and 'Croat', which used to be classified together as one and the same language, Serbo-Croat.

All this requires in-depth analysis, and I will be returning to these themes frequently in this book. What needs to be borne in mind right now is the fact that the notion of *language* is an abstract one; while useful for the linguist, its only basis is the regularity of certain characteristics and certain practices which can be found in the utterances of speakers, what Ferdinand de Saussure called, at the start of the twentieth century, *actes de parole,* acts of speech. Parodying Friedrich Engels, who wrote that 'the proof of the pudding is in the eating', we could say *that the proof of languages is in the speaking*. This way of putting it has the advantage of emphasizing a concrete reality (acts of speech, linguistic practices – the name we choose to give them is of little importance), on the basis of which the idea of language was created. So, on the first level, we have a group of *practices*, or *uses*, of which we can try to gain an overall, statistical picture (what we call a 'macro-approach'), or which we can study in the detail of their interactions within a small group, a family or across a restricted territory (what we call a 'micro-approach'). From these *practices*, which are very concrete, linguists have extracted an abstraction, *language*, a fact we could write as: *practices* > *languages*, to bring out the relation of production between these terms: it is practices which constitute languages.

But languages are not merely an invention of linguists, they also exist in the minds of speakers who say that they are 'talking one language or another', and know, or think they know, what languages are spoken in one country or another. Here we come up against a paradox: there is something which does not exist, which nobody can point to (unless you consider that a language comes down to books, a grammar and a dictionary, or to acts of speech, recorded or transcribed), and which yet does exist in the eyes of everyone. Languages exist because and since speakers believe in them, because they have ideas about them and images of them, ideas and images which constitute the second part of our system, namely *representations*.

Practices > *languages* and *representations*: this then is the framework within which I will be trying to describe the linguistic situation of our world, those 5,000 or so languages which coexist on the face of the earth at the beginning of our twenty-first century, sometimes peacefully, more often in a state of conflict. I will start from this plurality, and try to impose order on it, organizing it in accordance with a certain number of *models*. A model is never more than a metaphor, an abstraction enabling us to conceive more simply the way a complex set of elements functions. And linguistics, ever since its origin, has used – and used up – a certain number of metaphors. Thus it has talked successively in terms of the 'life of languages' (languages are born, live, grow old and die, so that there are dead languages and living languages), and 'families of languages' (Indo-European, Bantu, Semitic languages, etc.). Thus there are sister tongues and mother tongues, leading to a paradox which has cast a long shadow on research: this image has often led people to ignore 'father tongues' – in other words the idea of linear descent has been privileged at the expense of 'co-production', of which creoles are a good example. Linguistics has also described languages in terms of tools or instruments of communication, or as trees, and it has used economic metaphors (the linguistic market, language as labour), metaphors of warfare (the war of languages)[2] or biological metaphors (interbreeding between languages, 'mixed' languages), etc. By dint of using images, we risk forgetting their metaphorical nature, and it is important, right from the start, to underline this fact: languages are not alive, are not part of a family, and are neither instruments nor organisms external to those who use them; languages exist only in and through their speakers, and they are reinvented, renewed and transformed in every interaction, each time that we speak.

As far as I am concerned, I shall be using several interacting models in this book in an attempt to explain social communication in all its complexity:

1 A *gravitational model*, intended to account for the world linguistic situation, the macro-sociolinguistic relations between different languages.

2 A *homeostatic model*, intended to account for the regulation of linguistic situations and of languages.
3 A *model of representations*, intended to account for the way speakers, individually and collectively, perceive their practices and those of others.
4 A *model of transmission*, intended to account for the way in which situations and languages change.

These last three models have a fixed relation with the first: they will enable us to understand how change occurs in the world's languages as a whole. This does not mean that the first model is on the side of synchrony and the three others on the side of diachrony: synchrony does not exist, it is merely a convenient (and rather lazy) abstraction that enables us to describe the state of a language while seeming to ignore the fact that it is affected through and through by history. For there are two approaches to linguistic situations: one I will call 'contemporary', which is interested in what is the case, and the other 'historical', interested in what changes. But *existence and change are inseparable*: what is, changes, and what changes, is. The homeostatic regulation of languages and situations, their linguistic representations and the transmission of this regulation and of these representations are factors that constantly determine the evolution of forms and functions.

There remains, of course, a fifth element, which has been tackled many times: the 'linguistic' model, which allows us to describe grammars (or to 'invent' them, as we shall see). At the risk of shocking some of my readers, I will say that this model, which has given rise to the greatest number of studies, discussions and polemics, is in fact the least important. If the description of languages is indeed a necessary way into any linguistic analysis, its place is, all things considered, minor, for once again it deals with grammars and not with communication. On the other hand, the interplay between situations, practices and representations depends on a model of the complexity of social communication which still needs to be developed, and to which this book is devoted.

With this end in view, I will use as a general principle an *ecological* approach to languages and linguistic situations. I am not here taking the term *ecology* in its current sense, which is its political version (protection of the environment), but in its first sense, 'the science of habitat'. And if ecology is the science which studies the relations between organisms and their surroundings, linguistic ecology studies the relations between languages and their surroundings, i.e. first and foremost the relations between languages themselves, and then the relations between languages and society. Put this way, things seem simple, but the task is to construct a theoretical model that goes beyond the artificial opposition between linguistics and sociolinguistics, and to integrate languages into their social context – and we shall see that this programme is far from easy.

Einar Haugen was the first to use the phrase 'ecology of language',[3] admittedly without much success, as this formula was subsequently reused only five or six times. 'Linguists have generally been too eager to get on with the phonology, grammar, and lexicon to pay more than superficial attention to what I would like to call the "ecology of language" ', he wrote, adding: 'Language ecology may be defined as the study of interactions between any given language and its environment.'[4]

This environment is society, which uses language as one of its codes. In this way, the ecology of language includes its interactions with other languages in the minds of bilingual or plurilingual interlocutors, and its interactions with the society in which it functions. As for language itself, Haugen viewed it as a transitional model:

> The concept of a language as a rigid, monolithic structure is false, even if it has proved to be a useful fiction in the development of linguistics. It is the kind of simplification that is necessary at a certain stage of a science, but which can now be replaced by more sophisticated models.[5]

A *useful fiction*: this provocative definition brings out both the usefulness of the instrumentalization of language (i.e. the fact it helped in the construction of a certain kind of linguistics) and what it simultaneously concealed (the truth, often reiterated but rarely explored, that language is a social fact).

Haugen concluded by presenting a list of the 'ecological questions' which in his view needed to be answered for any given language:

1 How is it *classified* vis-à-vis other languages?
2 Who are its users?
3 In what domains is it used?
4 What other languages are employed by its users?

5 What internal varieties are present in the language?
6 What is its written tradition?
7 To what extent is this written form standardized?
8 What kinds of institutions support and foster it?
9 What are the attitudes of the speakers towards this language?
10 Finally, it would be desirable to draw up a typology of the ecological classification that would enable us to situate the language in relation to the other languages in the world, to say where it stands and where it's going.

Three authors have recently developed the idea of linguistic ecology: Peter Mühlhäusler, Salikoko Mufwene and Albert Bastardas i Boada. In the opinion of the first,[6] the ecology of language has met with little success because Haugen accepted a certain number of the key notions of the 'linguistic establishment', which led to his proposals being marginalized – in particular the idea that there is such a thing as a 'given language' and that its description, history, internal evolution, etc. are problems that can be studied by different groups of specialists. For Mühlhäusler, the notion of 'given language' is a problem for two reasons:

1 the absence of linguistic criteria enabling one to decide on the number of languages in a given ecology;
2 the difficulty of separating languages from other forms of communication.

I will return in detail, in my final chapter, to the problem of the limits to be set to languages and the relatively numerous cases in which linguists and language speakers disagree about the existence of one, two or three languages, in particular when it comes to 'Serbo-Croat' and 'Kituba'. For the time being, I will simply present two of Mühlhäusler's assertions:

1 The identification of languages and the way they are named are far from being an act of objective description and may constitute a very serious violation of the linguistic ecology of a given area.[7]
2 By formulating the problem of the disappearance of languages in terms of ecology, we open up not only new perspectives but also new possibilities for intervention.[8]

For him, an ecological perspective raises the question of the system that supports languages and their speakers and the links between the 'linguistic and non-linguistic inhabitants' of a linguistic ecology, which leads him to formulate several recommendations for a different kind of linguistics. Drawing on the study of linguistic phenomena from the Pacific zone and the way they are usually described, he emphasizes how, in the history of linguistics, we come across beliefs that had turned out to be quite useless in the study of the traditional languages of this zone: the belief that there are distinct classes of words, or that the same descriptive categories can be used for all languages, or that languages can be separated from non-linguistic systems and that there are such things as separate languages.[9] And he uses all this as a theoretical basis for the defence of imperilled languages, languages in danger of extinction – in other words, for a linguistic ecology in the usual sense of the term *ecology*: the defence of the environment. Letting those languages live, as it were. . . .

Salikoko Mufwene, in a paper delivered at the Society for Pidgin and Creole Linguistics,[10] emphasizes that linguists have been inclined to baptize different linguistic varieties as *creole* or *pidgin* without giving any real definition of these terms, and that the uncritical use of those inherited labels runs the risk of skewing our approach. For his part, he proposes tackling the problem from the point of view of the ecology of language, in other words, from 'the social environment in which a language is used', and goes on to raise the question of 'how this environment affects the language'. His purpose, clearly shown by the titles of his recent publications – 'Genèse des populations et genèse des langues' ['The genesis of populations and the genesis of languages'],[11] 'Creole genesis, a population genetics perspective',[12] 'The founder principle in creole genesis',[13] and 'Métissage des peuples et métissage des langues' ['Cross-breeding between peoples and cross-breeding between languages'][14] – is twofold: he wants to treat the problem of the emergence of so-called 'creole' languages, to which he devotes a significant proportion of his scientific activity, and also to formulate the question of the various different influences that govern cross-breeding between linguistic features.

In order to understand these influences, he first of all looks at the genesis of populations and the 'founder principle': the foundation of a new, isolated population, by a restricted number of individuals, ends up producing differences vis-à-vis the original stock and leading to a process of divergence. And in his view, languages should not be compared to *individuals*, but to *species*. This means that changes (in the species as in the language) can be explained 'by the ecological effects on the members of the community: it allows the characteristics of the individuals that it favours to win out, and little by little eliminates the characteristics of the individuals it does not favour'.[15] His conception of ecology, acting both within the species and outside it, leads him to propose an approach that accounts for self-regulatory processes both in languages *and* in the environment:

> External ecology is more or less the same as the ethnographic environment of a language, including the other languages with which the lexificatory language is in contact, the status of the speakers of these languages, the status of the lexificatory language itself, the nature of the relations that can be observed between the different speakers, and many ethnographic factors that are in a position to influence the use and ultimate destiny of a language. On the other hand, internal ecology denotes in particular the variation that occurs within the language/species itself, on both the idiolectal and dialectal levels.[16]

Turning to Albert Bastardas,[17] we find that his work, entitled *Ecologia de les llenguës* ('the ecology of languages'), is permeated by yet another musical metaphor: just as in an opera, for instance, the voices and instruments constitute an ensemble, and a melodic fragment played on one instrument is determined by its relations with the other sounds that simultaneously coexist, an 'ecodynamic landscape' must be considered as a harmony, and not a melody.[18] The musical form undergoes internal changes (a voice, an instrument) or external changes (the arrival of a new conductor who may modify the way the work is performed), and 'in the sociolinguistic aspects of a society, the arrival of a new population from other linguistic areas, or new political powers, can introduce fundamental modifications into the overall balance'.[19] He thus concludes that linguistic contacts and changes are the products of two principal factors, decisions taken by political powers on the one hand, and migratory movements between different linguistic areas on the other, which mainly leads him to analyse, from this point of view, the situation in Catalonia and the relations between Catalan and Spanish.

Of course, we may decide that these approaches simply produce one more metaphor. But in all three cases – and even if Mufwene,

Mühlhäusler and Bastardas are examining linguistic situations that in the final analysis are somewhat limited – it is the whole contemporary linguistic approach which is being questioned and, in the case of Mühlhäusler in especial, actually blown out of the water. Once this joyful act of iconoclasm has been registered, all that remains is to rebuild the theory. This book aims to propose a conceptual framework in which such a reconstruction is possible.

My approach will thus be first and foremost *theoretical*, aimed at explaining the communicative function of society. I will however be using a certain number of empirical studies to illustrate or test out my theoretical proposals. Here I have two aims in mind: a *description of different situations* and a *prediction of their evolution*, even if human behaviour is relatively unforeseeable and unpredictable. This is why the 'hard' sciences try to establish *laws*, whereas social sciences establish *probabilities* and *trends*. But the analysis of these trends has a twofold importance. On the one hand, it guarantees the scientific nature of our approach: a science must be able to predict what, in certain given conditions, will happen. On the other hand, it lays down the conditions of possibility of what I will call, broadly speaking, applied linguistics. Whether we are talking of the teaching of languages, for instance, or of linguistic policies, no *in vitro* conception is possible without a close understanding of *in vivo*, or *in situ*, practices and trends, since it is here, in the final analysis, that any attempt to affect language and linguistic situations is going to be put into practice.

In a state of ceaseless disequilibrium, and constant evolution, the blocks of noise we use in our – sometimes successful – attempts at communication are merely *variants*, and the convenient abstraction of language (or generative grammar) is one huge *variable*.[20] Variants are first and foremost signs of freedom, and variables can thus be considered as spaces of freedom. But this freedom immediately needs to be qualified. On the one hand, variants cannot go against the consensus or if they do, they then contribute to the appearance of a new consensus, a 'new language'. On the other hand, consensus implies a group, a community within which variants can be used as forms of identification. For example, 'Beur' speech, the way that children of immigrants from the Maghreb use the French language, is simultaneously dependent on an internal consensus (they recognize each other from the way they talk) that thus assumes the function of a mass language, and an external consensus (they are recognized from the way they talk) that thus assumes an emblematic function,[21] and exactly the same can be said of the English used by black Americans, for example. These forms of micro-consensus thus distinguish between sub-groups, relations between which are regulated in a homeostatic way. These problems are traditionally studied by what has been called sociolinguistics, a label whose main function is to keep everything concerning social life out of linguistics. But what is brought together around the concept of sociolinguistics (discourse analysis, interactions, polyglottism, contacts between languages, conflicts between languages, etc.) consists in each case of observing the problem through the wrong end of the telescope – and a different telescope each time. What I mean is this: everything that we can read under these different labels is both interesting and partial. It bears repeating: linguistics cannot manage without an overall theory of social communication.

Why and how do we communicate? Essentially because we think we have things to say, or because we need to say something. This need for communication is central, and what, for want of a better name, I will continue to call 'language' is a response to this need, which appeared at a given moment of the social organization of human beings. In every society there is a 'before' and an 'after' this need for communication and the response that it has found. And this response is not the same across the whole planet. The fascinating thing is that human groups have come up with different responses to this same need: in the same way that, as we have said, linguistic practices are variants, languages too are from a certain point of view variants. But variants of what?

To be sure, in claiming that languages are variants, I do not in any way wish to endorse Chomsky's theory, known as 'principles and parameters', which proposes that the world's languages are merely surface variants of one single innate grammar, a 'universal' variable, so that all human beings actually speak the same language. It is easy to see how the will to systematization led Noam Chomsky from the initial opposition between 'deep structures' and 'surface structures' to the idea that the different languages of the world are merely the surface grammars of *one* common deep grammar.[22]

This hypothesis of a universal grammar which, lodged somewhere in children's brains, supposedly enables them to learn their parents' language and subtends the grammars of all the languages in the world, has recently been presented by Steven Pinker in these terms: 'According to Chomsky, a visiting Martian scientist would surely conclude that aside from their mutually unintelligible vocabularies, Earthlings speak a single language.'[23] Let us leave aside the obvious paradox in the claim that human beings all apparently speak the same language while being mutually incomprehensible, and look at the argument in more detail. Why, Pinker wonders, are the world's languages different if their basic organization is the same? Because, he replies – to put it simply – human beings need to differentiate themselves from one another. And he takes up and develops Darwin's parallel between languages and species. In Darwin's words:

> The formation of different languages and of distinct species, and the proofs that both have been developed through a gradual process, are curiously parallel. . . . We find in distinct languages striking homologies due to a community of descent, and analogies due to a similar process of formation. . . . Languages, like organic beings, can be classed in groups under groups; and they can be classed either naturally, according to descent, or artificially by other characters. Dominant languages and dialects spread widely, and lead to the gradual extinction of other tongues. A language, like a species, when extinct, never . . . reappears.[24]

Thus French and Italian are as alike as a wolf and a fox, and differ from each other in the same way: in both cases what we have is an evolution from a common ancestor. This point is difficult to quarrel with: the existence of 'families' of languages is one of the established facts of historical linguistics, but the problem raised by Pinker lies at an earlier and more primordial level. No one denies the existence of Romance, Slavonic or Germanic families of languages, for instance, and the reconstruction of a hypothetical language, Indo-European, from which these three groups seem to originate, is in itself convincing. But, parallel to Indo-European languages, linguists distinguish other 'families': Semitic languages, Bantu languages, etc., and it is at this level that the problem becomes more complicated: is it true that beyond these families, earlier than them, there is some principle of which they constitute realizations, an innate grammar or indeed a single origin? German linguists, for instance, proposed at the end of the nineteenth century a reconstitution of the original form of Bantu, Ur-Bantu, the 'mother language' of the Bantu languages of our own time. The problem is that of knowing if there are relations – and if so, what they are – between Ur-Bantu and Indo-European, as the 'principles and parameters' theory presupposes.

In order to be acceptable, a theory must be falsifiable: that is, each point in its argument must be capable of being taken up and verified or criticized. The reconstruction of Indo-European or that of Ur-Bantu can be discussed and criticized in this way because these reconstructions exist, because the efficacy of the phonetic laws and the correspondences between the languages can be checked, and the evolution of Indo-European into Greek or Sanskrit can be reconstructed, etc. But Chomsky's postulate is quite different: it is based on an unfounded assertion. We can demonstrate that languages have become different, thanks to the action of linguistic variation, isolation and transmission, when we possess data we can compare. But when it is proposed, without any further proof, that there is an innate grammar, a step is taken that leads us out of science, unless concrete descriptions can validate what is a mere hypothesis.

Let us take one simple, quick example. Steven Pinker, having sketched a kinship between certain Bantu languages and English in regard to the dative construction in Kivunjo and English, pursues his argument by pointing to the existence of 'genders' in these two languages, explaining that in one case (Kivunjo) they refer to objects, animals, human beings, etc., and in the other (English) to sexes: 'The Bantu "genders" refer to kinds like humans, animals, extended objects, clusters of objects, and body parts. It just happens that in many European languages the genders correspond to the sexes, at least in pronouns.'[25] This means, according to Pinker, that there must be one principle, that of gender, which under the influence of certain parameters has been realized in different ways in different languages, such as in English and Kivunjo. But he does not seem to realize that this kinship stems merely from the fact that certain English-speaking linguists have baptized with the name 'gender' certain phenomena which they have seen as being akin for the plain and simple reason that, in both cases, they require grammatical agreement. In the case of Bantu languages, we have a series of couples of prefixes contrasting singular and plural: in Swahili for example ki/vi (*kisu/visu*: knife/knives), m/mi (*mwaka/miaki*: year/years), m/wa (*mtu/watu*: man/men), etc. And these prefixes are encountered throughout a phrase or sentence:

kisu/visu, 'knife/knives'

kisu kidogo/visu vidogo, 'little knife/little knives'

kisu kidogo kimoja
ki + knife ki + little ki + one, 'a little knife'

visu vidogo viwili
vi + knife vi + little vi + two, 'two little knives'

kisu kidogo kimoja kime anguka
ki + knife ki + little ki + one ki + auxiliary verb
'a little knife has fallen'

visu vidogo viwili vime anguka
vi + knife vi + little vi + two vi + auxiliary verb
'two little knives have fallen'

This phenomenon, generally called 'nominal classes' in French, is thus more a matter of number than of gender. And it is obvious that the question of whether classes of the *ki/vi* type and genders of the *le/la, il/elle* type in French or *he/she* in English have a common origin, or correspond to a common principle, depends on a typical semantic artefact: it is because they have been given the same name in English that they are seen as analogous. This example is limited, to be sure, but it speaks volumes: it springs from a vicious circle, and as everyone knows, the more you stroke a vicious circle, the more vicious it becomes.

The problem of the origin (and, as far as we are concerned, that of the origin of languages, or of the origin of the differences between languages) is, nonetheless, the one which is the greatest source of vexation for the scientist: when, how, where and why did human beings forge those codes that we have been using, transforming and reshaping for thousands of years? The study of cases of aphasia and the brain lesions that correspond to them has demonstrated the link between a capacity for language and the ability to stand on two legs: only the biped speaks, which in no way means that standing erect is a sufficient guarantee of language, but quite simply means that there is no language unless people first stood erect. As for the rest, we can merely formulate hypotheses that are endlessly modified and renewed in an attempt to answer these questions. Was language invented once and once only, in a single place, before going on to multiply like so many cells? Or did it appear independently in different forms and in different places? In the latter case, was there something innate in the human brain which conferred identical characteristics on all languages, at whatever depth this identity lies? I repeat: these questions are vexatious. What is certain, however, is that if there *is* one single innate principle behind all the languages in the world, it needs to be discovered and not just imagined.

But we have very few clues to guide us in our quest. Certain scientists study fossils, carry out archeological digs and can carbon date sites or objects with a pretty high degree of accuracy. Others, by comparing the DNA of tens of dogs and wolves, have managed to demonstrate that the different breeds of dog all come from wolves that were domesticated about 100,000 years ago. In comparison with this, the reconstruction of languages, the study of their history and the postulation of phonetic laws, all carry little weight: the linguist has little to go on when trying to solve the mysteries that face him. And the response that consists of drawing up a list of 'language universals' is not really convincing.

Steven Pinker, yet again, attempts to illustrate the 'principles and parameters' theory by drawing on an example often put forward by the proponents of generative grammar – and one that strikes me as being of stupefying naivety. Since principles are universal and innate, when children learn a particular language, they do not need to acquire long lists of rules, but merely the parameters that will actualize their innate grammar. Thus, the fact that in English the verb comes before the object while in Japanese it comes after, and that in English there are prepositions and, in Japanese, postpositions, does not constitute a difference between these languages but, on the contrary, brings them together: 'Japanese and English are looking-glass versions of each other.'[26] And since these two languages are symmetrical, gazing at one another in the mirror, children merely need to know which parameter their language possesses so as to be able to learn it.

> All they have to learn is whether their particular language has the parameter value head-first, as in English, or head-last, as in Japanese. They can do that merely by noticing whether a verb comes before or after its object in any sentence in their parents' speech. If the verb comes before the object, as in *Eat your spinach!*, the child concludes that the language

> is head-first; if it comes after, as in *Your spinach eat!*, the child concludes that the language is head-last.[27]

Further on, Pinker produces an even more radical formulation: children learning a language are like archeologists (sic) faced with the Rosetta stone, which presented a text in a known language and its translation in an unknown language. For the child, the unknown language is the one he is to acquire, and the known language is a mental language.[28] We are not told whether the child possesses an innate manual of generative grammar to help him in this task, or whether he is obliged to eat spinach – whether he is allowed to choose rice, or whether spinach is served with prepositional languages and rice with postpositional languages. . . .

More seriously, the problems discussed here do indeed have to do with two universal facts. *The first linguistic universal is the fact that man speaks*. It so happens that the human species has given itself certain oral codes and that a second universal results from this: *languages are linear*, quite simply because the human being cannot pronounce two sounds simultaneously but only one after the other. This linearity of phonemes, and consequently of the words that they compose and the phrases and sentences into which these words fit, is the catalyst of the first major difference between languages.[29] To mark the relations between discourse elements, speakers have selected two main systems. The first system is based on the fixed order of elements. In French, for example, the subject generally comes before the verb and the object afterwards; in Bambara (a language spoken in Mali), the subject precedes the object, which is inserted between the auxiliary and the verb, so the two orders are different but the principle is the same, consisting as it does of marking functions within a linear scheme by a fixed order:

French:	*il*	*achète*	*un cheval*	
	Subject +	verb +	object	
Bambara:	*a*	*bé*	*so*	*san*
	Subject +	aux +	object +	verb

The second system is based on a way of marking elements so as to indicate their function – what are called 'cases': in Latin, Greek, Classical Arabic, Russian or German, the order of words can vary because their function is marked by case endings. Thus in Latin, *rosam*, 'rose', can only be a direct object, whether it is placed before or after the verb. And in an Arabic phrase such as *dahala arajulu el dara* (the man went into the house), in which the verb (dahala) precedes the subject (rajulu), which precedes the object (dara), it is the -u which indicates the subject and the -a which indicates the object, and not the order of words in the sentence, which can vary. This major division between fixed-order languages and declined languages is purely synchronic. If we examine the evolution of languages, we discover that certain of them change in the course of history from one system to another: French and English have, in their earlier incarnations, both included declensions. For instance, in Old French there were two cases:

li murs (the wall, subject) *le mur* (the wall, object)

li mur (the walls, subject) *les murs* (the walls, object).

And the formal difference between subject and object could be more important than in the preceding example: *lerre/larron* (thief), *ancestre/ancessor* (ancestor), *cuens/comte* (a count), *trovere/troveor* (troubadour), etc.

In the same way, while Classical Arabic was an inflected language, all forms of contemporary Arabic (the 'dialects', as they are generally now called) are fixed-order languages in which the system of declension has been replaced by analytical constructions. Now, to my knowledge, there is no case of language evolution operating in the opposite order – no examples, that is, of a fixed-order language inventing declensions for itself. Thus, if we combine the hypothesis that all languages stem from a same basic innate scheme, and the fact that inflected languages show a tendency to evolve towards a fixed-order system, we are forced to conclude that the inflected system is closer to this hypothetical basic scheme and – why not? – that all fixed-order languages were, at an earlier stage, inflected.

How can such a hypothesis be tested? Nothing seems to confirm it in the case of, for example, Chinese, even though we have very ancient written documents. But the fact that ancient languages, those monuments of complications and irregularities, show a regular tendency to become more regular (to 'simplify' themselves), and that the same tendency is shown when a language spreads, suggests that there is, at the origin of languages, a large proportion of improvisation. We have the clear impression that communicational practices have, in the course of the centuries, 'polished' imperfect products. But the 'principles and parameters' hypothesis is not very good at explaining diachrony or the obvious fact that languages change: was the innate grammar modified, did the parameters vary, or do they actually lead to evolution? The linguist would like to go back in time, or live for ever, so as to be present in person as his object of study evolves. For, while we are able to be present millions of times over at the acquisition of a language by a child, we have never directly witnessed the birth of a language (except, but from something of a distance, in the case of creoles, a point to which I will be returning).

Let us go back to the Darwin quotation that Pinker uses. It is interesting, even if it contains false assertions (such as the one claiming that once a language has died, it cannot be reborn: the case of Hebrew obviously goes against this idea, even if in this instance a deliberate effort was made to bring it back to life – but a theory should be able to integrate this type of deliberate intervention). It is true, for example, that the expansion of dominant languages implies a trend towards the gradual extinction of other languages – a slow and not always inevitable trend: Berber, for instance, continues to be spoken in Algeria and Morocco in spite of more than ten centuries of Arabic colonization. Above all, the parallel between languages and species appeals to the imagination and leads us to another vision of things: not the affirmation of a common origin, or an innate grammar, which is an ideological way of looking of things, but an *ecological* point of view of the relations between languages. It is this point of view that I am going to try and establish in this book.

This approach, which thus situates 'languages' within their environment, implies that we take into account everything that is involved in communication. When linguistics came into being, it needed to define its field of study in order to guarantee its scientific status. This definition transformed and even hardened practices into an object, but while structuralist linguistics needed to invent language, it does not realize that it is now a prisoner of that invention. There is a sort of blindness in continuing, as do the supporters of functional linguistics or generative grammar, to consider artefacts as truths and practices as objects. Language is not an object that can be considered in isolation, and communication does not simply occur by means of sequences of sounds. Let us consider, for example, the following scene. Two people, a driver and his passenger, are in a car that has stopped at a red light and are chatting together. Suddenly the passenger says, 'It's green.' And the driver drives off. In this brief interaction, there is a succession of at least four kinds of communication:

- An electric apparatus makes a traffic light change colour from red to green.
- A person observes this transmission of meaning.
- This person communicates the same information to his neighbour verbally.
- His neighbour reacts to this information by behaving in a certain way: he lets in the clutch, engages gear and moves off.

In the name of what theory should we separate out, in this sequence of actions, the one which is communicated by the emitting of sounds? The answer generally given is that, on the one hand, there is the oral instrument of communication, namely language, and on the other there are facts that have to do with 'non-verbal' communication, or semiology. And this affirmation is characteristic of the trap into which the theory of language as an isolatable object, an instrument, has led us. What needs to be grasped here is this: the notion of language is a model, simultaneously useful and reductive, and we must take care not to allow ourselves to be imprisoned by the models that we use. Language is not a mechanism, even if such a vision is convenient to the analyst: it does not evolve through the intervention of a screwdriver or an adjustable spanner, it does not exist in isolation from social life; language (or at least what I continue, for the sake of convenience, to call language) is a social practice within social life, one practice among others, inseparable from its environment. It is on this basis that I am going to present my ecological approach to the languages of the world.

— 1 —

The Ecology of Languages

The reader will by now have realized that the presence of the term ecology in the title of this book did not mean that it was devoted to defending the rights of languages or our right to a certain language, the survival of languages threatened with extinction, etc., even if the analyses I am putting forward may ultimately be used for such aims. Certain authors have, however, tried to use the idea of ecolinguistics for militant purposes. Thus Celso Alvarez Caccamo criticizes Haugen for not focusing on these problems: 'Haugen's ecology is limited to the field of production of *knowledge* about a language, and does not add any proposal for *ecolinguistic action* aimed at the management of glottodiversity.'[1] But before proceeding to any potential reflection on the militant fallout of a particular scientific approach (and, in the case of Alvarez Caccamo, to the problem of the defence of Galician), that approach has first and foremost to be properly constituted – which is what I am attempting to do here. Referring to ecology is not synonymous with defending threatened species, but implies rather the quest for an explanatory *model*. We have seen that every model was a metaphor, and we are therefore going to begin by examining in broad terms what the ecological metaphor may mean in the linguistic domain.

The different levels of life can be presented as a series of embeddings: the simplest organism, the *cell*, then the *multicellular organisms* which constitute themselves into *colonies* or *societies* and then into *populations* (gatherings of the individuals of one particular species), gathered into a biological community or *biocommunities*. We can then identify the environment in which a biocommunity is established as the *biotope*, then the *ecosystem* or ensemble of biotopes and finally the *ecosphere*, the set of the whole planet's ecosystems. Ecology studies the higher levels of this embedding, which extend from populations to the ecosphere.

The ecology of languages likewise presupposes different levels of analysis. The higher level is that of the worldwide organization of the relations between languages: the gravitational model that I will develop in chapter 2 is an application of this approach. This worldwide system (corresponding, in our metaphor, to the ecosphere) is comprised of a hierarchy of lower systems (corresponding to ecosystems). In a linguistic ecosystem, the languages that coexist are interrelated in such a way that each of them is assigned to a certain *ecological niche*: the 'niche' of a language is constituted by its relations with other languages, by the place it occupies in the ecosystem, i.e. by its functions and by its relations with the environment – essentially, that is, by geography, which plays a defining role in the spread of languages.

The basic idea is thus that the practices which constitute languages, on the one hand, and their environment, on the other, form an *ecolinguistic system*, in which languages multiply, interbreed, vary, influence each other mutually, compete or converge. This system is in interrelation with the *environment*. At every moment language is subject to external stimuli to which it adapts. *Regulation*, which I will define as the reaction to an external stimulus by an internal change which tends to neutralize its effects, is thus a response to the environment. This response is first and foremost the mere addition of individual responses – variants that, over time, lead to the *selection* of certain forms, certain characteristics. In other words, there is a selective action of the environment on the evolution of language, which I will analyse in chapter 3.

Ecology employs the term 'valency of a species', meaning the capacity to populate a greater or smaller number of environments: this valency can be low or high, and varies under the influence of 'limiting factors'. A *limiting factor* is a factor favourable to the survival of a species, and it must be maintained within certain limits: if it is too high, or too low, the survival is threatened. From this point of view, the presence of a species in a particular environment is linked to the valency of its most sensitive stage within this environment. For example, an animal species will have a low valency at the larval stage and a higher valency at the adult stage. Likewise, a language may be rendered more vulnerable or more robust by a certain number of factors: the number of its speakers, its social functions (*in vivo*), its official functions (*de jure*), its relations with other languages, its standardization, etc. There is thus a swathe of factors, the one being dominant and the others limiting or correcting its effects.

If we consider for example that a language must, in order to exist, have speakers (which may appear obvious), then too great a drop in the number of these speakers threatens the existence of the language (which is also obvious). This is why the rate of transmission of a language, which I will be discussing in chapter 5, is an important element in the analysis of its ecosystem. But the concept of limiting factor also implies that too high a number of speakers threatens the existence of the language, which is much less obvious and may, on the contrary, seem paradoxical. However, history shows us that the expansion of languages bears within it the seed of their disintegration. If today there exist languages that we call French, Italian, Spanish, or others that we call Arabic, Egyptian, Tunisian or Moroccan, this is, after all, because Latin and Arabic spread out over vast areas, multiplying the numbers of their speakers, so that their 'number of speakers' considered as a limiting factor exceeded its tolerable upper limit. From this point of view, the ecology of languages would enable us to predict a tendency of widespread contemporary languages such as English, French and Spanish to disintegrate and take on a variety of new forms. This factor is however corrected by other factors. Thus a standardized, official, centralized language will be in a better position to resist the excessive number of its speakers than a less official language, or one that is less centralized.

Another factor that may correct the effects of the dominant factor is the way that speakers imagine languages, the *representations* that I will be studying in chapter 4. Let us merely take two brief examples. That of Fulani (Fulfulde) to begin with: the broad zone of expansion of this language means that it is everywhere in contact with other languages (Mandingo, Zarmasongay, Hausa) and that it thus appears in different linguistic ecosystems, which have of course left their mark on its form, in particular in the shape of its borrowings from neighbouring languages, but also on the representations of which it is the object. Thus Salamatou Alhassoumi Sow points out that, for the speakers he has interviewed in the Niger:

> the eastern branch of Fulfulde, Fulfulde-Hawsa, is considered as the Fulani of the Hausa because of its situation in Hausa territory and in Bornou, but especially because of the numerous borrowings from Hausa

> contained in the language (more than 30% of the lexicon). Fulfulde-Hausa does not enjoy a prestigious classification thanks to this fact. It is the area, they say, where Fulani is at its weakest.[2]

He adds that 'the Fulani that is next door to Zarma does not have the same status as the Fulani that is next door to Gourmantché in this region. The socio-historical prestige of the neighbouring people acts on the way the form of speaking is evaluated.'[3]

Another, equally eloquent example is the way in which the Wolof speakers of Dakar (Senegal), when describing languages or forms of languages, characterize their speakers, whom they distinguish on the basis of their linguistic behaviour, and who constitute a certain number of groups and sub-groups on the basis of either diachronic distinctions or social contrasts.[4] For example, during the colonial period, people made fun of those they called *tubaab jaxate*, i.e. 'white Jaxate', Jaxate being a typically Wolof family name.[5] The *tubaab jaxate* was anyone who, in his gestures, clothing and language, imitated white people to a ridiculous degree, and there was an expression that was used to make them seem even more ridiculous: *tubaab jaxate dàall sang kawas*, 'the toubab [white] Jaxate with his shoes and no socks'. The current version of the *tubaab jaxate* is what these days are called *doseurs* (pretenders): 'they roll their /r/ like Parisians', 'they talk Wolof with the French /r/', 'he can't speak Wolof without French').[6] In contrast to the *doseurs*, a distinction is drawn between the *booy-Dakars*, the children of Dakar, who speak a Wolof that is full of argot words, the *kaw-kaw* (peasants, country folk) and the *wàcc-bees* (new arrivals) who 'never mix in French words', a characteristic which may be judged positively ('they speak proper Wolof', 'it's the pure form of the dialect') or negatively ('they speak a complicated language', '*I* can't understand the Wolof that they speak').

Thus, linguistic representations organize the population of the city according to two kinds of contrast: a diachronic contrast that distinguishes between the 'old pretenders', the *tubaab jaxate*, and the 'young pretenders', the *doseurs*; and a synchronic and social contrast between *doseurs*, *booy-Dakars* and *kaw-kaw* or *wàcc-bees*. Thiam even notes, in connection with the *booy-Dakars*, that it is possible, on the basis of the districts they come from, to draw up a more precise and socially more discriminating classification between *booy-Plato* (coming from the Plateau, the posh district, the former colonial district) and *booy-Medin* (coming from the 'Medina', the more African district).

I will be examining this problem of representations at much greater length in chapter 4. For now, let me merely say for the sake of simplicity that, in a given *ecolinguistic system*, when faced with a *central*, and widely spoken, language, the speakers of *peripheral* languages[7] may behave in ways that express an attitude of rejection – a rejection stemming from considerations based on ready-made ideas: from ideology or even from the unconscious. This was for example the case of speakers of Czech, Hungarian, Polish, etc., vis-à-vis Russian before the fall of the Berlin Wall. Conversely, a language that is little spoken, but whose speakers nonetheless consider that it is important to keep it going (for emblematic or religious reasons, reasons of identity, etc.), can survive in a way that the mere number of its speakers does not allow one to foresee.

The reader will by now have grasped that the size of an ecosystem varies with the point of view of the researcher – it can extend from the size of a drop of water to the whole world, via a duck pond, a garden, a forest, a city, a whole country, etc. As far as we are concerned, the system of the world's languages will thus be analysed on different levels: languages (considered metaphorically as species) are organized into populations which are in constant relation with their environment, and evolve in reaction to the stimuli that come from that environment.

In the following pages I will be illustrating these principles, on which this book is based, with various concrete and limited examples, before returning, in the following chapter, to theoretical problems. For now, it is merely a question of showing what the ecological approach to languages can teach us.

The need for identity and its linguistic manifestations: endogenous and exogenous relexifications

Let us consider, to begin with, the following sentence, taken from a newspaper article:

Example 1
'Dans le pigeot', rigole Farid, 'ça sentait les pieds de Malik. C'est un gros hallouf, çui-là. La vie d'ma mère, j'repars pas avec lui.'

[In the *pigeot'*, chortles Farid, 'you could smell Malik's feet. He's a big *hallouf*, that guy. On my mother's life, I'm not travelling with him again!'][8]

Here we find a certain number of characteristics that differentiate this passage from standard French. A phonetic characteristic first of all (*pigeot* for Peugeot, the make of car), a word taken from Maghrebin Arabic dialect (*hallouf*, 'pig') and finally a structure (*la vie d'ma mère*) which is borrowed from Arabic. This evidence, associated with the name of the speaker (Farid), thus leads us to a simple interpretation: we are in the presence of a hybrid form of French, marked by the fact that Farid is an Arabic-speaker and is transposing into a second language, French, linguistic habits from his first language. However, a more refined analysis invalidates this first hypothesis. It is true that /œ/ does not exist in Arabic, and that Maghrebi people have a tendency to pronounce it as /i/, but neither does /p/ exist in that language, and it as often as not turns into a /b/: /baris/ for Paris, for instance. Now, Farid here pronounces the /p/ of Peugeot, but he also goes on in the rest of the sample to pronounce a whole series of /œ/, in particular in 'verlan' [reverse slang]: *meuf* for *femme* [woman], *teuf* for *fête* [party], etc.

Example 2
'Je vais rester une semaine ou dix jours, peut-être plus. Ça dépend si ça délire bien, s'il y a du soleil, des bonnes teufs et des petites meufs.'
['I'm going to stay a week or ten days, perhaps more. It depends if people are having a good time, if it's sunny, if there are some good parties and nice chicks.']

Example 3
'Téma les seins de la meuf, là, derrière la grosse. Sur la tête de ma mère, jamais ma meuf elle montrera ses ins comme ça.'
['Get a load of the breasts on the woman, over there, behind the fat one. On my mother's head, my wife will never show her breasts like that.']

This leads us to another hypothesis: the speaker is here knowingly modifying the form of the French language, and marking it in a particular way that places him as being of Maghrebi origin: *pigeot* is the archetype of the pronunciation of Maghrebi immigrant workers, a sort of caricature. And, to support this hypothesis, we need to consider the ecological 'niche' in which these examples are situated. Young French people who are the children of Maghrebi emigrants, and are born in France to parents who were themselves born in Morocco, Algeria or Tunisia, are in what I have elsewhere called an 'interstitial situation',[9] a phrase taken from the sociologists of the Chicago School. They are not really secure in the culture of their parents and still not secure in that of the welcoming country: they fail in school, do not have a firm identity, etc. Hence, in reaction to the surrounding environment and the image of themselves that it reflects back on them (racism, rejection, etc.), they respond by constructing an interstitial culture which they can call their own, and which takes the form of various marks of identity: a particular way of dressing, musical activities (rap, break dance), graphic activities (graffiti), sports activities (basket ball, whereas young people from the working classes tended to play football) and, finally, linguistic practices. In other words, these 'Arabisms' bear witness to a desire to transform French by adding a touch of personal identity to it, so as to recall origins that are little by little becoming mythical and thus become mummified, fossilized in a few words and expressions.

The function of these linguistic collages is thus to act as a marker of identity, something which is found elsewhere, in other communities, and which constitutes a practically universal fact: French speakers mark their origins (Provençal, Breton, *pied-noir* [French Algerian]) within the language by using words that are Provençal (*pitchoune*, *fan de*, etc.), Breton (*ken avo*) or . . . Arabic. And a *pied-noir* will use the word *hallouf* in the same way and with the same meaning as a young *Beur* [Arab] whose parents are immigrants from the Maghreb. From this point of view, Farid in example 1 is quite simply speaking what he considers as *his* French, just as people from Provence, Brittany or Algeria are speaking their French.

The 'identity-bestowing' French of young *Beurs*[10] is relatively simple to understand and describe, but other forms, that we can analyse in the same terms, are more complex. Let us consider example 4, in 'Nouchi',[11] a linguistic form used in the Ivory Coast first and foremost by juvenile delinquents, then by young people as a whole: its syntax is 'French' but its lexicon is composite. At Abidjan, two delinquents are brought before the courts for the theft of a wallet, and the magistrate asks them for an explanation. One of them replies:

Example 4
*'**Draman!** En façon que depuis deux jours nous on a pas **badou**, on est là se promener, voilà **gawa** qui est courbé, son **bé** est sorti. En façon que moi j'ai **gnou** le bé et j'ai donné ça à Périco. On est là **fagne, po baabiê** là est venu **djo** les gens. C'est ça on est là!'*

A speaker of standard French will pick up a few passages of this text but its general meaning will be beyond him, because of vocabulary items that he does not know (those in bold) and certain syntactic turns of phrase. What we find here, in fact, are French words used with a different meaning (such as *drap* [which usually means 'sheet'], taken from the expression *être dans de beaux draps* ['to be in a fine mess']), others in a truncated form (*po* for *policier* ['policeman']), words taken from other African languages (*Gawa*, in Burkina Faso, designates a region far away from the capital, thereby signifying 'peasant', 'bushman'; *baabiê* in Diola means '. . . of your mother'), and words whose origin it is difficult to trace (*badu*, 'to eat'; *fagne*, 'to run away'; *bedu*, or *be*, 'wallet'; *djo*, 'to catch'; *gnou*, to steal, etc.). Then the words of example 4 become easy to understand: 'Judge! [*homme*, 'man', who causes problems, *draps*]. We hadn't eaten in two days. While we were walking along, we saw a peasant bending over, and his wallet was sticking out of his pocket. I stole the wallet and gave it to Périco. We ran off, but that motherfucker of a policeman there came and caught us. And that's why we're here.'

That leaves unusual syntactic forms: *En façon que* ['so as that'], *qui est courbé* ['who's bent'], *c'est ça on est là!* ['that's it we're here!'] which probably constitute interferences from African languages. *En façon que*, for instance, seems to be a loan translation based on an expression in Diola, *cogo min* (*façon que*, or 'so that').

But these explanations, while allowing us to translate example 4, only answer one question ('What do these words mean?') and ignore another ('Why say it this way?'). One can of course adopt the hypothesis that we here have the result of a partial, imperfect appropriation of French – a hypothesis we must reject for at least two reasons. On the one hand, certain expressions are based on puns and linguistic jokes that indicate a rather good knowledge of the language: *drap*, based on *être dans de beaux draps*, in the example above, but also *une grosse* for a 25-franc coin (AFC [African Financial Community] currency) – a reference to its size; or a *tais-toi* ('quiet!') for a 10,000-franc note (AFC): when you show one to somebody, it takes their breath away . . . On the other hand, I have often heard, both in Paris and at the Senghor University of Alexandria, students from the Ivory Coast who can speak French perfectly well but actually use Nouchi amongst themselves. As some of them told me: 'It's our way of showing we are from the Ivory Coast while living abroad.' Then we are in a situation comparable to the one illustrated by examples 1 to 3. Nouchi (a word which originally designated juvenile delinquents in Abidjan and now designates their 'language') has been taken back by educated youth as a way of expressing their identity. It has become *the* language which shows their ethnic identity, and, especially when abroad, it affirms that they come from the Ivory Coast.

It is thus clear that in the two situations I have discussed there is an action of the environment on the language, and a problem of identity finds a response in a transformation of the signifier, of the linguistic form, which in turn reacts back on the environment: to speak like Farid, for instance, constitutes an assertion of identity and at the same time permits others to classify Farid into a certain category that can be rejected or accepted.

This approach to linguistic data allows us at the same time to theorize more precisely what happens in both situations. Pieter Muysken[12] has described in Ecuador what he calls a 'media lengua', which draws its functional categories from Quechua and its lexicon from Spanish. The Indian language is *relexified* by the colonial language, or, if you prefer, a Spanish vocabulary slowly replaces the original words in Quechua sentences: the media lengua (which its speakers call *utilla ingiru*, 'little Quechua') presents a lexicon of Spanish origin in a syntax that is undeniably Quechua. An example chosen at random will suffice to convey what I mean to the reader:

Example 5

media lengua	*Unu*	*fabur-ta*	*pidi-nga-bu*	*bin-xu-ni*
	a	favour	to ask	to come
	ACC		NOM-BEN	PROG
Quechua	*Shuk*	*fabur-da*	*maña-nga-bu*	*shamu-xu-ni*
Spanish	*Vengo para pedir un favor*			

It is clear how the Spanish words *un*, *favor*, *pedir*, *venir* are borrowed, phonetically adapted and inserted into an undeniably Quechua syntax. *Unu* (Spanish *un*) replaces *shuk*, *pidi* (Spanish *pedir*) replaces *maña*, *bin* (Spanish *venir*) replaces *shamu*, but the syntax and the morphology are Quechua. A knowledge of Spanish still does not allow you to understand this sentence, or any other in the language, and Quechua speakers, as Muysken points out, recognize that the media lengua is a rather strange version of Quechua and one that they find difficult to understand.

The fact remains that the way in which Muysken presents this 'little Quechua' raises a slight problem. He ponders its status and concludes that what we have here is a full-blown language, neither Quechua nor Spanish. His strongest argument is that we have here an intercommunitarian language. However, the name he gives it, and the title of his 1981 article, 'Halfway between Quechua and Spanish', suggest that he is basing his views on purely synchronic considerations and that this 'media lengua' constitutes, perhaps, an advanced form of Quechua. In other words, linguistic variation (from 'little Quechua' to Quechua) can here be analysed as evidence for the change – the evolution – of Quechua to a form more influenced by Spanish. The fact that his 'little Quechua' or this 'media lengua' is the means of communication of a given community does not at all imply that we here have a different form of Quechua or Spanish: the whole problem lies in knowing what 'halfway' means – halfway between *what*? Viewing it as a language halfway between two other languages is singularly reductive: 'language' is the product of a community and it is here a community which is halfway between two other communities, or is trying to find its way.

But in every language in the world there are phenomena which are akin to this kind of relexification: the entirety of what we might call argot or popular neologism.

Example 6
Le keum a cornanché son dabe
(The guy has killed his father)

Example 7
The Paddy is in the Black Maria
(The Irishman is in the police van)

We may not be able to understand the above phrases, but we will realize that example 6 is French and example 7, English. After all, the words *keum*, *cornanché*, *dabe* may not be known, but the conjugation of the verb, the article *le*, the possessive *son* [his], as well as the syntactic order, clearly show that example 6 is French; and *Paddy* or *Black Maria* may not be recognized by, for instance, a French speaker, but the article *the*, the preposition *in* and the conjugate verb *is* all indicate, for their part, that example 7 is English. It could of course be objected that I am here taking *relexification* in a somewhat extended sense, since in the case of argot we have only one language at stake (French or English in the above examples) whereas there are, in the example presented by Muysken, two languages (Quechua and Spanish). Furthermore, the situations are not, sociolinguistically speaking, comparable: the existence of the media lengua can indeed be viewed as evidence for the eventual disappearance of Quechua, whilst argot is merely one form of the language from which it comes. But if we wish to subsume all these examples, it is enough to consider that there may be two types of relexification, defined as a change in the phonetic form of the signs:

1 An *exogenous relexification*, when the new signifier comes from another language. This is, of course, the case described by Muysken (the Spanish lexicon relexifying Quechua), and it would be the case of French relexified by certain African languages of the Ivory Coast, or of *hallouf* used instead of *pig* in example 1.
2 An *endogenous relexification*, when the new signifier comes from the same language, via different transformations – originally in order to fulfil a cryptic function. This is the case with the various forms of slang. The slang of example 6 is not, after all, a language different from French: it is a French whose lexical elements have been transformed, either by the application of a rule (here, *verlan*, which turns *mec* [guy] into *keum*), or by the creation of a new word (*cornancher*, to kill, from *corne*, horn). And example 1 shows us that these two types of relexification may coexist: endogenous for *meuf* (the *verlan* form of *femme*, woman) and exogenous for *hallouf* (taken from Arabic).

The advantage of this extension of the notion of relexification lies not only in the fact that it allows us to consider the 'media lengua' and certain procedures of slang or popular neologism as being the products of a comparable phenomenon, but above all that it relates their differences to social phenomena. Relexification is a process of transformation that may be responding to different exterior stimuli. The 'media lengua' is the product of a glottophagic relation of force[13] and is a sign of the penetration of Quechua by Spanish, whereas slang is the product of a desire to be cryptic and Nouchi or *Beur* ways of speaking have the function of asserting one's identity. These different elements are linked: linguistic change, which proceeds in all these cases by modifying the signifier, is not triggered by the same phenomenon, and it is precisely this trigger which selects the type of relexification, exogenous or endogenous. The (lexical) evolution of the language can thus easily be seen in a perfectly ordinary formal change (here, a change of signifier), but this formal change does not respond to the same principles in accordance with the external factors that trigger this evolution.

This way of presenting things also has the advantage of reminding us that lexical modifications, however important they may be, do not change a great deal in the system of the language: the 'media lengua' is still Quechua, the *Beur* speech of example 1 and the slang of examples 6 and 7 are still, respectively, French or English.

The graphic environment

Another simple way of illustrating what we may learn from an ecological approach to linguistic situations is what I will call the graphic environment. We will be seeing in the next chapter that, in parallel with the gravitational system of languages, there is a gravitational system of writings: several people are digraphic, acquainted with the system that allows them to note down their own language and another system, which is as often as not the Latin alphabet. Now this digraphism can be seen on the walls of our cities, in inscriptions, posters, signposts. The plaques that show road names, for instance, are bilingual in Morocco (Arabic/Latin alphabets) or in London's Soho (Latin alphabet/Chinese characters), and the same system can also be used to write different languages in the same place (English and Spanish in the USA, for instance), with different relations between signs and sounds. A whole discourse can thus be seen on the walls of our cities.

Thus the walls of Paris demonstrate a coexistence of graphic forms and languages: the French language, first and foremost, and Latin graphic forms, both of them largely dominant. The Latin alphabet is also used to write other languages – English, German, Italian or Spanish, for signs that are generally meant for tourists (*English spoken, duty free, cambio, Wechsel* . . .). These non-French inscriptions do not appear at random. They are not found in working-class districts, but in the commercial districts of the city centre: the avenue de l'Opéra, the rue de Rivoli, the Champs-Elysées, etc. Other graphic systems can also be seen on the city walls: Arabic, Hebrew, Vietnamese and Thai alphabets; Chinese characters and Japanese kana and kanji. Here too, graphic systems do not appear at random: you come across Arabic, Chinese, Vietnamese and Thai inscriptions, as well as a few in Hebrew, in the working-class district of Belleville, and Chinese, Vietnamese and Thai inscriptions in the 13th arrondissement. Arabic, more often than not clumsily written and misspelt, indicates restaurants, hallal butchers, and grocers; Hebrew signals the sale of kosher products; and Asian languages indicate simultaneously restaurants, commerce, assorted dispensaries, travel agents, hairdressing salons, etc. Arabic is again encountered, this time more careful in its calligraphy, in the wealthy districts, but, like English or German, it then indicates bureaux de change or the sale of duty-free goods.

So we here have a linguistic niche that we to some extent read on a second level, via graphic transcriptions that show us the functions of and relations between languages. The Arabic written in Belleville more often than not tells immigrant workers that at such-and-such a butcher's they sell meat which has been slaughtered in accordance with Muslim ritual; in the avenue de l'Opéra the Arabic is addressed to rich customers from the Gulf. Again in Belleville, the contrast between inscriptions in Arabic and those in Asian languages is a sign of a significant difference in the social levels of migrants who speak these languages. The graphic environment is thus an indication – again on a second level – of the functions of languages, of the social situation of their speakers, and this synchronic vision leads to mutations, as is more clearly shown by the two examples that follow.

A sociolinguistic study carried out in the historic heart of Jerusalem[14] has brought out the 'trigraphism' of the old town, the coexistence of Arabic, Hebrew and Latin alphabets (the latter more often than not being used for English). The plaques that bear street names are also written in three languages (Hebrew, Arabic and English), but a more detailed analysis of this grouping of languages shows that what we have

Street signs in Jerusalem (from Bernard Spolsky and Robert Cooper, *The Languages of Jerusalem*)

here is not merely a synchronic fact (the presence of these three languages at the time the study was made) but a situation that is historical through and through, being evidence simultaneously of the situation's past, present and future.

Let us consider, for instance, the plaque that gives the name of Ha-Malakh Road in three languages, Hebrew at the top, then Arabic and English. If we compare it to the plaque to the right, which has the same content, we can see that the inscription in Hebrew has been added above an older plaque in Arabic and English. But the 'English' version is not the same: HA-MALAKH RD. in the first case, EL-MALAK RD. in the second. There is a simple explanation for this: EL-MALAK RD.

is a transcription in the Latin alphabet, with an English abbreviation (RD. for road), of the Arabic form of the street name, whereas HA-MALAKH RD. is the transcription of its Hebrew form. In both cases, the forms are 'English' only by virtue of the alphabet and the abbreviation RD. In fact, the plaque on the right dates from the Jordanian period (1948–67), in the course of which the two languages used were Arabic and English, in that order, whereas the plaque on the left dates from the ensuring Israeli period, and the addition of the inscription in Hebrew above the plaque was intended to 'normalize' the inscription. The order of languages is thus the same in both cases, but the transcription (of Hebrew or Arabic) is evidence of differences in the political situation. In the Jaffa Gate plaque the same languages are used in a different order (English, Arabic, Hebrew). It dates from the British Mandate (1919–48) and provides evidence of a different linguistic policy: three successive periods, English, Jordanian and Israeli, have left different traces in the graphic environment. Finally, the symbolic violence shown in the final plaque, on which the Arabic and 'English' text has been obliterated, is evidence of the vision that certain people have of the city's future.

These four photos thus come from one period and from many different periods. They demonstrate that history is present at all times and in all places, and that synchrony and diachrony are inseparable. Any Palestinian who sees the final plaque senses that there are people who would exclude him from Jerusalem, while any Israeli who sees the plaque at top right remembers that there was a time when his language was not officially present in the Old City. And the four photos raise a painful question for everyone: the question of Jerusalem's future.

It is also possible to read, in the graphic environment, the way ideologies have evolved – not simultaneously, as in the Jerusalem example, but consecutively. Thus a study of street names in a small town in Andalusia, Almonte, shows us how the political regimes that followed one another in Spain have left an imprint on its toponymy.[15] At the beginning of the century there was in Almonte a ring road called *Arenal* ('sandy') and a town-centre street called *Concepción*. In 1931 the Republicans rebaptized the ring road *Concepción Arenal*, after the name of a nineteenth-century Galician feminist writer, and the street *Cervantes*. In 1937 the Francoists decided to efface these democratic traces: *Concepción* street, with its obvious religious connotations, reappeared, but not at the same place, instead of *Concepción Arenal*, and

Cervantes became *Queipo de Llano*. Finally, in 1981, when democracy returned, *Arenal* and *Concepción* were given back the names they had had at the beginning of the century. In these repeated name swappings, both in Jerusalem and Almonte, we can thus read how power affected the graphic environment and toponymy.

In the Kabyle town of Tizi-Ouzou (Algeria), we find a situation that is similar to that in Jerusalem, insofar as the variations have to do with languages and writing systems, but at the same time very different, insofar as the variations are the effect not of power but of individuals. Three languages (Arabic, Kabyle and French) and three alphabets coexist, without there being necessarily any direct, one-to-one relation among them. While Arabic is written in Arabic characters and French in Latin characters, Berber may be transcribed into both of these alphabets or even into Tifinagh, the traditional Berber writing system. Rabah Kahlouche[16] has analysed the graphic environment in this town since the beginning of the 1990s, i.e. since developments in the political system (the end of the hegemony of the FLN [*Front de Libération National*, National Liberation Front], political pluralism, etc.) limited the application of the laws on Arabicization.

This relative democratization is demonstrated in Tizi-Ouzou both by the reappearance of French and by the emergence of Berber in the graphic landscape. Whereas in the rest of Algeria official signs are written solely in Arabic, in Kabylia they use three languages, Arabic, Berber and French, in that order, Berber texts being generally in Tifinagh. This is a result of the influence of the RCD (*Rassemblement pour la Culture et la Démocratie* [Rally for Culture and Democracy]), the majority party in the region, which has included in its programme the recognition of the Berber language and the teaching of scientific subjects in French. As far as commercial signs are concerned, one encounters 'monolingual signs in Arabic and in French (never in Berber), bilingual signs and trilingual signs'.[17] Kahlouche's study bore on the two main avenues in the town, one in the old town and the other in the new town, and the situation is summarized in table 1.1.

As opposed to those found on public buildings, these signs manifest the choice of the shopkeepers and show a clear overall trend: 'most of the owners of monolingual businesses in Arabic declared that their signs went back to the time of the FLN diktat, and that they would reintroduce French as soon as they renovated their shops'.[18] And, for Kahlouche, the bilingual signs in the old town illustrate a 'linguistic

Table 1.1 Commercial signs in Tizi-Ouzou

Language	Old town	New town
French	54.9%	90.4%
Arabic	22.9%	–
Arabic/French	19.4%	7%
Berber/French	–	2.6%
Trilingual	2.7%	–

Source: Rabah Kahlouche, 'Les enseignes à Tizi-Ouzou: un lieu de conflit linguistique'.

transition' that is made equally obvious by the relative positioning of the two languages: Arabic above French (50 per cent), French above Arabic (28.5 per cent) and Arabic and French on the same level (21.5 per cent).

A somewhat hasty observer might see in this type of situation nothing more than disorder, or the result of chance. However, this polygraphism is characteristic of the linguistic niche of Tizi-Ouzou. Behind the various uses of the three coexisting languages, we have, on the one hand, a difference between the *in vitro* graphic environmental policy (the trilingual official inscriptions reflect the choice of the RCD) and the *in vivo* practice of the shopkeepers (who show a preference for French). 'Arabic is for power; French is for my customers and me,' declares one shopkeeper. This presence of French is also illustrated by the fact that signs are more often than not conceived in French, then translated or adapted into other languages.

There is a paradox in this situation. On the political level, shopkeepers systematically show the support they give to Kabyle claims to self-identity (in particular by shutting up shop on the days when there is a demonstration), but they still choose to compose their shop signs in French and not in Berber, as if they separated linguistic problems from problems of identity. But the paradox is only superficial.

Kabylia, a majority of whose inhabitants are hostile to the policy of Arabicization, which implied the liquidation of their own culture, privileged French rather than Arabic because the official propaganda presented Berber as a factor of division. In other words, Berber has a strategic need of French, behind which it advances as if concealed by a mask. But, in this linguistic niche, the dominant limiting factor, the number of speakers, shows a tendency to favour Berber, and only secondary factors privilege French. This is why Rabah Kahlouche's conclusion seems unduly pessimistic:

> In this war between languages, set in the landscape of writing constituted by the town of Tizi-Ouzou, Berber and French appear as great allies. But it is an alliance in which the Berber partner is too strictly eradicated. The French language is in the process of supplanting Arabic and leaving merely an insignificant place to Berber.[19]

In fact, the debates on Arabicization in a newly independent Algeria offered no more than a choice between two functional possibilities: Arabic alone or an Arabic/French bilingualism. Berber language and culture were literally obliterated in this debate, and the sole issue for them was to prevent Arabic from imposing itself as the only language. But at the same time, French benefited from this situation and enjoys much more of a presence in the linguistic landscape in Kabylia than in the rest of Algeria. If in Kabylia the 'logical' bilingualism of Berber/Arabic is threatened by competition from Berber/French bilingualism, it is because, in this particular niche, there is a mutual dependence between the two languages. Berber and French need each other, just as mistletoe needs birds to eat it and spread its seeds; mistletoe nourishes the birds and the birds ensure the reproduction of mistletoe. This example, which I have taken from Charles Darwin,[20] is in fact more complicated. Mistletoe is, in fact, a parasite of the apple tree, from which it draws part of its sustenance. But if there is too much mistletoe on a single tree, the tree risks dying. The survival of a clump of mistletoe on a tree thus implies that there should not be too many clumps on the same trunk. At the same time, as we have just seen, mistletoe and bird are mutually dependent. Developing the metaphor, we can see that it is in fact Berber that corresponds to the apple tree. A certain ecological equilibrium may guarantee the existence of the apple tree, the mistletoe and the bird, in the same way that, in the Kabyle niche, another equilibrium may guarantee the existence of Arabic, Berber and French, as the graphic environment just described shows.

One might be tempted to consider that this graphic environment is merely a second-level system that allows us to read a situation via the transcription of languages. But the passage from phonetic to graphic levels and the choice of one or other system of transcription tell us more about this situation than the languages themselves. In Galicia, for instance, an autonomous region of Spain that is officially bilingual (Galician/Spanish), the city of Corunna is written as either *La Coruña* or *A Coruña*, in Spanish in the first case and in Galician, in 'normative' (official) spelling, in the second. These two ways of writing the name may in the first analysis be considered as evidence of official bilingualism. But you also come across graffiti or unofficial inscriptions which spell it *A Corunha*, using the system of Portuguese notation. And this slight difference between *ñ* and *nh* to notate the same sound is evidence of a political conflict between so-called 'reintegrationist' groups, who consider that Galician is Portuguese and that the 'normative' spelling is a colonial imposition, and those who accept this official spelling. *A Coruña* and *A Corunha* are pronounced in exactly the same way, but the graphic variation is heavy with symbolic meaning.

Another example of this reading of an ecolinguistic situation via the graphic environment can be found in the capital of Senegal, Dakar.[21] Extending from the south to the north, from the privileged districts (the Plateau) to the poorer districts (the Bissap estate, Ouagou Niayes) and passing through a buffer zone (Médina), the city can be read through its street signs. Myriam Dumont has shown that French was dominant on the Plateau and that the more one went northwards in the city the more one found business signs in Wolof and references to Islam, as conveyed by the use of the Arabic language or alphabet. In tandem with this, the types of signs change too, starting from modern, illuminated signs, often perpendicular to the wall, to more unsophisticated signs, often clumsily written, with texts painted on planks of wood or sometimes painted directly onto the wall. The ecological niche of Dakar, in which there coexist a good fifteen or so African and French languages, is thus filtered. The way business signs are written shows us that Wolof is imposed as the dominant African language rather than the official language, French, inherited from the colonial period. And the hesitation as to whether the Latin or the Arabic alphabet should be used to transcribe Wolof or Senegalese proper names is at one and the same time evidence of a historical fact (languages stemming from the oral tradition, whose spelling is not really fixed, as opposed to a language with a written tradition) and of the growing presence of Islam.

The graphic environment thus deserves a special theoretical treatment. In the above-mentioned work on the languages of Jerusalem, the authors propose to explain the choice of languages in public inscriptions on the basis of three rules:

- Rule 1: write in a language you know.
- Rule 2: write in a language that potential readers are supposed to be able to read.
- Rule 3: write in your own language or in a language with which you wish to be identified.

It is clear that between the communicative function of rule 2 and the symbolic function of rule 3 there may be a contradiction. The inscriptions in Arabic on the Muslim butchers' shops of Paris are, for instance, a response to rule 3, but not to rule 2 (most of the time, immigrant workers cannot read). At Tizi-Ouzou, respect for the law (which prescribes writing in Arabic) is a response to rule 1 (everyone learns Arabic at school) and thus to rule 2, but not to rule 3, and individual initiatives (which lead one to writing in French or in Kabyle) thus privilege the symbolic function shown in rule 3. Thus the graphic environment is not the mechanistic translation of a particular situation, but the illustration of subtle relationships, and of conflicts, between different functions (official, communicative or identity-asserting) which are embodied in the choice of transcription.

Dramatic change in a specific linguistic ecology: the example of Australia

In a large-scale collective work[22] we find, mainly in the sections written by Peter Mühlhäusler, an attempt to analyse the changes brought about in the linguistic ecology of Australia by the arrival of European colonizers.[23] The development of the situation can be symbolized by two figures: in 1788 more than 250 languages were spoken in Australia, today there are fewer than fifty, and 90 per cent of Aborigines speak English or a form of Aboriginal English. This summary of the situation suggests that in Australia, just as everywhere else, a colonial language (in this case English), endowed with all the means conferred on it by power, has won out over the local languages and threatens their survival. Arabic plays the same role in the Maghreb with regard to Berber; French has played the same role in France with regard to Breton or

Occitan and is playing the same role in Africa with regard to local languages, etc. We could therefore, returning to the case of Australia, consider that this glottophagous phenomenon[24] has predictably led from a plurilingualism worthy of Babel, a fragmented assembly of small languages without any possibility of interethnic communication, to a linguistic centralization based on standard English or a local form of English. But Mühlhäusler disputes the validity of this view. For one thing, he explains, the Europeans found, on their arrival in Australia, not a great diversity of isolated languages, but a complex and highly-organized network of communication.[25] And for another, contact with the Europeans generated a certain number of changes, the fallout from which has had important effects on the linguistic situation. For example:

- the introduction of illnesses (in particular smallpox) which killed a great number of Aborigines, thereby reducing the size of traditional linguistic communities and making certain languages no longer viable;
- the displacement of Aborigines from the fertile lands they occupied towards less fertile lands, with the result that they went from a status of self-sufficiency to a status of dependency;
- the overturning of intercultural relations (nomads gathering around mission settlements, contacts between groups that had traditionally not been in contact, etc.);
- a policy of assimilation, in particular ensuring that children attend boarding schools (where they were principally taught in English), and a hostile attitude towards local languages;
- more recently, the introduction of new technologies of communication (radio, TV, IT) in English.

These modifications to the ecology have thus had an impact on linguistic situations, which have to be analysed in several stages: first region by region, then in the relations between neighbouring regions and finally at the level of the entire country. So I will be dwelling successively on New South Wales, South Australia, Queensland, Western Australia and the Northern Territory (see map).

In January 1788 a British penal colony was set up in Port Jackson (now Sydney) in New South Wales. It comprised 1,024 persons, 74 per cent of them convicts. At first they had little contact with local populations. Things started to change in April 1789, as a result of a

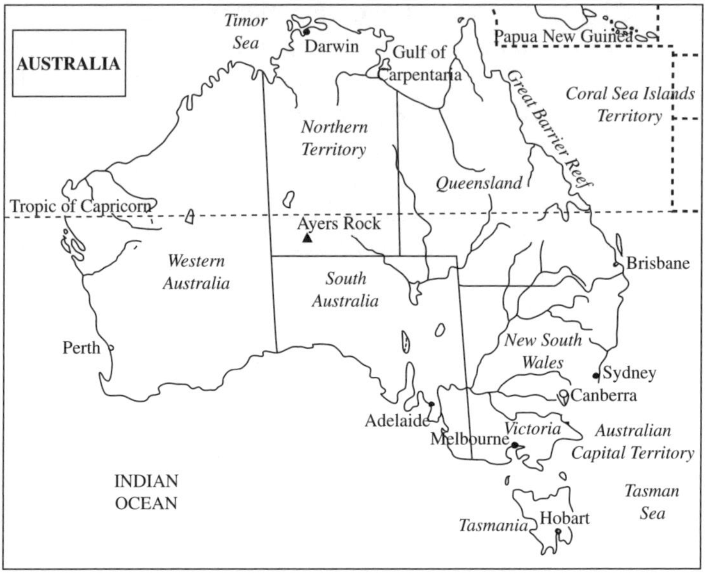

smallpox epidemic that led to numerous deaths. To begin with some Aboriginal orphans were taken into the care of British families who taught them English. Then, in 1790, adult Aboriginals came to settle in Port Jackson, and from the relations between them and the colonists there emerged a contact language which spread through the region, New South Wales Pidgin.[26] This pidgin, the result of contacts between Aborigines and Britons, then spread northwards into Queensland,[27] where it gave birth to Queensland Pidgin English, and westwards into Western Australia.

Right at the start of the nineteenth century, this area was inhabited by seal hunters of various origins (English, French, Maori, Portuguese, Tahitian, American, New Zealand, etc.) who settled in the south of Australia, on Kangaroo Island. There were some fifty of them, in 1820, living with about a hundred women and children. These Aboriginal women came mainly from Tasmania but also from certain coastal areas (numerous judicial documents prove that these women were most often kidnapped).[28] Among these hunters, their women and the whale hunters who sailed the neighbouring seas, conditions conspired to produce a 'nautical jargon', the first vehicular language of the region. Later on, at the end of the 1830s, religious missions were established in the Adelaide region, and these missions opened schools in which Aboriginal children, far from the influence of their parents, were educated in English and sometimes (in one particular German mission) in the Kaurna language. In the 1840s migrants from Cornwall settled in the region and worked in the silver and copper mines. They were followed by immigrants from Pakistan, China and Germany. The result was the appearance of a 'pidgin' (South Australian Pidgin English), influenced by its neighbouring New South Wales version, which went on to spread westwards (to the Perth region), via the Trans-Australian Railway Line, at the time of the Kalgoorlie Gold Rush. The first European colonists to arrive in the Perth region in 1830 had encouraged the use of the languages of the Nyungar group. From the relations between English and Nyungar, and under the influence of South Australian Pidgin English, there emerged a new contact language, South Western Pidgin English.[29] In tandem with this, the Northern Territory was a place of contact between Asian languages (Chinese Pidgin English imported by Chinese, Macassan imported by sea-slug fishers from Indonesia) and the pidgin of New South Wales. As a result, two 'creoles' appeared, Northern Territory Creole and Torres Strait Broken, which slowly replaced the indigenous languages.

This apparently simple example in fact raises numerous questions for linguistics. One cannot, for instance, envisage any one of these different languages existing on their own. Between the situation preceding the arrival of the colonists, insofar as we are able to reconstruct it, and the present situation, a certain number of modifications took place in the environment and triggered a set of chain reactions. The relations between language and territory were completely transformed by the arrival of the whites (essentially by the displacement and regrouping of populations), which led to the adoption of the pidgin English used in contacts between English-speakers and Aborigines, who, to begin with, preserved their own languages. Things changed when these Aborigines were displaced to other places and, above all, found themselves mingling with speakers of other languages. Different solutions were then put into effect: the adoption of a dominant Aboriginal language as vehicular language (for example at Aurukun, in Queensland, Wik Mungkan replaced the other Aboriginal languages); the formation of a koine stemming from traditional languages; a move to English or Aboriginal English, etc. This Aboriginal English, the result of the first pidgins which, as we have just seen, developed in different areas of the territory at the start of colonization, was first of all used for contacts between Aboriginals and colonists. It went on to become the vehicular language of the Aborigines regrouped in government reserves and missions, and finally became a local dialect of English.[30] This expansion can be clearly seen from history of grammatical and lexical facts. We find for instance the use of *been* as an aspect marker in New South Wales in 1826, in Queensland in 1842, in South Australia in 1890, in Western Australia in 1883. In tandem, the expression *black fellow* (with the sense of 'native') appeared in 1801 in New South Wales, in 1838 in South Australia, in 1842 in Queensland and in 1845 in Western Australia.

This brief overview of recent Australian history shows what can be learnt from the ecological analysis of a linguistic situation, how a change in linguistic ecology and the networks of intercultural communication have transformed the linguistic landscape. We start out with a *system* in which more than 200 languages coexist – a system that is evidently linked with the *milieu*, determined by geography – which is dramatically transformed by the introduction of new languages, by displacements and regroupings of populations, by the reduction of certain groups, etc. The response to these external stimuli, the *regulation* of the ecological system, is eventually the appearance of different regional pidgins, simultaneously influenced by each other and marked by local circumstances, in particular by other languages from neighbouring islands or from Asia. These pidgins first served as a means of communication with colonists, and the Aborigines preserved their own languages for inter-communal communication. But, each time they were displaced towards new areas by the colonists, brought into contact with groups speaking different languages, and discovered that their languages no longer allowed them to communicate with their new neighbours, the pidgins tended to change function and become the native vehicular language.

The political frontier and the ecolinguistic system

An ecolinguistic system can be modified by two types of factors:

- on the one hand, the habits of the speakers: the movements of population, the acquisition of a dominant language and the non-

transmission of the dominated languages from one generation to another, etc.
- on the other hand, the actions of the state power: the choice of linguistic policies, schooling, literacy, the media, etc.

From this last point of view, the first intervention of the state on ecolinguistic systems is the one which consists of tracing its territorial limits, imposing on the weave of peoples, ethnic groups and languages a division which initially has nothing to do with peoples, ethnic groups or languages. Political frontiers, after all, rarely correspond to linguistic frontiers, and political divisions can have important knock-on effects on ecolinguistic and sociolinguistic situations: gravitation towards the language spoken in the capital, the introduction of diglossic relations, borrowings on the part of the dominated language from the dominant language, the slow imposition of the central language, etc. The frontier is thus a good example of external intervention on an ecolinguistic niche in the sense that it reorganizes all inter- and intra-linguistic relations: the gravitational system is modified, a language can be torn between two sources of attraction, coexist with different languages and be marked by them, enter into different diglossic relations.

On a very simple level, this may concern the system of borrowings which one and the same language is going to make on both sides of the frontier, from different languages. Thus, Wolof is spoken in Senegal and Gambia, a small country that is a kind of enclave in the former, but Senegal was colonized by France and still has French as its official language, whereas Gambia was colonized by Great Britain and still has English as its official language. Despite the geographical proximity of the two countries, their Wolofs have slowly diverged on the lexical level, especially in the towns: the Wolof of Dakar is stuffed with borrowings from French, whereas that of Bathurst has borrowed from English. In other words, the same language, introduced by a political process into two different diglossias, into two different gravitational systems, is modified both in its attraction and in its form.

We have a comparable situation in the border zone between Uruguay and Brazil. Here the ecology has already been modified by the border and could be modified again, but in the other direction, by the linguistic policies of MERCOSUR, the Common Market of the South.[31] When Uruguay was created in 1828, its population was composite: European migrants in the south (Italians, Galicians, French, etc.), constituting linguistic minorities vis-à-vis the Spanish-speaking majority, and Portuguese speakers in the north and north-east, who hitherto had been in a majority in this region but were henceforth to be in a minority thanks to the establishment of the Uruguayan state. The 'law of common education' adopted in 1877 became the spearhead of a voluntarist linguistic policy tending to unify the country around Spanish.[32] The languages of migrants, in the south, rapidly disappeared before the advance of Spanish, whereas the border dialects were to resist better thanks to their more long-standing implantation (Brazil was integrated with Portugal as early as the end of the sixteenth century) and the 'logistical' support provided by speakers who had settled on the other side of the border, in Brazil. But 'there Spanish clearly became the language of prestige, whereas the Portuguese dialects were little by little considered to be stigmatized variants',[33] which generated a great linguistic insecurity among the speakers of the dominated varieties. We thus have, today, a country that is linguistically unified in the south and partly bilingual in the north, the situation of the Portuguese dialects spoken there being comparable with that of Alsatian in France: in both cases, a low variety in a diglossic situation whose high variety (Spanish, French) has been imposed by the capital (Montevideo, Paris), and in both cases the standard form (Portuguese, German) is found on the other side of the border.

These frontier vernaculars have been only partly described, in extremely traditional terms, and without their sociolinguistic and ecolinguistic conditions being taken into account in any meaningful way.[34] The few studies available emphasize for instance phonetic facts such as the pronunciation as [o] of the final [u] in Portuguese verbs such as *tenho*, *canto*, etc., or interferences between Spanish and Portuguese in the semantics of verbs. Furthermore, the works of Barrios and Behares,[35] which give us a good idea of the overall picture in sociolinguistic terms, do not give us any concrete description of the form of these dialects. It appears, however, that the border dialects, forms of Portuguese marked by the domination of Spanish, cut off from their 'natural' linguistic base (the standard Portuguese of Brazil), are in a situation which could lead to their eventual disappearance. But the recent creation of MERCOSUR and the planned linguistic policies associated with it (the teaching of Spanish in Brazil, of Portuguese in Argentina, Uruguay and Paraguay) may make the situation develop in a different direction. In particular, the reappearance of Portuguese as an official language could reinforce and revitalize the dialects and lessen the linguistic insecurity of their speakers. The situation would thus be paradoxical, since Uruguay, which established itself linguistically by struggling against languages other than Spanish – in particular against Portuguese in the border zone – should now be led to promote this very same Portuguese: 'To achieve linguistic uniformity, the Uruguayan state struggled for decades, more or less explicitly, against Portuguese: today it is expected to encourage people to learn it and use it.'[36]

In 1971, discussing the 'spiritual exercises' of Ignatius Loyola, Roland Barthes analysed them as 'the invention of a language' whose practice involved the establishment of a 'field of exclusion' and a 'linguistic vacuum'. 'All these protocols have the function of creating in the exercitant a kind of linguistic vacuum necessary for the elaboration and for the triumph of the new language: the vacuum is ideally the anterior space of all semiophany'.[37] In 1974, in *Linguistique et colonialisme*, I used this text, albeit adding a slight twist to its meaning. Barthes saw in Loyola a question (how to speak to God?) and his reply (by getting rid of all previous languages by means of the spiritual exercises). I transformed this in the following way: 'The question is no longer "How to speak to God?" but, depending on the situation, "How to speak to the capital?" when you are in Brittany, Occitania or Corsica, "How to speak to the metropolis?" when you are in North Africa, Black Africa, Indochina, etc.'[38] For me it was a matter of describing the imposition of a means of communication which, in colonial situations, implied that one set aside local languages in order to speak to the metropolis and used an exclusive language, the colonial language.

The border situations I have just been discussing show us, depending on the situation, a conflict of 'fields of exclusion' or the replacement of one 'field of exclusion' by another. The swapping over of exclusive languages (French/English for Senegal and Gambia, French/German for Alsace, Spanish/Portuguese for northern Uruguay) that happens at a frontier leads to a series of modifications in the ecolinguistic system (change in the source of attraction, change in the nature of the diglossia), and this transformation of interlinguistic relations leads to transformations in the form of coexisting languages (systems of loans, phonology, etc.). In other terms, the political frontier has transformed the ecolinguistic niche of Portuguese dialects in Uruguay/Brazil or of Wolof in Senegal/Gambia (remember that I have defined the niche of a language as the set of its relations with other languages, the place it occupies in the ecosystem, i.e. I have defined it by its functions and by its relations with its milieu), which, in a second stage, leads to a formal and functional modification of these languages that may in certain cases even entail their extinction.

The influence of the horse on European languages

One need merely glance at the linguistic history of Europe to realize the foundational role played in it by migrations. We do not know very much about the languages spoken in Europe some 7,000 or 8,000 years ago, but the reconstruction of Indo-European and archaeological traces show us that the current situation is the product of a great movement of populations travelling, in André Martinet's words, 'from the steppes to the oceans'.[39]

Since the first reconstructions of Indo-European, at the start of the nineteenth century, our knowledge has developed greatly. After proposing, via the hypothesis of phonetic laws, a reconstitution of that 'mother language', scholars attempted to reconstitute, through vocabulary, the systems of thought and the social systems of Indo-Europeans; hypotheses based on the linguistic approach have been confirmed and made more precise by archaeology, and, more recently, an attempt has even been made at a 'pragmatic' approach to Indo-European.[40] We know that around 4,500 BCE, people from the Volga basin reached as far as the steppes to the north of the Black Sea; they buried their leaders under tumuli, which in Russian are called *kurgan*, with servants and concubines probably immolated to accompany them in death. So, following Marija Gimbutas,[41] these invaders have been baptized the 'Kurgans'. The archaeological traces constituted by these tumuli, as well as the later study of certain ceramic techniques (globular amphorae, corded ceramics), have enabled us to retrace the successive invasions of these semi-nomads, their movements and the directions they took. After the first wave in the fifth millennium there was another around 3,500 BCE, coming from the northern Caucasus, which extended as far as what is today the Ukraine, Poland, Germany and northern Italy. Then, around 3,000 BCE, a third invasion brought the Indo-Europeans to Central Europe.

But it would be extremely reductive to think that this migration, which happened in several stages, in several waves, had merely linguistic results, and went no further than the importation of a language which later gave birth to the great majority of present-day European languages. The successive intrusions of the Kurgans between 4,500 and 2,500 BCE and their settling in Europe did in fact lead to numerous dramatic cultural and social changes, of which the linguistic inheritance is merely one aspect.

So while we know more or less when these Kurgans moved westwards, and the traces they left in different domains, two questions remain: why and how did they come? It would be wrong to imagine these Kurgans as having originally been a people of warriors, armed to the teeth and spoiling for a fight with their distant cousins in the west, and it would be wrong to consider the Indo-Europeanization of Europe as the invasion of an aggressive people imposing its law on a pacific people. In fact, the Indo-European vocabulary of weapons practically always designates, to begin with, agricultural weapons that have been to some extent hijacked from their original function to be used first of all as hunting weapons.[42] It seems that in the Bronze Age there was a crisis which led these men to transform their ploughshares into hunting weapons.

> There were changes in subsistence patterns with a greater reliance on hunting than on farming and a shift from burial to cremation. It is possible that the Kurgan reliance upon herds disrupted the ecology of Old Europe through one of the two mechanisms, or a combination of both. Overgrazing may have strained arable resources beyond acceptable limits forcing the human population of both traditions to seek supplements in hunting.[43]

In 1968 Jacqueline Manessy-Guitton wrote that 'the two techniques, of linguists and historians respectively, seem quite unable to meet'.[44] Since then things have developed considerably, and all the archaeological and linguistic research, which it would take too much time to mention here, shows that there was not a peaceful people on the one hand, and a warrior people on the other. This dual approach, mixing linguistic reconstruction and archaeology, provides us with a first answer to our questions: if the Kurgans moved west, it was because they were seeking pastures and game.

That leaves the second question: how did they manage to travel such distances? The answer partly resides in a fundamental difference between the Kurgans and the Europeans they were about to invade: the former had domesticated the horse, which gave them great mobility, whereas the Europeans were essentially a sedentary agricultural people. The Indo-European horse, as archaeology has been able to reconstitute it, was small in size, used as food and then as a mount (from 4,000 BCE) and finally as a draught animal (from 2,300 BCE).[45] It thus constitutes the first factor that shook up the European ecolinguistic system: without this mount, the Kurgans would probably have remained in their original steppes and the Europeans would today speak different languages. Mounted and armed, they found it possible to cover vast distances, and between 4,400 BCE and 3,000 BCE they invaded the whole of Europe in several waves, as we have seen. But the horse did not merely carry the Kurgans and their language, it also 'transported', so to speak, a patriarchal society organized into three classes ('breeders-farmers', 'warriors', 'priests') and four circles ('family', 'clan', 'tribe', 'country'), a society with its religious beliefs and its pantheon of heavenly gods corresponding to the three classes (as opposed to the Europeans, who apparently worshipped a chthonic goddess). The early development of Europe was therefore the product of a hybridization between two symbolic and social systems. We can thus see a whole set of dramatic changes; one of them was linguistic, but the invasion of the Kurgans, and the consequent Indo-Europeanization of Europe, profoundly modified the continent: 'The clash between these two ideologies and social and economic structures led to the drastic transformation of Old Europe', writes Gimbutas.[46]

This example, which demonstrates the importance of migrations in the evolution of ecolinguistic systems, can be analysed in an original and productive way within the framework of chaos theory. The physical sciences call 'chaotic' those phenomena that apparently occur at random but are in fact ruled by a certain determinism: the simplest example, within the field of meteorology, is that of 'Lorenz's butterfly' which, by beating its wings on one side of the world, can create a meteorological catastrophe on the other. In other words, the behaviour of such systems cannot be *predicted*, but it can be explained a posteriori: they are not random nor totally predictable; they are erratic, and their behaviour may amplify tiny variations in unforeseeable ways. Didier de Robillard has suggested that this theory could enable us to explain linguistic changes (in particular on islands):

> A slight change in the system of a language, amplified by social factors, can lead to important changes in the system, by a boomerang effect.

> Conversely, one can imagine very small changes in the social field which are amplified by 'systemic effects' and lead to linguistic landscapes being dramatically and significantly affected.[47]

The domestication of the horse, 7,000 years ago, fits the second part of his suggestion and is comparable with this 'butterfly effect'. From the point of view of the history of Europe, this domestication by the Kurgans, in a far-distant place, was a product of chance and had no relation with the linguistic situation. It did, however, ravage the ecolinguistic niche, because it enabled populations to be displaced towards Europe, populations whose languages would over the centuries impose themselves and replace those that existed there. What we see, then, is the amplification of a social variation (the domestication of the horse) whose effects we are still living with, 6,000 years later. And, more generally, we can consider the evolution of ecolinguistic situations in the same way: it is neither totally predictable, nor totally random, since these two terms (determinism and chaos) are not opposites. I will return to this point in chapter 5, which focuses on the transmission of languages and linguistic situations.

A false conception of linguistic ecology: Bickerton's simulation project

In ecology there is a practice which involves simulating the way systems function. First, a model representing the system under consideration is created (this implies the determination of variables, of the relations between these variables and of parameters); then its evolution is studied on the computer. One is strongly tempted to carry out the same kind of experiment on languages: is it possible to produce, *in vitro*, in a laboratory, the birth of a language?

In 1990 Derek Bickerton imagined an approach of this kind when he proposed the 'experimental creation of a natural language',[48] with the support of three scientific consultants, Steven Pinker (MIT), Jurgen Meisel (University of Hamburg) and Talmy Givon (University of Oregon).

His project started out from a certain number of questions that I mentioned in my introduction: How do people acquire languages? Do they follow the structures of a pre-existing grammar, or can they create a new grammar on the basis of different, disorganized materials? And so on. The project was also motivated by Bickerton's interest in creoles. In his view, creoles as different as those of the Indian Ocean and the Caribbean present striking similarities which cannot be mere coincidences: serial verbs, for instance.[49] Now, he continues, these similarities cannot be explained by the influence of West African languages, which play no more than a limited role in the genesis of creoles of the Indian Ocean. The only explanation, in his view, is to postulate 'a biological capacity for creating languages that is shared by all the members of our species',[50] i.e. the innate grammar I discussed in my introduction. To try and verify this hypothesis, he suggested bringing together, in a closed environment (he thought first of all of a desert island, then a château in Provence), for a period of twelve months, native speakers of four mutually unintelligible languages, without any shared language between them, and giving them a basic vocabulary of 200 words (invented by Bickerton) so as to study, directly, the strategies involved in creating a new language. With this aim in mind, a team of observers (seven persons) was to be permanently present on the site of the experiment, noting and recording everything that would happen. The adults (two couples per language) were to be between 18 and 25 years old, the children between 2 and 5, so that the total number of 'guinea pigs' would be 16 adults and between 8 and 16 children.

The guinea pigs, whose languages would be typologically very different (Basque, Dutch, Finnish and Greek), were meant to learn the vocabulary before the experiment began. Everything was then planned out in advance, in minute detail: the guinea pigs' schedule (on arrival, a competition in the use of the vocabulary; ethnic songs, dances, maintenance of the site, cooking, etc.), the presence in the scientific team of a speaker of each of the four languages, the contract that the guinea pigs were to sign, their remuneration (which increased every month, from 50 to 600 dollars, with a final bonus of 6,100 dollars, i.e. an overall payment, for those who stuck it out to the end of the experiment, of 10,000 dollars), etc.

The project was never carried out, partly because it could not get financial backing. But, insofar as it consisted in creating a *milieu*, an artificial linguistic ecology, it cannot fail to interest us. Bickerton spoke in his text of a 'deliberate manipulation of the environment', and 'the creation of a natural language under controlled conditions', thereby placing himself, perhaps unwittingly, or at least without saying so explicitly, within the perspective of ecological simulation. I am not here going to set out the moral reasons for which such an experiment strikes me as unacceptable (the choice of the phrase *guinea pigs* is enough to convey my feelings), but I will try to explain why it could not, in my view, succeed.

This apparent reconstitution of the linguistic situation of slaves (Bickerton, we must not forget, has essentially worked on creoles), apart from the deontological problems it poses, first and foremost demonstrates a singular failure to understand the real relations between language and social life. What characterizes the birth of creoles, in fact, the adaptation of languages to new milieux (see chapter 3), is above all a power relation: whites speaking a European language, and dominating the blacks who speak different African languages. In a situation such as this, the process of learning the language could happen only in one direction: the whites did not acquire the slaves' languages. Bickerton's project was thus already compromised: what he was proposing was the simulation of something which he had invented – and nothing proves such a situation has ever existed. The four languages brought together would in fact have been in a relationship of equality: an equality that was statistical (the number of speakers), emblematic (none of them enjoyed an aura of superiority over the others) and statutory (none of them would have had, in this artificially created milieu, functions superior to those of the other languages). Bickerton had expressly excluded English from the experiment, whereas the only plausible situation would have consisted in taking guinea pigs who did not know English and imposing this language on them – it would have been the language of the scientists in charge of the experiment. But perhaps it would have been necessary to provide these experimenters with whips, and shackle the feet of the guinea pigs. . . .

The catalyst chosen was a vocabulary injected into an artificial milieu, a vocabulary presented by Bickerton as having no link with any real language. Now, paradoxically enough, this is the only interesting point in the project. What we have here is a perfectly simple and obvious question: is a human being capable of inventing words that have no link with any real language? At all events, it seems that a linguist is quite incapable of doing so. In Bickerton's list, the links between certain 'invented' words and real languages are immediately apparent: *doso* ('back', French *dos*), *riko* ('beans', French *haricot*), *biri* ('beer'), *fundu* ('bottom', French *fond*), *pane* ('bread', Italian *pane*), *broko* ('break'), *hundu* ('dog', German *Hund*), *peshi* ('fish', Italian *pesce*), *ale* ('go', French *aller*), *montu* ('hill', French *mont*), *sabe* ('know', Spanish saber), *lota* ('many', English *a lot*), *pisi* ('piece'), *dodo* ('sleep', French *dodo*), *fema* ('woman', French *femme*), *kidi* ('young', English *kid*), etc. In other cases, the relations are slightly different: *kubu* (a metathesis of the English word *book*), *bruno* (a metathesis of to *burn*), *kopu* ('coffee', which recalls the English *cup*), *mayo* (*can*, says Bickerton, as in *to be able*: but it also evokes the term *may*, which has a meaning that is close to this), etc.

These evident sources do not matter, Bickerton would no doubt retort, since the guinea pigs selected were to be monolingual and, in particular, were not to have any knowledge of English. But is it imaginable that a Dutch person, a Basque, a Greek or a Finn would not know a single word of English? Is it thinkable that he might never have seen the word *beer* on a bottle, the word *mount* on a map, etc? All of this is, of course, devoid of interest, since the experiment never took place. But the absence of inventivity demonstrated here is significant. A computer could have been entrusted with the task of forging this vocabulary at random (the French car company Renault created the name of one of its models, the *Twingo*, this way), even if the programmer would doubtless have left his trace in the system. But the fact that Bickerton was influenced, in his lexical creations, by the languages he knows, leads us to surmise that the guinea pigs in turn would have been influenced by their languages or by one of them (the phenomena of charisma in particular might well have led to the language of one of the guinea pigs establishing itself more than the others, so that they all ended up communicating in some approximate form of Greek or Dutch, for instance). The human factor is here fundamental, and the four languages (or the four groups of speakers) could not remain in a relationship of equality for long. Above all, if they really had created a composite language, it would have been the result of a complex job of *bricolage*, performed on the basis of whatever had been introduced into the test tube of languages and individuals. *Bricolage* – in other words an improvised adaptation to the milieu, with structural approximations, regulation, etc. The fact that this simulation was not in fact envisaged in terms of computing is itself eloquent testimony: the aim was to verify the hypothesis of an innate grammar, and for that they of course needed human brains, for which no one has yet constructed a model. But man is not simply a brain, and the total absence of sociological considerations in this project leaves one perplexed. If I have discussed it, it was to emphasize the fact that the *ecology of languages*, their relations with their milieu, are something much more complex than Bickerton seems to have thought, and, once again, that methodology is rarely neutral: it impacts back on the image it gives us of the facts being studied. This fallout should be controllable, but the more numerous the factors in play, the more difficult this control becomes: languages are not well-oiled mechanisms independent of their environment.

Conclusions

I can thus summarize everything I have just said as follows. We consider languages as practices that are inscribed within a worldwide *gravitational* system, itself organized into *constellations* (see chapter 2), within which every language has its *niche*, defined by its relations with other languages and by its functions in the *milieu*. Every language (i.e. every set of practices, in a given social and historical context) possesses a *valency*, a capacity to populate a larger or smaller number of milieux and to transport itself into a given milieu (see chapter 5), a dominant *limiting factor* (the number of speakers) and secondary factors among which *representations* play a central role (see chapter 4). In its turn, the milieu acts on languages by stimuli to which languages respond in the mode of *regulation* (see chapter 3). This set of complex relations defines what I have called the *ecology of languages*, a framework in which I intend to operate. An ecological approach to the linguistic situations of the world thus implies that we take into account, vis-à-vis a given situation (whatever its size: from a small group of *Beurs* to the whole of the planet, via an island or an international organization), the relations between sets of practices and the effects on these practices of external stimuli.

These linguistic practices, or these practices > languages, are not considered here as organisms[51] but as populations, i.e. sets of variants (in the sense in which I defined this term in the introduction) which constitute the variable that I consider as a population. On this basis, just as the genetics of populations studies the aptitude for the reproduction and mutation of individuals of the same species cohabiting in the same geographical zone, I will be studying the transmission and change of 'languages' in their ecological niches.

— 2 —

The Galaxy of Languages

A large proportion of humanity is confronted, every day, by several languages and learns to speak some of them. A more limited proportion of this same humanity is confronted by choices of communication: which language to write a book in, or record a song, which language to make a film in or compose a tender for offers, etc. These choices, of course, are not gratuitous and rest first and foremost on the quest for efficiency. The Senegalese shopkeeper in Brazzaville, the capital of the Congo, who learns Munukutuba or Lingala does not choose, a priori, a language because it is 'beautiful', or 'pleasing', but because it is 'useful' and will enable him to carry out his job, i.e. he chooses a language spoken by his potential customers. The novelist from Martinique who decides to write in creole or French chooses in the first case to demonstrate his identity and in the second to reach a considerably wider public, just like the Swedish or German rock group who decide to record in English.

These choices, these strategies, cannot be explained by traditional linguistic typologies (genetic, structural, functional). One might imagine, in the light of genetic typologies, that the speaker of a Romance language would tend to acquire another Romance language, that it would be 'easier' for him than English or Chinese, just as one might imagine that the speaker of a Semitic language such as Hebrew would tend to acquire as a second language another Semitic language, such as Arabic, with comparable syntactic structures, but this is not what generally happens: these speakers, if they learn a language other than their own, will select from the linguistic environment, from the field of possibilities, the one which plays an interesting and useful role for them. And this 'selection' is relatively limited: human beings are not always able to choose their languages, their choice is determined first and foremost by the milieu in which they find themselves, by the languages that coexist in this niche and then by their needs, and very little by the typological situation of the coexisting languages.

In fact, these diverse typologies, all of which have their use and their function, have the drawback that they atomize the totality of the world's linguistic reality. How can this reality be presented in such a way that the relations between languages – between all languages – are respected? This is what I am going to attempt in this chapter, using a gravitational model initially developed from the suggestions of Abraam de Swaan,[1] which I will, as the reader will see, be modifying and fleshing out.

Constellations of languages

Starting out from the point of view of political sociology and political economy, de Swaan considers the set of the world's languages as a vast galaxy, and suggests that these languages are linked among themselves by bilingual speakers. In this galaxy, sub-groups are thus constituted by 'peripheral' languages that are not linked to each other but are all *linked by bilingual speakers* to a central language, a situation which can be represented as in diagram 2.1.

This quite simple diagram is to be interpreted as follows: the speakers of languages L2, L3, L4, etc., also usually speak language L1, and this confers on the latter a special place at the centre of this little

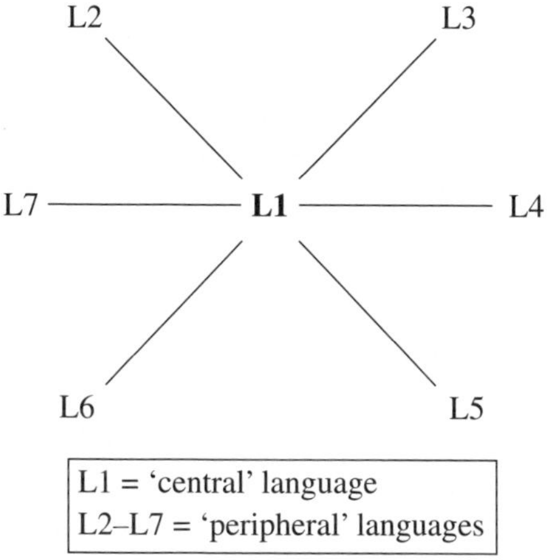

Diagram 2.1

'constellation'. Thus, in the former USSR, bilingual individuals usually had Russian in their repertory, and this language was thus the keystone of a constellation, just as Arabic, between Maghreb and Mashrek, is the keystone of another constellation, and French the keystone of a third constellation in part of Africa. I will restrict myself for the time being to this simple model, but things can be more complicated, in particular because, as we shall see, one and the same language can be present in two different constellations – central in one place and peripheral in another.

In this simple model, the link between the central language and the peripheral languages may be considered as a sort of gravitation, an attraction felt by the speakers of the peripheral languages towards the central language, and thus a tendency to bilingualism that is oriented towards the centre. In Morocco or Algeria, for instance, a person who is bilingual in Arabic and Berber has every likelihood of having Berber as a first language, and this pronounced tendency illustrates this attraction. Gravitation is generally defined as a phenomenon by which two bodies attract each other with a force proportional to the product of their mass and inversely proportional to the square of the distance between them. It is more or less the same for linguistic constellations: in certain peripheral points, one may see a lesser attraction towards the centre, or indeed a conflict of attraction, whereas the central languages (those whose 'mass' is significant) attract each other. In their turn, the central languages of these sub-groups may not be linked to each other (by bilingual speakers) but may all be linked to a super-central language, and the super-central languages may in their turn be linked in the same way to a hyper-central language, the keystone of the 'linguistic gravitational system'. We thus have a provisional four-level model:

Level 1 a hyper-central language
Level 2 ten or so super-central languages
Level 3 one to two hundred central languages
Level 4 four to five thousand peripheral languages

I propose to characterize bilingualism, which is thus the cement of this system, by two factors: its mode of acquisition and the direction in which this acquisition occurs. We need to distinguish between, on the one hand, the *programmed learning* of a language, that which happens at school, for instance, and, on the other hand, its *spontaneous learning*, or informal learning, which happens via social practice (learning 'on the job'). Furthermore, this learning may have as its object a language on the same level, as per our model, and I will call this a case of *horizontal bilingualism*, or else a language on a higher or lower level, and this I will call *vertical bilingualism.*

On level 1, we thus have a single language, currently English: those speakers for whom English is their first language show a distinct tendency towards monolingualism.

On level 2, we have ten or so languages (Arabic, Russian, Swahili, French, Hindi, Malay, Spanish, Portuguese, Chinese): people who have one of these languages as their first language show a tendency either to monolingualism or to bilingualism with a language on the same level (horizontal bilingualism) or with that of level 1 (vertical bilingualism). These languages are, of course, among the most widely spoken in the world, but the high number of speakers is not enough to confer the status of super-central language on them: German and Japanese, for instance, which both have over a hundred million speakers, do not fulfil this role.

On level 3, we have 100 or so languages (Wolof, Bambara in Africa, Quechua in South America, Czech, Armenian in eastern Europe, etc.): the speakers of these languages show a tendency to bilingualism with a language of level 2 (vertical bilingualism).

On level 4, we have languages whose speakers show a tendency to horizontal and vertical plurilingualism.

What we have here are tendencies and not laws, tendencies that are confirmed by numerous empirical studies. But we have to emphasize that in vertical bilingualism there is a general tendency towards the acquisition of a language from an immediately higher level. Thus, to take a Senegalese example, a speaker of a level 4 language (Serere or Diola) first acquires the level 3 language of its constellation (Wolof) and then the level 2 language (French) and in some cases, finally, the hyper-central language (English). We thus have four cases, shown in the matrix.

	Spontaneous acquisition	Programmed acquisition
Of a language on the same level	1	2
Of a language from a higher level	3	4

To take each cell in turn:

1 This is the case, for instance, of a Diola from Casamance who acquires Manjak, or of a Dogon from Mali who acquires Fulani.
2 This is the case of a French schoolchild who is studying Spanish.
3 This is the case of the Diola from Casamance who acquires Wolof, or of the Dogon from Mali who acquires Bambara or French 'on the job'.
4 This is the case of a French schoolchild who is studying English, or of the same Diola from Casamance who is learning French at school.

In other words, we have on a first level a certain number of linguistic constellations which gravitate around the hyper-central language (English) (see diagram 2.2).

In each of the constellations, other languages gravitate around the super-central language (for example, French) (see diagram 2.3).

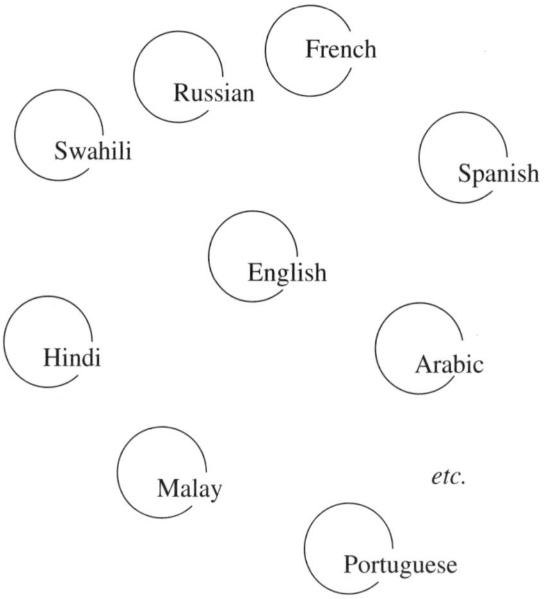

Diagram 2.2

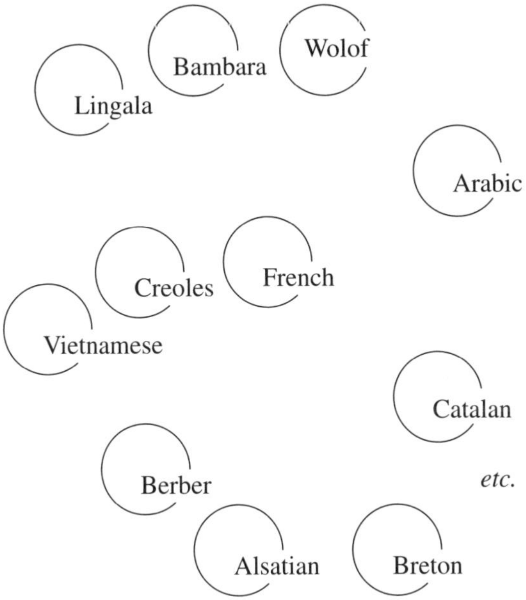

Diagram 2.3

Finally, certain of these languages are in their turn the centre of a constellation: we will later on be looking at a concrete example, that of the 'Bambara constellation'.

That leaves the problem of the dynamics of this system (in the sense in which we speak of a solar system): how do the relations between languages and between groups evolve? Demography, of course, plays an important role here, as do conquests, the expansion of religions and conversions, trade, etc. But, just as the saying goes, 'to everyone that hath shall be given', there is an internal dynamic which means that the more value a language has, the more it acquires. Language, as I said earlier, is at once a collective product and a collective property: no individual can create it or maintain it alone, no individual alone can prevent its creation or suppress it. And this collective property partly defines its value: the more users a language has, the more it increases in value. But this is not the only engine of change, and we shall see for instance, in chapter 4, how evolution is perceptible in the transmission of languages and situations, and, in chapter 5, the role that representations play in this evolution.

The galactic model and linguistic policy: the example of the European Community

This gravitational model also enables us to tackle the possibilities of intervening *in vitro* on linguistic situations – linguistic policies, as they are called. The types of link that exist between the languages of one and the same constellation are such that it is difficult to imagine that an intervention on a peripheral language can change anything at all in its relations with the central language: no action on Breton, for instance, can change the central situation of French. On the other hand, if linguistic policies are unable to act separately on peripheral levels, we can ask whether a *collective* international linguistic policy, bearing on a language that is less widely spoken than that of a dominant language, can modify the system: for example whether a language such as Fulani, peripheral in several different constellations, can benefit from an action across constellations.

A good example of these problems of linguistic policies, re-examined in the light of the gravitational model, is that of Europe. The basic principle of the linguistic policy of the European Parliament is that all the national languages of the member states are *ipso facto* working languages, which in the state of things in the 1990s gave us eleven languages (this figure was, of course, revised upwards as other countries came to participate in the European Union), in other words more than twice what was the case at the UN or UNESCO (six languages). Among these eleven languages we had:

- a hyper-central language: English
- super-central languages: French, Spanish, Portuguese
- central or peripheral languages: Italian, Greek, Dutch, Danish, Swedish, German, Finnish

The logic of our model would thus mean that those whose first language is English should be monolingual, that those of French, Spanish and Portuguese mother tongue should either be monolingual or should have acquired one of the two other languages and/or English, and that speakers of Italian, Greek, Dutch, Danish, Swedish or German should first of all acquire one of these three languages (French, Spanish, Portuguese) before acquiring English.

We do not have any precise studies on European multilingualism that would enable us to verify whether this is really the case, but a few selective surveys can give us a certain amount of information. Thus, a questionnaire survey on around 5,000 civil servants of the European Commission[2] shows that three languages are essentially used in internal communication:

- For oral communication, French (62%), English (31%) and German (6%)
- For written communication, French (64%), English (35%) and German (1%)

The predominance of French, which may come as something of a surprise, can be explained by the fact that Great Britain joined the European Community very late, so that French had time to establish its status without competition – and we also find here, at the same time, an illustration of the fact that latecomers tend to adopt what is already in place. But this situation cannot last.[3] Thus, at the beginning of 1996, 171 MEPs were taking private lessons, the languages studied being, in order of frequency, English, French and German.

The projection of the worldwide gravitational system onto Europe makes it a place of intersection and conflicts between different constellations which extend far beyond it. Thus the 'Spanish constellation' draws strength in particular from Latin America, the 'French constellation' in particular from Africa; Swedish and Danish belong to the 'English constellation'; and German is caught between two constellations, French and English, with a greater attraction towards the second.

This plurilingualism of the European institutions does of course raise problems: translation represents more than 3 per cent of the Parliament's total budget; translation booths occupy about 45 per cent of the space of assembly rooms; there are not enough competent translators for all the language combinations; and to translate from Dutch to Greek, for instance, it is sometimes necessary to pass by one or even two intermediary languages, etc. There are two possible solutions: reducing the number of working languages (in December 1994 the French Minister, Alain Lamassoure, suggested limiting them to five: English, French, German, Italian and Spanish) or adopting a 'neutral' language such as Esperanto. Beyond these suggestions, there is another possibility, which I have baptized 'planning by default':[4] this consists in doing nothing, or in adopting a laissez-faire attitude, which seems to be the present trend and which can only lead, sooner or later, to reinforcing the *de facto* status of English.

What solution can our model suggest? We are here at the intersection of an abstract model (the gravitational model) and a concrete reality (the European territory). From the first point of view, we find that the fields of gravitation interfere with one another: Italian and Greek, for instance, have a (strong) link with English and a (weaker) link with French; Swedish and Danish have a (strong) link with English and a (weaker) link with German, etc. From the second point of view, these languages also have geographic links and shared frontiers: French for instance is in contact with German in the east, Spanish in the south-west, and Italian in the south-east; Spanish is in contact with Portuguese and French; Italian with French, German, Greek and Slovene, etc. One can thus imagine a linguistic policy that plays on the border links that occur at the intersection of constellations. It is, for instance, by systematically privileging Italian in the schools of the south-east of France, Spanish or Catalan in the south-west, German in the east and Dutch in the north, *before* moving on to English – i.e. by *having an impact on the bilingual speakers who hold it all together* – that we can hope to have any impact on the system. After all, I stated earlier that languages were linked by bilingual speakers, and that learning languages was an activity that could be either *programmed* or *spontaneous*. Now, if it is by definition impossible to act directly on spontaneous learning, it is altogether possible to act on spontaneous learning, via educational policies that are obviously in the remit of the state. But these educational policies are also influenced by representations, in particular those of pupils' parents. If the French, Italian, Spanish (etc.) states privilege the learning of English in their schools, this is also because parents do not understand how it could be any other way. Action on the linguistic gravitational system, or on one of its constellations, thus happens via an action taken on their different constituents, not just languages but also systems of bilingualism and linguistic representations. It is on this condition that a linguistic policy can be developed in an effective manner and, in particular, that the European Community will be able to move from planning by default to planning in an effective and deliberate way.

The Hindi constellation

In an analysis of the contact situations between the languages of India Grant McConnell starts out from a distinction between 'majority languages' and 'minority languages', and this enables him to define three types of contact situation by reference to the geographical limits of the states that constitute the federation:

- a type that has no single pole, with several minority languages but no majority language;
- a unipolar type, with several minority languages and one single majority language;
- a multipolar type, with several minority languages and at least two majority languages.[5]

McConnell goes on to define three characteristics of languages: the attraction that languages experience towards a given language (linked to the percentage of bilingual speakers of these languages in the language under consideration); the demographic weight of a language (linked to the number of mother-tongue speakers); and the dependency of a language (linked to the number of speakers of this language who are bilingual).

By combining these three types with these three characteristics, he finds that in the unipolar or multipolar types, the attraction is 'almost exclusively associated with the linguistic poles, whereas in the types without a pole, languages all have the possibility of attracting each other mutually', that 'the poles have a less significant weight' and that 'minority languages are rather dependent on the poles, whereas in the type without a pole languages ought to have different levels of dependency'.[6]

This enables him to represent the relations between languages, state by state, taking these three factors into account, which for the states that are in a unipolar situation gives us the table shown.

We thus see that in the state of Bihar, for instance, where Hindi is the pole language, 70 per cent of Tamil speakers also speak Hindi, while only 2 per cent of Hindi speakers speak another language. We also see that the pole language is systematically the least dependent and the one which has the greatest weight and (with the exception of Manipur) the most attraction.

Table 2.1

State	Pole	Language with most attraction	Language with most weight	Most dependent language	Least dependent language	Pole attracted towards
Bihar	Hindi	Hindi	Hindi	Tamil 70%[a]	Hindi 2%[a]	Sanskrit 52%[b]
Himachal Pradesh	Hindi	Hindi	Hindi	Sindhi 87%	Hindi 10%	English 73%
Haryana	Hindi	Hindi	Hindi	Punjabi 37%	Hindi 7%	Punjabi 48%
Kerala	Malayalam	Hindi	Malayalam	Bengali 75%	Malayalam 18%	Hindi 92%
Madhya Pradesh	Hindi	Hindi	Hindi	Punjabi 66%	Hindi 3%	Sanskrit 67%
Manipur	Manipuri	Hindi–English	Manipuri	Assamese 77%	Manipuri 19%	English 71%
Rajasthan	Hindi	Hindi	Hindi	Malayalam 74%	Hindi 2%	Sanskrit 33%
Tripura	Bengali	Bengali	Bengali	Sanskrit 93%	Bengali 10%	English 91%
Uttar Pradesh	Hindi	Hindi	Hindi	Marathi 57%	Hindi 2%	Sanskrit 76%

[a] Percentage of bilingual speakers.
[c] Percentage of bilingual speakers with this as their second language.

Source: Adapted from Grant McConnell, 'Analyses et comparaisons des situations de contact en Inde'.

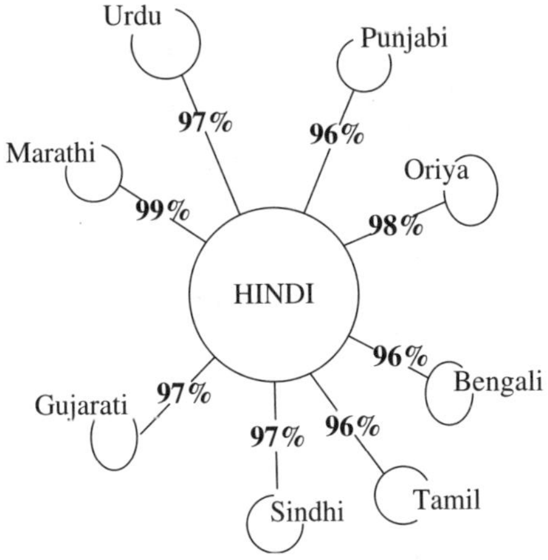

Diagram 2.4 The Hindi galaxy in Uttar Pradesh (in bold, the percentage of bilinguals in peripheral language/Hindi)
Source: Adapted from Grant McConnell, 'Analyses et comparaisons des situations de contact en Inde'.

Now, this description of linguistic situations is a perfect illustration of our gravitational model. Consider, for example, the state of Uttar Pradesh, which, following McConnell, can be presented in the form shown in diagram 2.4.[7]

We see that around the central language, Hindi, there gravitate eight peripheral languages, whose speakers are almost 100 per cent bilingual, whereas, on the other hand, Hindi speakers speak only Urdu (16 per cent) and Sanskrit (76 per cent – this language does not appear in the diagram as it is not a first language). But from the earlier table we also see that one of them, Bengali, is in turn a central language in the state of Tripura, and that we have here, as in our model, an embedding of constellations of languages. This is even more evident if we consider the situation of a state considered by McConnell to be 'multipolar', that of Andrah Pradesh (see diagram 2.5).

We see that two central languages (Hindi and Telugu) share a certain number of peripheral languages (Gujarati, Malayalam, Marathi) and have their own peripheral languages, whereas their speakers are generally bilingual (95 per cent of Hindi speakers speak Telugu, 80 per cent of Telugu speakers speak Hindi). So here we have, as in the case of the European Community, an intersection and conflict between

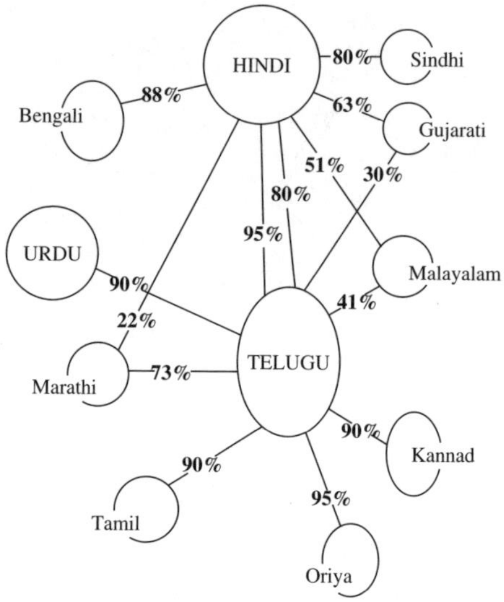

Diagram 2.5 Languages in Andrah Pradesh
Source: Adapted from Grant McConnell, 'Analyses et comparaisons des situations de contact en Inde'.

different constellations – of which either Hindi or Telugu is the central language – with, for instance, a greater attraction of Gujarati towards Hindi and of Marathi towards Telugu.

In other words, McConnell's geographical and statistical approach produces the same type of result as the gravitational approach that I have been developing on the basis of the work of Abraam de Swaan, which it thus both illustrates and confirms.

The Bambara constellation

Bambara, a Mandingo language that is spoken in Mali as the first language of part of the population and the vehicular language of the whole of the south of the country, is one of ten national languages but statistically the most significant. I would here like to analyse its relations with the other coexisting languages, starting out from a number of recent empirical studies.

Let us consider, to begin with, a work published in 1994 which sets itself the task of describing communicative strategies in Mali.[8] In fact, the title (*Stratégies communicatives au Mali*) is deceptive, as part of the territory is not covered by the studies brought together here – a fact to which I shall return. But this work, to which I will add two more (Barry, 'Étude du plurilinguisme au Mali' and Calvet, 'Les langues des marchés en Afrique'), nonetheless enables us to test out our model by presenting a constellation of which Bambara is the central language.

The region of Koutiala

Situated south-east of Bamako, not far from the border with Burkina Faso, this region – in which the first language of the majority of speakers is Minyanka (from the northern branch of Senufo, one of the country's ten 'official' languages) – is the site of a significant coexistence of other languages: different Malian languages, Bambara, French and Arabic.[9]

According to the survey I am using (carried out on a school-age public), there are in Koutiala fourteen first languages including some (Minyanka, Bambara, Fulani, Bobo, French, etc.) that are also second languages.

We see from the table that there are languages which are not shared, i.e. those which are only first languages, such as Bozo and Samogo, and others which are not significantly shared, such as Khassonke, More, Sarakole or Malinke; and the presentation I have adopted, placing the proportion who use these languages as a vehicular language in decreasing percentages, shows that the hierarchy here demonstrated cannot really be analysed in accordance with the levels suggested by Swaan. If French, here the most widely used vehicular language, is a level 2 language, and if Bambara is indeed a level 3 language, then Minyanka, Fulani or Bobo (which have a certain percentage as vehicular languages) should be classified in the set of 'peripheral' or level 4 languages in the same way as Bozo or Samogo, which do not rate as vehicular languages at all.

The Khassonke country

As in the preceding case, we here have a survey of school-age children which was carried out in Kayes, to the north-west of the capital, near the border with Senegal.[10] Generally speaking, the following table

Table 2.2

	1st language	2nd or 3rd language	Total	Proportion using it as a vehicular language, in %[a]
French	2	246	248	86.70
Bambara	188	82	270	28.67
Fulani	7	16	23	5.59
Minyanka	55	15	70	5.25
Bobo	5	11	16	3.85
Senufo	10	9	19	3.15
Songhay	6	9	15	3.15
Dogon	–	3	3	1.05
Malinke	6	3	9	1.05
Sarakole	1	2	3	0.70
More	–	2	2	0.70
Khassonke	2	2	2	0.70
Bozo	1	0	1	–
Samogo	2	0	2	–

[a] Calculated by Dombrowsky as the relation between the number of second- or third-language speakers and the total number of those questioned. So what we have here is not the rate of vehicular language, but the percentage of those questioned having a given language as their second or third language.

Source: Klaudia Dombrowsky, 'La situation socio-linguistique du sud du Mali'.

shows that 69.93 per cent of the population surveyed have Bambara as their first language; 30 per cent of this same population show bilingualism (Bambara as well as their own other African language) and 100 per cent show either trilingualism (Bambara plus one other African language plus French) or a bilingualism in Bambara plus French.

As in the preceding case, the hierarchy of vehicular languages here means that it is difficult to classify in the same 'peripheral' group languages such as Khassonke or Soninke and others such as More or Diakhanke. Furthermore, the presence here of Wolof, a vehicular language with a percentage rate of 7.69 per cent, raises another problem, that of its proximity to another constellation in which the functions of languages are inverted: on the other side of the border, Wolof is the central language and Bambara a peripheral language.

Table 2.3

	1st language	2nd or 3rd language	Total	Proportion using it as a vehicular language, in %
French	–	143	143	100.00
Bambara	100	43	143	30.06
Khassonke	12	36	48	25.17
Soninke	3	31	34	21.67
Fulani	10	26	36	18.18
Malinke	13	14	27	9.79
Wolof	–	11	11	7.69
Songhay	1	7	8	4.89
Bore	2	2	4	1.39
Minyanka	2	1	3	0.69
More	–	1	1	0.69
Diakhanke	–	1	1	0.69

Source: Valentin Vydrine, 'Études sociolinguistique en pays Khassonké'.

The Djenne region

Situated to the east of Bamako, not far from Mopti, the city of Djenne presents a complex linguistic situation.[11] Here again, different languages coexist: Bambara, Fulani, Bozo, Dogon and a form of Songhay called Koyra Ciini, or, in Bambara, Jenekakan ('language of Djene'); in Fulani, Jeneenkoore; and in Songhay, Jene.

These three surveys have certain characteristics in common. First, there is the existence of a dominant local language, Minyanka in Koutiala, Khassonke in Kayes and Koyra Ciini in Djenne, and the presence everywhere of Fulani as a vehicular language, which goes against many preconceptions.

Second, there is the fact that these three places, and indeed the region of Kita which I will be mentioning later on, are in the zone of influence of Bambara: it is not Mali that we are dealing with, despite the title of the 1994 work by Dumestre, but the 'Bambarized' Mali, or the Mali which is gradually being 'Bambarized'. We are here in the south of the country, and nothing is said about the situation in Gao or Timbuktu, and even less about the situation in the Great North, the territories of the Tamasheq. Surveys carried out in the markets of

Table 2.4

	1st language	2nd or 3rd language	Total	Proportion using it as a vehicular language, in %
Bambara	51	103	154	66.8
Koyra	53	78	131	50.6
Fulani	39	48	87	31.1
Dogon	6	1	7	0.6
Bozo	4	10	14	6.4
Soninke	1	2	3	1.2

Bamako, Mopti and Gao[12] show, for instance, that the further east one goes, the less Bambara is spoken: 78 per cent of the interactions in Bambara were observed in the markets of Bamako, 46 per cent in the markets of Mopti and 9 per cent in the market of Gao, whereas, in comparison, Songhay passes from 2 per cent in Bamako to 13 per cent in Mopti and 77 per cent in Gao. This is why we have to view with great caution the claims made by Dumestre that 'Bambara is no longer an ethnic language but a neutral and unmarked language', that its expansion is evidence of the emergence of a 'Malian ethnic identity' and, finally, that there are no inter-communal tensions in Mali.[13] A survey carried out in the north would certainly produce quite different results.

Furthermore, being based on Bambara, the studies of Vydrine and Dombrowsky tell us nothing about the micro-constellations of which Minyanka or Fulani in Koutiala, and Khassonke or Fulani in Kayes, are the centre. It is just as if the researchers had pre-empted the great sociolinguistic movements by focusing on the dominant Malian language, and the precision of the descriptions bears witness to this. The very subtitle of the work I am drawing on is indeed perfect witness to this bias: 'Langues régionales, bambara, français' ['Regional languages, Bambara, French'], whereas a year previously the very same Dumestre had published with Cécile Canut a study entitled 'Français, Bambara et langues nationales au Mali' ['French, Bambara and national languages in Mali']. In the second case, Bambara was viewed as being on the same level as the other languages ('national' languages), which is *de jure* the case, whereas in the first title these languages are relegated to the rank of 'regional' languages, Bambara thus having a special status, between 'regional' languages and French, which is *de facto* the case. But this move from what is in principle correct to what is in fact the case – this variation in the stratification of languages – is not made explicit, and we have the impression that there is a certain absence of neutrality.

However this may be, Koutiala, Kayes and Djenne, by reason of their geographically specific situations (south-east, north-west, east) and their linguistic situations (Songhay, Khassonke, Minyanka) provide clear evidence of both the variety of linguistic situations and the unifying role played by Bambara. We are here in the 'Bambara constellation', a constellation which, moreover, does not necessarily correspond to the borders of the country, though its centre is situated in the capital, Bamako. The following table summarizes, for these three places, the percentage rate at which the principal languages operate as vehicular languages, i.e. the percentage of bilingual speakers.

Between Koutiala and Kayes, there are languages that are not directly related to one another: Senufo, present in Koutiala, is not spoken in Kayes, while Khassonke, significant in Kayes, is practically not spoken in Koutiala, etc. And the gravitational model is altogether relevant in attempting to explain this situation, so long as we remember that we have to increase the number of levels, that there is a 'level 5' in which languages that are peripheral with regard to Bambara can, in turn, be central.

Furthermore, the case of Kayes, with the sudden appearance in the system of a language from elsewhere – Wolof – shows us that every constellation has zones of instability at its edges, and that its power of attraction is variable: Bambara is at the centre of one constellation,

Table 2.5 Percentage rate of use as vehicular language

KOUTIALA	Bambara 28%	KAYES	Bambara 30%
	Fulani 5%		Khassonke 25%
	Minyanka 5%		Soninke 21%
	etc.		Fulani 18%
	DJENNE	Bambara 66%	
		Koyra 50%	
		Fulani 31%	
		etc.	

Wolof at the centre of a neighbouring constellation, and their status varies in two respects:

- Horizontally, the central language of one constellation is becoming the peripheral language of a neighbouring constellation.
- Vertically, the central language of one constellation is becoming the peripheral language of a higher-level constellation, a situation described in the following diagram:

French

Bambara			**Wolof**	
Minyanka	**Khassonke**	**Songhay**	Jola	**Khassonke** etc.
Fulani	**Fulani**	**Fulani**	Manjak	**Bambara**
Bobo	**Wolof**	Dojon	**Fulani**	**Fulani**
Songhay	Bobo		(Casamance)	(river region)
	Bozo			
(Koutiala)	(Kayes)	(Djenne)		

Sketch of the Bambara constellation and the Wolof constellation (in bold, the languages which appear in both systems or sub-systems).

The galaxy of writing systems

The systems of language transcription – writing systems – may not be as numerous as the languages themselves, but they can be counted in their hundreds. It is not my intent here to describe their history or typology, but to test out my gravitational model on them.

Writing was born at least three times over, independently, in three different parts of the world: in Mesopotamia (cuneiform scripts), China (Chinese characters) and the Yucatan (Mayan glyphs). The languages transcribed in these ways – those of the Sumerians, the Chinese and the Maya – were in no way akin, but they had at least one point in common: the words in them were essentially monosyllabic. And this characteristic is perhaps not unlinked to the appearance of graphic systems which, although extremely different, had in common the fact that they transcribed syllables. The Mayan graphic system is no longer in use; the Chinese system is still being used and has been borrowed and adapted several times (to transcribe Korean, Vietnamese and Japanese); as for the Mesopotamian system, it has slowly evolved to give birth to the set of alphabets of the western world. If, then, there are on the surface of the planet several hundred different alphabets, they all have the same origin: the alphabet was invented once and once only.

We could in consequence present this set of graphic systems 'genetically', bringing out the family connections: starting from a proto-Sinaic origin, three lines of descent (which I have suggested baptizing 'Greek', 'Indian' and 'Arabic') have led, via a series of successive transformations and adaptations, to all the alphabets in the world.[14] But my purpose at present is different: in order to present the relations between these different systems, I will be claiming that, just as languages are linked together by bilingual speakers, writing systems are linked together by 'digraphic' writers, i.e. that there are, pretty much across the whole world, individuals capable of reading and using two or more than two writing systems. Thus, in Arabic countries, part of the population can read both the Arabic alphabet and the Latin alphabet; a proportion of Russian speakers, who read the Cyrillic alphabet, also know the Latin alphabet; cultivated Japanese know both the kanas, of course, and also a certain number of Chinese characters (kanji) used to write their language and enabling them thus to decipher a simple text in Chinese, as well as the Latin alphabet; the Greeks, who use the Greek alphabet, practically all know, in addition, the Latin alphabet, etc.

The coexistence in a single person or in a single place of two or more writing systems may correspond to the coexistence of two or more languages. We saw in the previous chapter how, in the Maghreb, the Arabic alphabet is used to transcribe the Arabic language and sometimes Berber, whereas the Latin alphabet is used to transcribe French and sometimes Berber, and the Tifinaghs transcribe Berber; or how in Israel the Hebrew and Latin alphabets transcribe, respectively, Hebrew and English or other foreign languages. But different graphic systems can also correspond to a single language. Thus Chinese, which is written in characters, can also be transcribed thanks to a system of romanization, pinyin; whereas a language such as Berber can, as we have just seen, be written in three languages, the Tifinaghs, the Arabic alphabet and the Latin alphabet; and certain languages, such as Swahili and Malay, have been successively transcribed into Arabic and then Latin characters.

In this set of graphic systems, one alphabet is dominant: just as, in the gravitational system of languages, English is at the centre of a set of

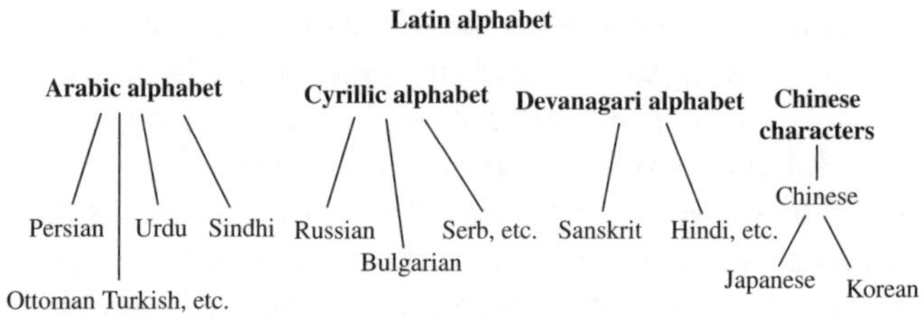

Diagram 2.6

constellations which themselves are constituted by peripheral languages gravitating around a central language, so likewise the Latin alphabet is at the centre of the galaxy of writing systems, linked to other alphabets or to other graphic systems by digraphic writers (see diagram 2.6).

We thus have a hyper-central system (the Latin alphabet), central systems (the Arabic, Cyrillic and Devanagari alphabets and Chinese characters) and peripheral systems, adapted from the previous ones, as users of the peripheral systems have a tendency to bigraphism and trigraphism (a peripheral system, a central system and the Latin alphabet) whereas the users of central systems have a tendency to bigraphism (their system plus the Latin alphabet); only the users of the Latin alphabet have a tendency to monographism.

But the central writing system, the Latin alphabet, is a variable semiology, in which the relations between sound and grapheme sometimes change. In other words, one can use the same alphabet to transcribe different languages with, on each occasion, different correspondences between sounds and letters: the series *ch* for instance is not pronounced the same way in French, Spanish and German, the *u* is not pronounced the same way in Italian and French, etc. But what we have here is a general characteristic of writing systems: the Arabic alphabet is modified in order to transcribe Persian, and the Chinese characters used to transcribe Japanese (the kanji) are not pronounced the way they are in Chinese, etc.[15]

Here I want to emphasize a striking parallel between the two systems: the hyper-central language, English, is transcribed with the help of the hyper-central system, the Latin alphabet, and the four central systems are used to transcribe at least one super-central language: Devanagari transcribes Hindi, the Arabic alphabet transcribes Arabic, the Cyrillic alphabet transcribes Russian, and Chinese characters transcribe Chinese. But the Latin alphabet remains clearly dominant, to such an extent that one can wonder whether the use of another graphic system does not constitute a brake on the expansion of languages. The presence of languages on the Internet, for instance (more than 90% English at the time of writing, with French, German and Spanish comprising most of the rest) is, of course, a by-product of the system of languages but also, to a lesser extent, of the set of writing systems. Indeed, it is worth noting that the super-central languages which are transcribed by another system than the Latin alphabet encounter several difficulties on the information 'highways' and, more generally, when it comes to their use in IT. This stems, of course, from the fact that the Internet was first conceived for English – hence, for example, the problems that had to be resolved for the accents on French vowels – but this 'imperialism' in the domain of IT is only one of the effects of the gravitational organization of the relations between languages and between writing systems.

The gravitation of writing systems is, like the gravitation of languages, a product of history, a moment in evolution, and it is altogether plausible to imagine that it too evolves. Thus, at the end of the fourth millennium BCE, the language of the south of Mesopotamia, Sumerian, and its graphic system, cuneiform, underwent a significant expansion, one that at the time was no doubt considered durable. Cuneiform writing was adapted to transcribe Akkadian, which then appeared in two dialect forms, Assyrian in the north and Babylonian in the south. It was Babylonian which was to become, around 1500 BCE, the region's vehicular language, whereas Sumerian, which was no longer spoken, remained the language of written culture: all scribes were bilingual in Sumerian and Akkadian. Thus, in 1269 BCE, the treaty of Kadesh (signed between the Hittite King Hattusilis and the Pharaoh Rameses II) was composed in Akkadian, the major language of that area in that period. Everyone abandoned his or her language (Hittite, Ancient Egyptian) and writing system (Hittite and Egyptian both had their own systems) in favour of the hyper-central language of this ecolinguistic niche at the time in question: Akkadian.

After the Aramaean invasion of the end of the second millennium, Aramaic replaced Akkadian as vehicular language, but Akkadian and Sumerian continued to be used in written texts. Then, with the conquest of Alexandria, it was Greek which became the most widespread language. In three millennia, there was thus a shift from the dominance of Sumerian to that of Akkadian, which disappeared in favour of Aramaic, which itself was replaced by Greek as the dominant language in the region; at the same time, the dominant writing systems were changing. And these two constellations continued to evolve: Latin replaced Greek, then was replaced by French and finally by English in the centre of the constellation of languages; and the Latin alphabet replaced the Greek alphabet at the centre of the constellation of writing systems. It is thus quite possible to imagine that the current situation will also evolve, both as regards languages and as regards graphic systems.

Conclusions

The first model that we used, or the first metaphor, thus enables us to represent the worldwide organization of languages in a rigorous hierarchy, held together by bilingual speakers. But this hierarchy is, at each point, prone to variation, to modification, even, indeed, to complete transformation: the gravitational system of languages is affected by history through and through, as are languages themselves, and just like these languages the system also undergoes local adaptations. Thus political events in Rwanda or Zaire in the 1990s show us that, in tandem with a civil war or a regime change, there sometimes occurs a linguistic change not all of whose effects we are so far in a position to gauge, a movement swinging from French to English, or, on a more local level, from Lingala to Swahili. (I will come back to this case in chapter 5.)

In the rest of this book I will study the factors for change which are working away at this system, and examine how a given linguistic ecology can evolve or be completely transformed. To begin with I am going to use my next chapter to focus on the regulation of linguistic systems, this time using a different model – the homeostatic model.

— 3 —

Regulation and Change: The Homeostatic Model

I have already in another work[1] presented the benefits of the cybernetic approach for the analysis of linguistic systems. When Norbert Wiener published his work on cybernetic systems in 1948,[2] his aim was to explain all phenomena which brought into play the treatment of information. For him, automatized mechanisms and living organisms had in common that they functioned like homeostats in the mode of self-regulation: the system receives information from outside and retroactively responds to those stimuli. In this way, a homeostat thus has the function of keeping things (body temperature, for example) as they were. In fact, since then, cybernetics has broadened its scope: it is no longer concerned merely with studying control and communication in animals and machines, but with the whole set of systems from the point of view of control and communication. In this sense, society can be considered as the object of study of cybernetics. The homeostat is no longer merely a system of conservation, it is no longer immune from conflict and change, and the *homeostatic model*, or *self-regulatory* model, implies a process of response to external stimuli – a response which may generate change: *regulation is a reaction to an external stimulus by an inner change which tends to neutralize the effects of this stimulus*. In this way, a linguistic constellation, as I defined it in the last chapter, is not something that is given once and for all; it is adapted and modified in response to the communicational demand, and it may lead to the disappearance of certain peripheral languages, or to the changing of the central language. Transposed into the linguistic domain, this model thus implies that a distinction is drawn between *the linguistic needs of society* and the *social functions of language*, and that the opposition between languages and society functions as a homeostat, a self-regulated system.

The notion of the *linguistic needs of society* is not new; it appears in a 1929 work by Henri Frei. In this, he wrote: ‘Society acts on language mainly by the way it determines the relative proportion of linguistic needs – from one language, social class or period to another'.[3] This notion thus implies that language is the response to a social need; formulated in this way, the idea is too general to be really worth discussing. But Frei went further, suggesting that the central factor was the extent (both geographical and social) to which a language was used. His point of view was simple: he distinguished between 'languages of small communication' and 'languages of great communication'. The first, used by small groups (he mentioned 'inferior, savage societies', professional milieux, sects, etc.), fulfil a function that I have labelled *mass*, as in *mass languages,* and Frei emphasizes 'the enormous role played by the need for differentiation and conformism: the swarming of lexical differences, the scarcity of generic terms, the plethora and complication of grammatical categories, etc.' The second, used much more widely (Frei said they were 'used by civilizations which are characterized by the force of their interrelations') tend towards a function that I have called *vehicular* and, in Frei's words, they are characterized by 'a very strong tendency to economy (brevity and invariability)'.

The opposition between mass and vehicular is both functional and formal, it initially defines the social functions of languages but at the same time implies that function retroacts on form. From our – ecological – point of view, these phenomena are explicable in terms of adaptation to the environment. As everyone knows, species which occupy the same or a similar environment show a tendency to morphological convergence. For instance, in cold climates, heat loss through the skin is proportionally greater in small animals than in larger ones, which makes homeothermia (the maintenance of a constant inner temperature) easier for the latter. Thus, polar animals are big in size, and palaeontology shows us that during the ice ages, the animals which resisted longest were the large ones.

What does 'adaptation' mean in linguistics? Our problem can be formulated in the following terms: what are the effects of a given ecology on a language when the latter is introduced into a new environment? Let me add a related question: what are the effects of introducing this language on the other languages present in that environment? Of course, climates here have no role to play; the environment of a language is constituted by social organization, the size of groups of speakers, the functions of languages, the social role of their speakers, the degree to which they are multilingual, etc. – factors which may have an influence on the form of languages.

One example of the influence of environment on the form of languages is provided by the various types of AIPE – American Indian Pidgin English. Emanuel Drechsel has compared three of them: 'Mobilian jargon' in the south-east USA (the Mississippi Valley), Chinook in the north-west and Delaware in the north-east. In all three cases, between the eighteenth century and the beginning of the twentieth, we have vehicular forms of different languages used by Indians for communication among themselves and with Europeans: given the geographical distance between them, they have no genetic relations. In each case, their phonology, their syntax and their lexicon are consequently very different – influenced by local Indian languages which are also very different. But Drechsel, without denying this fact, simultaneously underlines that there are striking convergences between Mobilian, Chinook and Delaware, both on the linguistic and on the extra-linguistic level. Among the linguistic convergences he points out, the most important for my purposes are:

- a mixed vocabulary, derived essentially from the different Indian languages with a small number of borrowings from European or non-American languages, used to name cultural borrowings;
- a syntax based on a fixed order to mark out the functions of words, with few inflections and few morphosyntactic redundancies;
- traces characteristic of the languages indigenous to the area under consideration when it comes to word order, without any apparent influence from the languages of post-Columbian migrants;
- simple sentences, with some traces of subordination and complex constructions;
- a clear influence of the primary languages on lexical and phonological variation.

And, among extra-linguistic convergences:

- the presence of a language of gesture, at least in the case of Chinook and Mobilian – something which is rarely found in the primary languages;
- the use of these vehicular languages in inter-tribal contacts, for commerce, political alliances and relations with Europeans;

- the use of these vehicular languages for needs that go beyond mere communication: narration, poetic forms of expression, etc.;
- the coexistence of these forms with other means of communication: the bilingualism or plurilingualism of speakers in local languages, the use of interpreters or the use of European languages for relations with migrants;
- numerous signs which tend to prove that these vehicular forms have a pre-European origin.[4]

The geographical distance between these three forms and the typological differences between the languages found in the three areas mean – to repeat my point – that we cannot interpret these convergences by resorting to the influence of local languages. 'The source languages for these pidgins were historically and structurally too divergent to produce similar linguistic compromises simply by chance.'[5] So we are left with nothing other than ecolinguistic conditions. Drechsel emphasizes for instance that we have, in all three cases, coastal situations (the Gulf of Mexico for Mobilian, the Pacific for Chinook, the Atlantic for Delaware), which suggest contacts with overseas peoples, and it can be supposed that the convergence of functions and environments has led to a formal convergence. That would also explain why the different creoles in the world present a certain number of points in common in their syntactic structures. There is no need at all to understand these convergences by postulating a common African origin, which historical studies in any case do not always enable us to demonstrate, since creoles share historical conditions of emergence, functions and usages which explain these resemblances at least as well as their genealogy. In other words, the ecological situation (the environment, the functions) selects certain developmental possibilities from among the set of possibilities that are all present. But the fact remains that certain forms of French creole also appear in working-class forms of French, and we thus simultaneously need to explain the *internal regulation of the language* and the *social regulation of linguistic situations*.

Let us take a quite simple example. I often ask my students to *invent a French verb*, i.e. to produce a verb which does not exist in the language but is acceptable within it. The result is always the same: their imagination applies itself to finding an original root, the name of a person, a friend or a teacher, that of an action which has not created any verb, etc. But they always go on to produce a verb of the first group type, with an infinitive ending in –er: *biérer* ['to beer'] for 'to drink beer', for instance, *piper* ['to pipe'] for 'to smoke a pipe', etc. Now, we find the same phenomenon in the French spoken in Africa, in which numerous verbs are formed on the same principle: *siester* for 'to have a siesta', *gréver* for 'faire la grève' ['to go on strike'], etc. There are, however, other verbal forms in French, certain of which are very common – in –ir (*tenir*: to hold), –ire (*dire*: to say), –endre (*prendre*: to take), –oir (*vouloir*: to want), etc., but the first-group paradigm is the most regular, the easiest to conjugate,[6] and one no longer creates any verbs outside this group (the last was probably *alunir*, to land on the moon, based on *atterrir*, to land [on the earth]). This neologistic activity is thus the product of two factors: a factor within language, a tendency to create verbs on a certain model, and an external factor, a social demand, the need to name an action.

We thus have an opposition between language and society, both terms being subject to internal pressures: language changes under social pressure but it does not change in any old direction; linguistic situations evolve, but this evolution is not mechanical, resulting from the opposition between supply and demand; it is simultaneously the product of internal and of external forces. The opposition between supply and demand, borrowed from the vocabulary of economics, has been used in particular (at the same time as the opposition between costs and profits, also borrowed from economics) in the domain of linguistic planning.[7] It is useful in helping us to understand two things:

1 the fact that the future of languages partly depends on the relation between a social need (the demand) and the functional potentialities of the existing languages (the supply).
2 the fact that this supply and this demand can be modified by human intervention on the two terms of the opposition.

It is easy to illustrate these two propositions with examples. First, each time that a newly independent country raises the question of its national, or official, language, it shows a need (a demand) to which it will respond by choosing from within the existing languages (the supply) the one which best seems to it to fulfil this need. But – and this is my second proposition – this opposition is not static, and it is possible to modify both the supply (by 'equipping' languages – giving them the means, for example the lexical means, to respond to any need; if one wishes to use, for the purpose of teaching, a language which has no mathematical or grammatical language, one can forge such a language) and demand (by formulating federalist plans, for example, which no longer necessitate the choice of *one* national language but of *several* regional languages, or by deciding to preserve as the official language the language inherited from the colonial era). In other words, the homeostatic vision of the evolution of linguistic situations is not mechanistic, and it integrates human action into the description of the linguistic environment. We must thus postulate simultaneously a self-regulation on the part of linguistic situations and an internal regulation of languages. It is this latter regulation that I will examine first.

An example of internal regulation: vernacular variants of French

'*We're* having fun': some tendencies of the verbal paradigm

Philippe Martinon already pointed out, in 1927, the tendency in French to use *on* ['one', as in 'one doesn't do that kind of thing'] instead of 'all other pronouns, even in the spoken language',[8] and Henri Frei, in 1929, commented on this tendency with these words:

> The great advantage of this mobile French word *on* is that it makes not just persons but also genders and numbers interchangeable. It fills other functions too; it avoids, for instance, the fortuitous repetition of the same syllables: *nous, nous nous amusons* [we're having fun] > *nous on s'amuse* [same sense, but with *on*]. And above all, it allows us to do without the verbal ending: nous nous amus*ons* > on s'amuse.[9]

The alternating pronouns *on/nous*, frequent in vernacular French, does indeed lead to a parallel alternation of the verbal ending VØ/Võ for regular verbs and the disappearance of one of the forms of the paradigm. Thus, in examples such as

- *on s'en va* ['we're off'] for *nous nous en allons* ['we're off', more formal] (or *nous partons* ['we are leaving'])

- *on mange chez moi* for *nous mangeons chez moi* ['we're eating at my place', less formal and more formal respectively]
- *on fait quoi?* for *qu'est-ce que nous faisons?* ['what shall we do?', ditto], etc.,

the forms *allons*, *mangeons*, *faisons* seem doomed to disappear, a tendency which Françoise Gadet comments on in these terms: 'It is perhaps possible to predict a time when only *vous* ['you', plural/polite] will constitute an exception to the rule according to which the personal suffix is missing in the French verb'.[10]

Now, this French word *on* used in the first person plural is not just a fact of vernacular speech in metropolitan France. If we broaden our field of observation to peripheral forms of French, we observe that this usage is systematic in Louisiana French, while the third person tends to be expressed in a unique form, both in the singular and the plural. This gives us, for verbs of the first group:

	singular	plural
1	je V	on V
2	tu V	vous V-ez
3	i V	i V

In Acadian French, the same system is found, sometimes with a strengthened form as in *nuzot on* [a version of metropolitan standard French 'nous autres, on'] at the same time as the strengthening of *vous* into *vuzot*:

	singular	plural
1	je V	on/nuzot on V
2	tu V	vuzot V
3	i V	i V

as in Missouri French:

	singular	plural
1	je V	on V
2	tsu V	vuzot V
3	il/i V	i V[11]

The same is true in the majority of French creoles: a form of the type *zot* as pronoun of the second (and, in Réunion, sometimes the third) person of the plural.

These different elements are all evidence of a tendency, in vernacular French, towards the unification of the verbal root:

- For the verbs in the first group (infinitive in –er).
  Present: je tu i on i [*parl*], with the exception of *vous/vuzot* [parle].
  Imperfect: *je tu i on vous/vuzot i* [parle].
- For verbs of the second group (infinitive in –ir).
  Present: *je tu i on i* [fini] with the exception of *vous/vuzot* [finise].
  Imperfect: *je tu i on vous/vuzot i* [finise]. The future is most usually expressed by *aller* [to go] + infinitive.[12]

These elements are also evidence of a comparable tendency in peripheral versions of French and French creoles. In other words, what is noted separately in the descriptions of different regional forms of French is reducible to a single principle, a single direction of change. There are thus points of the system at which the language always evolves in the same direction, whatever the external differences, the ecological differences, may be in other respects.

This evolution is thus the product of the linguistic system, in this case the French system. What we have, in fact, in the set of the world's languages are two great principles that are clearly differentiated. On the one hand, there are systems in which the person is marked by a pronoun, while the verbal root can remain invariable: this is the case with languages which are in other respects as different as Chinese, English or Bambara, to mention just a few examples. And, on the other hand, we have systems in which the verb endings render pronouns unnecessary: this is the case of Spanish or Italian, for instance. Thus, in contrast with the pronominal Chinese paradigm *wo, ni, ta, women, nimen, tamen yao* ('I, you, he, we, you, they want') we have, in Spanish, a verbal paradigm *canto, cantas, canta, cantamos, cantais, cantan* ('I, you, he, we, you, they sing'). In the first case the root (*yao*) is bare, and so the pronouns are necessary; in the second case different endings are added to the root for each person, which means that pronouns are unnecessary. French combines these two principles, or rather is halfway between them: *je, tu, il, on, ils* [chant], *vous* [chante]. Furthermore, in the Channel Islands, and more widely throughout Basse-Normandie, one finds an alternation which clearly illustrates this double tendency. The first person plural is formed either in the form V + õ (for example *je mangeons* [we – in the form of the pronoun 'I' – eat] with the determinate meaning 'I plus you'), or in the form '*nous* V' (*nous mange*, with an indefinite sense).[13] In other words, to demonstrate a distinction between 'definite *nous*' and 'indefinite *nous*', the language uses either verbal inflection in the 'Spanish manner', or the pronominal paradigm 'in the Chinese manner'.

The facts I have just described thus illustrate a tendency to the regularization of an irregular system, which some have analysed as the product of language learning,[14] but which are evidence above all of a self-regulation of the system, a change whose mainsprings are internal to the language.

Parisian French and Marseilles French

The descriptions of different types of vernacular French often seem to be studying the same thing, especially in the domain of syntax, even when they intend to present regional variations. I will here refer briefly to two of them. The first, published in 1920, focused on *Parisian dialect*,[15] while the second, dating from 1931, discussed *Marseilles dialect*.[16] So what we have here are places that are not just geographically separate but also sociologically very different: on the one hand, the capital, in which the legitimate form of the language is brought into being and, on the other hand, the result of a diglossia between French and Provençal, marked, furthermore, by a very high number of foreigners – essentially, in the period under discussion, Italians – through waves of migrants whose languages left their mark on the local dialect, in particular its lexicon.

The situation in Marseilles and its history can indeed be easily read in the vocabulary. For example, in Marseilles there is a vernacular form understood by all and used by a large proportion of the population: *mettre le pàti* ('make a mess', 'muck things up'), *quel pàti* ('what a mess!'), etc. The word *pàti* at first designated in Provençal the place where the herds were kept, hence expressions such as *sèmblo un pàti* ('it looks like a cowshed') or *curo-pàti* (dustman) – examples given by Mistral.[17] The word also took on the meaning of 'toilet', and then that of mess, on the model of the French *planter la merde, mettre la merde* [both meaning 'to mess things up']. But in the 1990s other synonymous expressions appeared and, among young people, replaced the previous ones. In these, *pàti* alternated systematically with *ouaille* (spelt in different ways: *ouaille, oai, oaï . . .*): *mettre le ouaille*, *planter le ouaille*, etc. This term seems to have been launched in 1991 by the group Massilia Sound System in a song (*lo oai*) whose refrain proclaims: 'You put *oai* everywhere'. Furthermore, the lyrics provide us with this definition: '*Oai* is a sort of revolution, participation and information. . . . Don't seek any further: *oai* is the solution.'

In fact, *oai* is not a creation of Massilia Sound System, and we need rather to conclude that the group launched an already available word, in the same way that in the 1970s the Renaud song *Laisse béton* (back slang for 'Laisse tomber', i.e. 'drop it') had already foregrounded the procedures of *verlan* that were already in existence but not very well known.

To return to Marseilles, where did the term *oai* come from? Is it of Provençal origin? Frédéric Mistral gave this definition in his dictionary: '*ouai*: interjection which expresses surprise and aversion, displeasure and pain'. But it is not easy to see the semantic link between this definition and the above-mentioned uses. The solution to this etymological mystery can in fact be found elsewhere. The word comes from the Italian *guaio*, 'woe', in the form *uaio*, frequent in the south (Naples, Italy): *che uaio!* ('what a mess!'), *Mi hai messo nei uai* ('you've got me in a real mess').[18] And so we find, in the evolution from *pàti* to *ouaille*, in the superimposition of Italian influence on Provençal influence, the lexical trace of a moment of the city's history: the weight of Italian migration can be read in the variation *pàti/oai.*

Then, at the end of the 1990s, another word appeared, *khra,* sometimes in the form *khla*, firstly in the texts of the city's other big musical group, IAM: 'We're making *khla* here [in the night-club]' (i.e. 'we're making a mess'). The usage then spread widely among the young people in the northern districts in the city, in which there is a dominance of migrants of Maghrebi origin. Unlike *oai*, for which a Provençal origin might be supposed, *khra* in no way suggests a Romance root: the word is a loan from Arabic *khra*, 'shit', sometimes pronounced *khla*, and the sequence *pàti* > *ouaille* > *khra* demonstrates, in the regional French of Marseilles, the successive influences of Provençal, Italian and Arabic influence.

The three terms coexist, but their usage denotes either a contrast between age classes (*pàti* versus *ouaille* and *khra*, the first being used by older people than those who use the two others), or a contrast between different districts and origins (*ouaille* versus *kra*, the first being more used in the southern districts and connoting a reference to 'Provençal identity', even if, as we have seen, the word is of Italian origin; the second being more used in the northern districts and connoting a reference to 'Maghrebi identity', even if everyone uses this word). In this sense, this brief example shows us how much the eco-linguistic niche of Marseilles produced lexical change: none of these three terms is used or understood in Paris, Toulouse or Lyons. And we could, of course, multiply the examples, from either Paris or Marseilles, that would show us how these two niches produce a different lexicon.

But, whereas the two forms described in 1920 by Bauche (in *Le Langage populaire*) and in 1931 by Brun (in *Le Français de Marseille*) were of course different lexically and phonetically, the same was not true as regards syntax – with the result that the impression was sometimes created that the same examples and the same commentaries could be found in both works. Thus Brun emphasizes that 'whatever the form of the relative pronoun, *qui, que, dont, à qui, où,* required by grammar, here we always see *que*' (p. 57), whereas for Bauche, '*que* is used on every occasion in the vernacular, even when irrelevant' (p. 104). And their examples are strictly parallel:

- 'C'est vous que vous avez sonné?', 'Is it you who rang?' (Brun) with duplicated 'que'. 'C'est vous que vous venez?', 'You are coming?', ditto (Bauche).
- 'Cet homme que je ne sais pas son nom','That man whose name I don't know' (Brun). 'La chose que j'ai besoin', 'The thing I need' (Bauche).
- 'Je lui empêcherais bien de recommencer', 'I'd stop him doing it again' (Brun). 'Je lui ai empêché de partir', 'I stopped him going away' (Bauche). *etc.*

The two authors point out the confusion between *être* and *avoir* [used as auxiliary verbs in the present perfect], and propose examples whose parallelism is, once again, striking:

- 'Je suis été malade', 'I've been ill' (Brun, p. 62). 'Je suis été', 'I've been' (Bauche, p. 131).

- 'J'ai entré', 'I've come in' (Brun, p. 63). 'Il a rentré ce matin', 'He came back this morning' (Bauche, p. 133).
- 'J'ai sorti sur le tantôt', 'I went out just now' (Brun, p. 63). 'J'ai sorti le tantôt', 'I went out just now' (Bauche, p. 133).

The same goes for the negation *ne . . . pas*, reduced to its second element: 'The elimination of *ne* in the formulae *ne . . . pas*, "not", and *ne . . . jamais*, "never", etc., is more or less definitive in the French of Provence: "*j'ai rien vu, j'ai guère mangé, j'ai pas sorti* de *tout le jour*", "I saw nothing, I hardly ate, I have not been out all day"' (Brun, p. 77). 'The "ne" is almost always omitted in the vernacular' (Bauche, p. 146). *etc.*

In any case, Auguste Brun is aware of these convergences. 'In reality, the *incorrect forms* that we have pointed out are not proper to Provence or Marseilles: they bear on points of French morphology or syntax that have always been the *weak points*, the ones where the language has always shown a certain hesitation'.[19] And he returns, in conclusion, to the same theme, after quoting Bauche:

> The French of the Marseilles area does not present, either in morphology or in syntax, any innovation properly speaking: there is nothing really new either in conjugation or in sentence structure or in word order. No spontaneous creation occurs. The grammatical system as a whole resists; only the fragile parts are attacked, those which are tricky to handle, those in which the language, in the course of history, hesitated, those in which the grammarians multiplied their prescriptions. On these points, the vernacular, in Marseilles as much as in Paris, deliberately contravenes the official code and the rules, and obeys its simplifying tendencies.[20]

In addition, Patrice Brasseur has noted a similar phenomenon for creoles and marginal varieties of French in North America (from Newfoundland and Saint-Pierre-et-Niquelon): 'Several phenomena are constantly found, at different levels, in marginal varieties of French and creoles. . . . It seems that these modifications, which may, in the case of creoles, entail profound restructurings, both syntactic and morphological, are inherent in the nature of the system of French'.[21]

The 'weak points' of the language, its 'fragile parts': Brun's intuition here is interesting, and as we can see, he has thus isolated the points at which the system is seeking equilibrium. In these examples, as in that of conjugation that I mentioned above – and unlike the sequence *pàti* > *ouaille* > *khla* – we thus find ourselves facing the phenomenon of internal self-regulation and the way the language develops as it attempts to regulate itself. I will now move on to analyse cases of self-regulation produced by the relations between a language and its milieu.

Of ships and languages: from Christopher Columbus to lingua franca

In the rich mythology devoted to pirates there are two figures of interest to the linguist – Misson and Lewis. In a work published in 1724, *General History of the Robberies and Murders of the most notorious Pirates*, a work that was at the time anonymous and is now attributed to Daniel Defoe, we find the figure of Lewis and a long discussion of 'the story of Captain Misson and his crew'. Lewis 'had a great aptitude for languages, and spoke perfectly well that of the Mosquil Indians, French, Spanish, and English. I mention our own, because it is doubted whether he was French or English, for we cannot trace him back to his origins.'[22] As for Misson, Defoe alleges that he himself composed his memoirs in French. Born into a well-off Provençal family, Misson was a successful student, but rather than entering the musketeers, as his father wished, he preferred to set off in search of adventure, took ship at Marseilles and in Italy met an unfrocked monk, Carrocioli, who became his adviser. Finally, on the shores of Madagascar, in the bay of Diego Suarez, he set up a sort of Utopian community called Libertalia. In his desire to fight racism and prejudice, considering as he did that the differences between languages were at the origin of the division between men, Misson apparently went on to try to return to the times before Babel and create a single language on the basis of a multiplicity of coexisting languages. He wanted to mix together the different languages so that there would henceforth be only one.[23]

In both cases, the historical reality of the figures is uncertain. There is a single source for Lewis, and it is repeatedly mined: for example, practically the same text as Defoe's is found in a later work, one that is clearly indicated as being different from its predecessor.[24] There is also just one single source for Misson – and we are told that this name was a pseudonym, a fact that I have been unable to verify. It was Gilles

Lapouge, in his work on pirates, who compared these two figures. He begins by presenting Misson in these terms:

> His instinct did not deceive him. If the appearance of separate languages was indeed a consequence of original sin, we need to go back before the Tower of Babel, to those ages when nature could be read like a book on which the finger of God had imposed its signature. Misson knows perfectly well that this innocent reading of the world is now lost and the transparency of souls clouded. But one can at least make an effort towards regaining the lost unity by recreating a synthetic language: so Misson invented an Esperanto of the tropics, a pirate Volapük.[25]

He then turns to Lewis:

> Two features bore evidence to the fact that Lewis was possessed by evil. The first was that he announced to his sailors the hour of his own death – a death which did indeed come. The second was that he had a gift for languages. This lad, without a father or a country of his own, spoke English, French, Spanish and Caribbean fluently. A gift for languages is granted in especial by the Holy Spirit: it is, indeed, one of his specialities. The story of Lewis tells us that the devil also has them in his gift, and it was already known that the witches of the Renaissance were often polyglots.[26]

And Lapouge concludes:

> The two purest figures of piracy, Misson and Lewis, thus reveal their secret kinship. Both of them have an unusual relation to language. Misson, who is Good, endeavours to resurrect the lost unity of human languages. Lewis, who is Evil, merrily tolerates the dispersion of languages – and why should it bother him, since it is his master who, thanks to the virulence of original sin, has fragmented both Being and languages? Lewis thus accepts the multiplicity of languages but he obtains from his patron the privilege of being able to speak them all.[27]

We are clearly here faced with an interpretation of history that owes everything to dreamy speculation and little to a critique of the sources; but the literature devoted to Corsairs and pirates provides us with several real examples of polyglot Corsairs or pirates. To mention just a couple of cases, Barbarossa, according to his biographer, spoke

Arabic, Turkish, Italian and French;[28] and Edward John Trelawny presents us with another polyglot pirate:

> De Ruyter . . . was familiar with all the out-of-the-way corners of the most irregular of towns, and entered into many dark abodes without ceremony. He conversed, on these occasions, with the natives, in their varied tongues with equal ease, whether in the guttural, brute-like grunting of the Malay, the more humanized Hindostanee, or the softer and harmonious Persian.[29]

And he attributes comparable abilities to himself. He hailed them in six different languages, but they replied only with shrill cries.[30]

We could give even more examples of this kind, but they would all indicate the same thing. For what emerges from all of them is the image of extraordinary individuals, capable of communicating in several languages.

But the reality behind the myths is both fascinating and problematic: how did men behave, linguistically speaking, in the closed community of a ship? What type of communication was established between different ships? And between these ships and the ports at which they called? For example, Trelawny gives us a particularly multilingual inventory of a ship:

> We had fourteen Europeans, chiefly from the dow; they were Swedes, Dutch, Portuguese and French together with a few Americans. Then we had samples of almost all the sea-faring natives of India; Arabs, Mussulmans, Daccamen, Cooleys, and Lascars. Our steward and purser was a mongrel Frenchman, the cabin-boy, English, the surgeon, Dutch, and the armourer and master-of-arms, Germans.[31]

How did the members of this community communicate, representing as they did a dozen or so mother tongues?

Sociolinguistics teaches us that, in such situations, there are only two possibilities: either one of the languages present assumes the dominant role in communication, or else this function is constituted by a composite language, borrowing from the different kinds of speech present. But this *in vivo* response to the problem of a multilingual community can only emerge over time. And in this case, things are made more complicated by the fact that these crews were not fixed: new members were brought on board all the time, and others put ashore. Furthermore, we should doubtless distinguish between (1) the languages of command, (2) the languages thanks to which the NCOs transmitted the captain's orders to the crew, and (3) the languages of communication between the crew members. Indeed, in the first and second cases, a passive understanding of the captain's languages was adequate, whereas in the third it was of course necessary for there to be mutual communication, requiring the adoption of a common code.

I will be tackling these questions in the context of the Mediterranean, considering ships as social micro-communities immersed in a much wider linguistic ecosystem, and investigating the productions of these systems both internally and externally through an examination of their effects on individual behaviour and unified linguistic forms. With this aim in mind, I will be taking two cases: that of an individual, Christopher Columbus, and that of a more or less unified form that served as a widespread language in the Mediterranean, namely lingua franca.

Christopher Columbus is a good example of the effects of such an ecosystem on the behaviour of an individual. The corpus at our disposal is made up of several manuscripts: several autographs (letters, reports, annotations on books) and, above all, logbooks copied shortly after his death in the *Historia de las Indias* by Bartolomé de las Casas[32] and in the *Historia* attributed to his son, Fernando Columbus. These texts, almost entirely written in Spanish (with occasional annotations in Italian and Latin), constitute an extremely interesting source for the linguistic practices deployed by the navigator, the languages he spoke and the way he spoke them; and the analysis of their syntax, their lexicon and their spelling enable us to reconstitute what may have comprised his linguistic system. These texts have, of course, been frequently studied by historians, but much less by linguists: there is one study by Menéndez Pidal, another by J. Arce and the long introduction by Juan Gil to the complete edition of his texts.[33] There is also a recent article in French on this theme,[34] but its authors, obviously working at second hand, attribute Juan Gil's introduction, whenever they cite it, to Consuelo Varela, date Menéndez Pidal's study on *La lengua de Cristóbal Colón* to 1944 when it was in fact first published in 1940[35] and, above all, completely bypass the main interest of these documents, namely the way in which Columbus's linguistic biography explains the form taken by his written (and, probably, spoken) Spanish.

Why did Columbus write in Spanish? When and where did he learn that language? Different answers to this question have been proposed. Some have suggested that he was born to Spanish and/or Jewish parents, others that he was a Galician. Menéndez Pidal convincingly demonstrates that while the admiral did indeed write in Spanish before coming to Spain, his language is in no way that of a native speaker: there are numerous traces of Judeo-Spanish and numerous Portuguese elements which, as I will be showing, are not at all evidence of a Galician origin: whenever there is a significant difference between Galician and Portuguese, the forms used by Columbus are clearly Portuguese.[36]

When he writes in Spanish, he sometimes uses Portuguese (*deter* instead of *detener*, *fugir* instead of *huir* for example) or Italian terms, and in particular his writing demonstrates a Portuguese pronunciation. Thus he almost systematically transcribes:

- the diphthong *ue* by *oe* (*poerto* instead of *Puerto*, *soerte* for *suerte*, *coerpo* for *cuerpo*, etc.);
- the diphthong *ie* by *e* (*quer* for *quier*, *pensamento* for *pensamiento*, *intenda* for *entienda*, etc.);
- the final *–o* by *–u* (*deseu* for *deseo*, *correu* for *correo*, etc.);
- the final *–n* is labialized as *–m* (*um* for *un*), etc.

Juan Gil concludes that 'the great navigator does not express himself correctly in any language',[37] and his explanation is simple: Columbus was above all else a sailor, who '*estaba acostumbrado a chapurrear mil lenguas sin lograr expresarse bien en ninguna*' ('who was used to speaking a thousand languages badly without being able to express himself well in any of them'). In his view, Columbus had learnt Spanish by going to Spain after his stay in Portugal, which would explain the Portuguese turns of phrase that we have just seen.

Menéndez Pidal, meanwhile, divides Columbus's life into three main periods.

Born in 1451 or 1452, in Genoa, to a weaver father, he stayed there until August 1473 and, during these first twenty years, acquired, apart from his first language (Genoan), the commercial Latin (spoken and written) of the period, and perhaps a little Italian. 'We can suppose that in Genoa, in order to fulfil his duties, Columbus was able to learn commercial Latin, that Latin which the Spaniards humorously called *Genevesco Latin*, and was able not only to speak it but also to write it.'[38]

In the second period, from 1473 to 1476, Columbus travelled round the Mediterranean working as the commercial agent for a Genoan firm. This point is confirmed by Marianne Mahn-Lot, according to whom Columbus entered 'big Genoan firms that sold wool and bought alum, spices and sugar; he sailed across the Mediterranean basin and even as far as England'.[39] During this period, he might have picked up Spanish in the Mediterranean ports, but Menéndez Pidal emphasizes that we find no trace of Andalusian in his language.[40] On the other hand, it is probable that he learnt another language at that time. 'In his youth, the Admiral had to communicate with his friends in the jargon known at the time as "Levantine", i.e. the language of the Levant and the Mediterranean in general', writes Juan Gil.[41] I will come back to this point later.

The third period started in 1476, when Columbus moved to Portugal, and lasted until 1485, when he settled in Castile. But he had learned Spanish before that last date, as is shown by the letters that he composed in that language. It was in fact, as Menéndez Pidal explains, in Portugal that the Admiral learned Spanish. At that time the dominant mode was for Castilian forms, with several poets writing in Spanish (and making, furthermore, 'mistakes' that are remarkably similar to those of Columbus), the nobles affecting to speak this language, etc. So it is altogether to be expected that Columbus's Spanish was marked by the place where he had learned the language: the Spanish he picked up was that of a Portuguese.

The linguistic biography of Columbus is thus an accumulation of Romance languages acquired one after the other. As he was born in Genoa, Genoan was his mother tongue; then he learned to speak and write commercial Latin. Going on to travel across the Mediterranean, he picked up a little Italian and, probably, lingua franca. Settling in Portugal, he learned Portuguese and Spanish, which was to be his second written language (after Latin). So in his texts we find a Christopher Columbus who, when writing in Spanish (the accounts he wrote of his travels were meant for the sovereigns of Castile), allows his spelling to be somewhat marked by his linguistic biography and shows in his lexicon the fact that he sometimes mixes up the different languages he has spoken. In addition, we have an interesting piece of evidence on his way of speaking, that of Garcia Ferrando who met him in 1491 and declares that, when Columbus arrived at the convent of La Rabida with his son Diego, he spoke Spanish like a foreigner. Menéndez Pidal comments: 'In other words, in 1491, when this scene occurred, Columbus – who had spent five years at the court of Castile – showed as soon as he opened his mouth that he was not a native speaker.'[42] When he wrote, his spelling revealed this linguistic practice, but he used what he considered to be Spanish, a written Spanish, admittedly often incorrect, but a Spanish that he was obliged to use, as our navigator was addressing sovereigns and could not report to his masters in anything other than their own language. Juan Gil makes an interesting observation about Columbus's Spanish:

> After all is said and done, the most characteristic feature of Columbus's writing is the economy of his language, which always seeks the form best understood in the greatest number of languages, knowing as he does that his interlocutors or readers will easily resolve any ambiguity. For this reason it is difficult to say whether the use of *per* constitutes an example of Portuguese or Italian influence.[43]

And this idea of economy, the seeking of forms common to several languages, constitutes a perfect transition to the point I now wish to tackle.

We have seen that, during his first Mediterranean voyages, Columbus probably communicated via a quite different linguistic form. This 'jargon', known as lingua franca,[44] which seems to have existed from the eleventh or twelfth century to the middle of the nineteenth,[45] must have spread at the time of the Crusades, when the speakers of Romance languages first encountered Arabic and Turkish speakers. We have few documents on the dialects of that period, but it is probable that it was born 'from the contact of Romance-speakers with non-Romance-speakers'.[46] Hugo Schuchardt presents it in these terms: 'Lingua franca is the communicative language formed of a Romance lexicon that arose in the Middle Ages between Romans and Arabs and subsequently Turks.'[47] And he adds that 'the geographical mid-point of this essentially uniform lingua franca is formed by Algiers, though not due to the fact that it was here that Italian and Spanish spheres of power came into contact, but because it was here that there was a firm citadel where a network of piracy spread over the Mediterranean.'[48]

Among the sources that have come down to us on this language is Diego de Haedo[49] who enables us to read a sort of 'basic Spanish' used in Algiers, with a few Italian or Sicilian words mixed in: '*Mira cane como hazer malato, mirar como mi estar barbero bono, y saber curar, si estar malato, y corer bono. Si cane dezir doler cabeça, tener febre no poder trabajar mi saber como curar, a Fé de Dios abrusar vivo; trabajar, no parlar que estar malato.*' ('Look, dog, how you are pretending to be ill. See what a good doctor I am and how I can treat you. If you are ill, you will be able to run well. Dog, if you say that you have a headache, that you have a fever and that you cannot work, I know how to treat you, in faith [literally: by the faith of God] I will burn you alive. Work, and do not say that you are ill.')

It is not always easy to attribute these lexical elements to a particular language: *mira* can be Italian (*mirare*) or Spanish (*mirar*), just like *corer* (*correre/corer*), *abrusar* can be Spanish or Venetian, but *cane, curar, parlar, malato* are obviously Italian in origin, and *cabeça, hazer, barbero, saber, doler, trabajar* are clearly Spanish. As we see, the syntax is considerably simplified: just one form of personal pronoun (*mi*, *ti*, etc.), verbs used in the infinitive, etc. According to Schuchardt, this infinitive was used for the present as well as the past (*mi andar* = 'I go', 'I went'; *mi sentir* = 'I understand, I understood') and the future was sometimes marked by the use of *bisogno* (*bisogno mi andar* = 'I will go'). In his comedy *Le Bourgeois Gentilhomme,* Molière gives us two passages in this language, perhaps provided by his friend Laurent d'Arvieux, who was minister plenipotentiary at Tunis.[50] In the course of the play first of all: '*Si ti sabir ti respondir, si non sabir tazir tazir, mi star Mufti, ti star ci? Non entendir, tazir, tazir.*' ('If you know, answer, if you don't know keep quiet. I am the Mufti, who are you? If you don't understand, keep quiet.')

And in the appendix to the play, the Mufti says to the Bourgeois Gentilhomme: '*Se ti sabir ti respondir, si non sabir tazir tazir*', and the latter has to reply, '*Mohametta per Giourdina, mi pregar sera é mattina, voler far un Paladina de Giourdina.*' And we find in these passages the same systematic use of the infinitive and the same pronouns (*mi, ti*) as in the examples provided by Haedo.

A century later, in 1761, Goldoni, in *The Impresario of Smyrna*, also uses lingua franca, and this limited corpus is now considered by certain linguists as reliable and as constituting proof of the autonomy of lingua franca vis-à-vis its source languages.[51] As the following extracts show, the main principles have barely changed: verbs are still in the infinitive, prepositions are still largely absent, but the system of personal pronouns has become somewhat more extensive (*io, me, mi*).

- *Si voler andar Turchia, io ti mandar Constantinopoli.* ('If you want to go to Turkey, I will send you to Constantinople')
- '*Star omo o star donna?*' ('Are you a man or a woman?')
- '*Andar diavolo! Seder presso di me! Non mi romper testa!*' ('Go to the devil! Sit next to me! Stop bothering me!')

Closer to our own age, General Faidherbe provides us with some examples of what is called 'sabir':[52] 'Moi meskine, toi donnar sordi' ('I am poor, give me money'), 'Sbanioul chapar bourrico, andar labrisou' ('the Spaniard has stolen a donkey, he will go to prison') 'Quand moi gagner drehem, moi achetir moukère' ('when I've earned some money, I'll buy a woman'). And he points out that, 'by using this language, the trooper is convinced that he is speaking Arabic, and the Arab is convinced that he is speaking French'. This 'sabir' then slowly disappears, though it does leave traces in the vernacular French of North Africa (such as *moukère*, from Spanish *mujer*, *makache bono*, with a negative verb form of Arabic origin and an adjective of Romance origin, etc.).

But is there a real continuity between these different forms? Paul Siblot is completely opposed to this view. For him, it is a mark of 'confused thinking' to suppose that lingua franca, 'a rudimentary mix of Romance languages, Greek, Turkish and Arabic used for commercial transactions', has anything to do with the Algerian 'sabir'. And he supports his point by referring to the definition of 'sabir' given by O. Bloch and W. von Wartburg in their *Dictionnaire étymologique*: 'A jargon that mixes Italian, Spanish, French and Arabic, spoken by the natives of North Africa when they wish to converse with Europeans.'[53] But, curiously enough, the quotation he gives us has been truncated. The authors do in fact, a few lines further on, compare 'sabir' to the Frankish language, 'a jargon of the same kind spoken at the time in the states of Barbary', and give as an example an extract from *Le Bourgeois Gentilhomme* . . . Before Siblot, Robert Hall Jr had defended the same position: the medieval lingua franca was, in his view, based on Provençal, and what is later presented as 'lingua franca' was in fact a Spanish pidgin in the seventeenth century and a French pidgin in the nineteenth.[54]

Be that as it may, many others incline to the continuity hypothesis. This is the case, for instance, with Keith Whinnom, who refutes Hall's thesis, essentially on the basis of arguments of internal linguistics: the texts at our disposal, some of which have been quoted above, demonstrate the features (pronouns and the system of conjugations) shared by the different states of the language.[55] The same is true of Salvatore Santoro, for whom lingua franca 'was a stable language with the morpho-syntactic simplifications common to many restructured languages'.[56] He emphasizes this characteristic in the following terms: 'Lingua franca, like any other language, evolved and underwent changes, during the course of at least eight centuries, a remarkable period of time for a contact language'.[57]

It is true that no language can stay the same over several centuries. If the excerpt from Haedo that I quoted earlier presents a lexical mixture that is essentially based on Italian and Spanish, the French language is then described by other authors as a mixture of Italian, French and Spanish,[58] or French, Romany and Spanish.[59] However, in every case, it presents a syntax reduced to the minimum, a sort of lowest common denominator of two or three Romance languages. To this we can add that between the examples given by Haedo (beginning of the seventeenth century), those provided by Goldoni (mid-eighteenth century) and those of Faidherbe (end of the nineteenth century), the sociolinguistic conditions of usage evolved to a considerable degree. But the ecolinguistic niche stayed the same overall, and we have to remember that there was constant variation in the continuity. Throughout its history, lingua franca ceaselessly shifted around the Mediterranean, being adapted and relexified: it was probably based on Low Latin to begin with, and then included within itself Venetian, Genoan and Provençal words, and then Spanish and French words, as it slowly moved from east to west to end up in North Africa under the name of 'little Moorish' or 'sabir' and in a form that was essentially Franco-Arabic. Faidherbe's corpus – a mixture of words mainly French and Arabic (here *meskine*, 'poor'; there *bezef*, 'much', or *maboul*, 'crazy') or Arabic phonetic characteristics (*sbanioul, labrisou*, forms explicable by the absence of /p/ in Arabic) – shows that the Frankish language was now reserved for communication between French and Arabs, more especially in Algeria. These fluctuations suggest that what we have here is a 'variable geography' lingua franca, which, depending on situations and periods, could be adapted and modified as its users required. Its form and final function ('sabir' for the form, Franco-Algerian communication for the function) show that its existence was linked to the fact that the French did not at the time speak Arabic, nor the Arabs French. The progress of the French language in Algeria would lead to the retreat and then the disappearance of lingua franca, which was replaced by the colonial language.

So what we have here is a highly idiosyncratic ecolinguistic system, whose ever-changing situation leads us to think in more detail about the conditions of mutual understanding between the speakers of different languages. I will start out from the following hypothesis: in the situations mentioned above, a rough-and-ready form of minimal and immediate understanding was initially achieved via the lexicon, i.e. by words whose reciprocal recognition necessitated a phonetic 'negotiation', and the quest for a common standard form, a sort of formal shared territory. It was only later, when things moved towards a potentially more precise and more nuanced communication, that the problem of syntax arose. I am aware that I thus seem to be flying in the face of a widespread view which sees language as the place in which a conceptual system, and indeed a whole culture, is made manifest. Far be it from me, however, to deny the links between language and cognition, I simply wish to underscore the fact that there are different levels of 'communication' and that to each of them corresponds a more or less elaborate form. A long experience of investigations carried out into multilingual markets has taught me, for instance, that on the technical level a handful of words, a knowledge of figures and two or three syntactic structures are more than ample for bargaining, buying and selling.[60]

Now, the same was probably true of navigation: we can suppose that a minimum composite language gradually came into being, and that this vocabulary circulated from ship to ship, port to port and island to island. Ships did indeed play a role as the diffusion vectors of this lexicon. Raymond Arveiller has shown, for instance, the tortuous itinerary of words such as the French *ananas*, pineapple (from Guarani via Portuguese): 'We believe it is possible to conclude that the word under study belonged to the (international) vocabulary of commerce used by sailors in quest of refreshments both in the Greater and Lesser Antilles and in Brazil.'[61] In his section devoted to the word *banana*, we can see that the first attestations of the word are found, geographically speaking, in the Indian Ocean and the Antilles. Elsewhere we see that the word *caiman* (cayman) appears almost simultaneously in texts referring to the Antilles, Guiana and Mexico, and then Guinea and the

Congo; the word *ouragan* (hurricane), appearing in the Antilles in 1640, was used in reference to Mauritius from 1679 onwards; the word *canot* (dinghy, fishing boat) was used simultaneously for ships from South America and Canada; and *caye* (key, coral reef) was used both of the Indian Ocean and the Antilles – and so on. Certain terms seem to have been borrowed in tandem from an Indian language and from Spanish or Portuguese, while others were both borrowed and translated. We here encounter what Robert Chaudenson has called 'the vocabulary of the islands',[62] those terms that were found practically at one and the same time in Réunion and in the Antilles, for example, and were transported from island to island by the ships of the West India Company which, from the seventeenth century onwards, monopolized trade 'from Cap Blanc to the Cape of Good Hope'.[63] Thus *habitation*, with the sense of 'farm estate', appeared simultaneously in the Indian Ocean and the Antilles; *ajoupa*, 'a hut made of wood or leaves', was found in Réunion, Louisiana, Haïti and Martinique; *pistache*, with the sense of 'peanut', was used in Réunion, Martinique and Haïti, etc.

This lexical circulation thus had ships and sailors as its carriers. The few brief examples I have just mentioned concern two far-removed geographical zones, the Caribbean and the Indian Ocean, and it is thus easy to understand how, in a closed space like that of the Mediterranean, this circulation should have been even more intense. After all, the etymology of the word 'Mediterranean' indicates its principal characteristic: 'in the middle of the land'. This geographical situation is the basis for what I have been trying to bring out. From port to port, from language to language, travellers accumulated lexical items, phonetic forms and syntactic formulae. The initial result was a set of personal practices: those of each individual involved, at a given time, in this ecosystem – practices that could vary with their history and their linguistic biography. That is what we traced through the writings of Christopher Columbus – the impact of a given ecolinguistic system on a given linguistic competence (here, Spanish). But, at this same time and in this same place, the interactions between individual practices produced, by self-regulation, an area in which these different practices could overlap, allowing communication in a microsystem (the ship, the port) or in a wider system (the Mediterranean): lingua franca. The latter evolved, adapted to new conditions, responded to new social demands and simultaneously bore the marks of history.

The description of Algiers presented by Haedo at the start of the seventeenth century is, from this point of view, quite characteristic. He distinguishes between five different communities (Turks, renegade Christians, captive Christians, Jews and Moors) representing some fifteen or so languages, with lingua franca as the sole shared language: 'Lingua franca is in such general use that one cannot find a house in which it is not spoken. Turks, Arabs, Berbers, great and small, men and women, and even the children, all use it to some extent, but the majority speak it very fluently indeed'.[64] Lingua franca was thus in a state of constant re-creation, undergoing constant modifications, reflecting the relations between different languages, i.e. the role played by the countries in which they were spoken. Italiano-Spanish to begin with, it thus evolved, in four or five centuries, into a more Arabo-French form. Between the texts provided by Haedo and those of Faidherbe there seem to be few links, but it was indeed the same communicational function that was embodied in this ever-changing form. It would be pointless to try and discover in it the trace of some 'bio-program' or other, or of any innate linguistic structures. It was rather a kind of *bricolage* that was operative here, both on the individual level (as in the case of Christopher Columbus) and on the social level (lingua franca). From this viewpoint, this Mediterranean lingua franca is an excellent example of the way in which an ecosystem *produces* the linguistic material it needs.

Vernacularization as ecological acclimatization: varieties of French in Africa

In his 1979 preface to a work on the lexicon of the French language of Senegal,[65] Léopold Senghor made a slight alteration to its title: 'Preface to the lexicon of French in Senegal'. We can see in this change from '*of*' to '*in* Senegal' the evidence of a debate on the status of the forms which the French language has assumed in Africa. Should we consider these, broadly speaking, as African variants of the French language, or are we faced here with the appearance of local types of French – the French of Senegal, Mali, Cameroon, the Ivory Coast, Gabon, etc.? In other terms, does the 'French of Africa' bear the same relation to standard French as the French of Marseilles, for example (i.e. the same language with a few regional particularities)? Or do the 'French languages of Africa' constitute the first fruits of a new generation of languages that will be to French what French, Spanish, Italian or Roumanian now are to Latin?

Ever since the publication in 1983 of the *Inventory of the Lexical Particularities of French in Black Africa*,[66] studies on the lexicon of French in Africa have grown ever more numerous: Prignitz (1984) for Burkina Faso, Wenezoui-Déchamps (1988) for Central Africa, Queffelec and Niangouna (1990) for the Congo, Féral (1993) for Cameroon, etc. It is possible, on the basis of these different works, to sketch out a typology of the lexicon of the French language in/of Africa based on its modes of creation. We thus find:

1 French coinages based on French roots, i.e. neologisms that respect all the rules of derivation of this language but do not exist in the French spoken in 'metropolitan' France: Hence we have *gréver* ('faire la grève' = 'to go on strike'), *siester* ('faire la sieste' = 'to take a siesta'), *couiller* (from French 'couille' = 'bollock', so 'to ball', i.e. 'to make love'), *essencerie* (from 'essence' = 'petrol', so 'service station'), *doucherie* (from 'douche' = 'shower', so 'shower corner' or 'shower compartment'), *alphabète* ('someone who can read and write'), *cigaretter* ('to give a cigarette'), *misérer* (from 'misère' = 'poverty', 'wretchedness', so 'to live in poverty'), *boyerie* ('place where the domestic servants – the "boys" – live'), etc.

2 French coinages based on African roots: Hence, from the Mandingo word *dibi*, 'pieces of meat', the Senegalese created a word designating the place where people sell grilled meat, namely *dibiterie*. This is a very productive model (*bijouterie*, 'jeweller's', from *bijou* = 'jewellery'; *épicerie*, 'grocer's', from *épice* = 'spice'; more recently, *animalerie* and *croissanterie* for places selling animals and croissants respectively), and, perhaps, by crossing it with the verb *débiter*, 'to retail' ('to retail meat in chunks'). In the same way, in Zaire they have forged the word *ziboulateur*, 'bottle-opener', from a Kikongo word, *ko zibula*, 'to open'. Another example: from *toubab*, a word of Arabic origin designating, in Mali or Senegal, 'a white man', they have created *toubabesse*, 'a white woman', *se toubabisser*, 'to have a tendency to behave like the whites', *toubabisme*, etc.

3 The use of French words with a different meaning from that which they have in standard French: *gagner* ('to have' or 'possess' instead of 'to gain'), *ambiance* ('merriment, party', instead of 'ambience', 'atmosphere' – hence *ambiancer*, 'to party'), *interner* ('to send

to boarding school' instead of 'to intern'), *mazout* ('a cocktail of Coca-Cola and whisky', instead of 'fuel oil'), *maquis* ('more or less clandestine restaurant' instead of the 'scrubland' as used by the French Resistance), *connaître* ('to know a fact' instead of 'to know a person' or 'to know by acquaintance' – standard French *savoir*), *gâter* ('to ruin, destroy', instead of 'to spoil'), *torcher* ('to light by a torch', instead of 'to wipe'), etc.

4 The use of words or expressions borrowed from African languages, such as *abana* ('it's over', from the Bambara), *karamoko* ('marabout', from Bambara), *borom* ('boss', from Wolof), *tchapalo* ('millet or sorghum beer', from Senefu), etc.

Some of these terms are used throughout French-speaking Africa, such as *gagner, connaître, gâter, grever*, etc. Others have a more restricted use, in a few countries or in just one: *brin* (a 'match', e.g. for lighting a fire, rather than a 'scrap' of material); *dibiterie* or *filiation* ('identity') in Senegal; *caillasse* ('money', 'coins': standard French meaning = 'loose stones') in Niger; *communiste* ('dishonest person') in Rwanda; *matabiche* ('a tip') or *cigaretter* in Zaire and the Congo; *payé-cousu* ('a ready-to-wear item of clothes': standard French *payé* = 'paid for' and *cousu* = 'sewn') in Cameroon, etc. And others, finally, can have different meanings in different countries. Thus the verb *tailler* (in standard French, 'to cut', with *la taille* meaning someone's 'height' or 'stature') means 'to take someone's measure' in Senegal, but 'to jilt a suitor' and 'not to reply to someone' in Cameroon.

This rapid typology would need to be refined, of course, but it already suggests the lexical and semantic variation that characterizes the French of Africa. In addition, demographic conditions and migrations have an influence on this lexicon and sometimes give it differentiated local forms. The example of Gabon, where migrants from the various African countries are particularly numerous, is revealing from this point of view. According to the 1993 census, 15.19 per cent of the country's population were foreigners; 22.3 per cent in the capital, Libreville:

- 10 per cent from French-speaking West Africa;
- 7.6 per cent from Central Africa;
- 3.1 per cent other Africans;
- 1.6 per cent non-Africans.

Now, we find in the lexicon of the French spoken in Libreville an unusual number of terms used to designate these foreigners:

- *Aofiens* to designate migrants originally from Western Africa, the AOF (= FWA, French West Africa) of the colonial period; these are also called *ouestafs*, *haussas*, *yoros*, and *popos*;
- *arranger-arranger* for the Ghanaians, often cobblers, who speak French badly and hail their potential customers saying, '*arranger, arranger*';
- *équato* for the Equato-guineans from Equatorial Guinea;
- *kalaba* for the Nigerians, who are also called *Naïdjés*, an abbreviation of the English form *Nigerian;*
- *malien* (or *maloche)* for the migrants from West Africa, in particular the grocers and especially those who do not sell alcohol.

All of these words have racist connotations, and the names a foreigner is called in Libreville are strangely similar to what happens in France: the presence of a significant number of migrants in an ecolinguistic niche thus generates the appearance of a varied and unpleasant vocabulary to name them, a vocabulary that is not encountered in such proportions in Mali or Burkina Faso, for instance, where foreigners are much less numerous.

But we cannot restrict a language to its vocabulary and, in order to reply to the question that is preoccupying us here – the status of the French language(s) of Africa – we also need to consider problems of phonetics and syntax. An investigation carried out by Marie-Louise Moreau, Ndiassé Thiam and Cécile Bauvois[67] provides us with interesting data on the phonetic aspect. The authors first made a tape of sixty-seven segments of twenty seconds extracted from sixty-seven interviews with speakers of university-level education from eight different countries (Benin, Burundi, Cameroon, Ivory Coast, Niger, Rwanda, Senegal and Zaire). Nothing in the contents of these segments enabled the origin of the speakers to be identified: the interviews were all about the reform of spelling in France, and passages had been chosen in which there was no reference to their nationality and no specific vocabulary was used. In the second stage, the authors played this tape to 104 students from the University of Dakar. They were told that the sixty-seven people recorded were all native speakers from French-speaking Africa and asked to say what their nationality was. The results of this research can be summed up in a few figures:

- 84.3 per cent of Senegalese speakers were recognized;
- 71.4 per cent of non-Senegalese speakers were recognized;
- the nationality of the non-Senegalese speakers was very difficult to identify;
- the ethnic origin of the Senegalese was also very difficult to identify.

So those questioned found it easy to identify their compatriots and foreigners, were unable to guess the exact identity of the latter and, above all, were unable to situate the ethnic origin of their compatriots. As the authors emphasize, 'the identity that the people recorded express first and foremost in their French seems thus to be on the level of national group and not on the level of ethnic group'. This would appear to indicate the appearance of a typically Senegalese way of speaking French, recognizable from phonetic criteria and not marked from a geographical and/or ethnic point of view; whether they are Fula, Sereer, Diola or Wolof, Senegalese speakers are recognized as Senegalese but not as Fula, Sereers, Diolas or Wolofs. We can thus postulate the existence in Senegalese university circles of a local norm of French, which is partly the product of the town. The urban factor in the constitution of national norms is a well-known fact: the intermixing of populations, different languages or local forms of one and the same language plays a part in the emergence of a vehicular language that gradually takes over from the other languages present.[68] This urban factor also plays on the ability of those questioned in the survey to distinguish the national origin of speakers: 'The listeners who spent their childhood and adolescence in an urban milieu are better able to distinguish the Senegalese from the non-Senegalese.' The authors conclude the presentation of their survey by emphasizing that this endogenous norm is of a nature to 'reduce the linguistic insecurity of the speakers and to bolster the feeling that French is now part of the Senegalese patrimony'. Of course, similar surveys would need to be carried out in other African countries to verify whether there are such clear endogenous norms elsewhere, but we here have, at least as regards Senegal, a highly interesting theory.

The problem then arises of knowing how to classify these varieties. The term pidginization is often used to describe them, though the authors do not always specify exactly what they mean by that word. In 1979, in a discussion of what he called 'the regional varieties of French in Africa', Gabriel Manessy emphasized the fact that 'pidginization tends to make the language more functional . . . i.e. to increase its efficiency as an instrument of communication at the expense of the other functions that language is usually expected to fulfil', while *creolization* consists rather in 'the multiplication of indices with a metalinguistic meaning'.[69] His pairing of pidgin/creole was meant to distinguish between the purely communicational use of a language and its use as a badge of identity, 'when this mode of language became the property of a socio-cultural group sufficiently stable and sufficiently particularized for its members to be aware of its singularity'.[70] Returning to the same problem in 1985, he postulated a parallelism between the appropriation of French by slaves (of which creoles were the result) and the *vernacularization* of French in Africa,[71] a notion that he defined several times over in different ways – for instance in 1994: 'The set of phenomena that are produced when a collectivity of speakers becomes clearly aware of the bonds that exist between its members, the interests that unite them and their common expectations to such a degree that the collectivity is led to singularize itself by its linguistic behaviour'.[72]

In every case, this *vernacularization* is a phenomenon that consists of manifesting in the form of a language the shift from a communicational function to one that proclaims identity, and we can postulate that it is this shift that we have observed in the types of French spoken in Africa. Manessy has suggested that this formal manifestation is not syntactic, as a persistent 'rumour' would have it, but *semantactic:* 'I am using this hybrid term "semantax" deliberately, to show that my intention is not to resurrect the naïve interpretation that defined creole as the result of a combination of a European vocabulary with an exotic grammar.'[73] In his view, the important thing is the particular colouration given to the French language(s) of Africa by a certain number of semantico-syntactic facts. I will not venture into the details here,[74] but simply mention one single tendency: the multiplicity of meanings assumed in Africa by French verbs or substantives that are normally less polysemic.

In the clearest of his texts on what he calls *semantax*, the title of which is also very suggestive ('the subversion of imported languages'), Manessey emphasizes that we often find, as we flick through dictionaries of African languages, long lists of the most varied meanings for the verbal entries,[75] an organization that we find echoed in the treatment of French terms. For instance, I pointed out above the different senses of the verb *gagner* ('to win', as in standard French, but also 'to obtain', 'to possess', 'to find', 'to receive', 'to have', etc.) or the verb *gâter (*'to spoil, destroy, ruin, disorganize, soil', etc.). There are also semantic patterns that sit a little oddly with the logic of French, such as the verb *pardonner* which can mean simultaneously 'to ask for' and 'to grant' pardon, but also 'to cancel a debt' and 'to bargain', or the verb *prêter* which, together with its standard meaning ('to lend') can also mean 'to borrow'. As for nouns, we can point to the different meanings of the word *ventre*, meaning 'stomach' or 'belly' in standard French ('part of the body but also heart, soul, seat of the emotions, genitals') and the numerous turns of phrase in which it plays a part: *avoir un ventre* ('to have a belly' and thus 'to be pregnant'), *avoir le ventre amer* ('to have a bitter stomach' i.e. 'to be resentful'), *avoir le ventre sec* ('to have a dry stomach' i.e. 'to be constipated'), *dire son ventre* ('to tell of your belly', i.e. 'to announce that you're pregnant'), *gâter le ventre* ('to spoil the belly', i.e. 'to have an abortion'), etc.

Manessy's hypothesis is that, over and beyond the interferences (i.e. the projection onto the foreign language structures of one's first language) that are usual in learning situations, these particularities are the trace of ways of seeing and organizing things that are foreign to French culture – the properly African 'semantax'. If we take a more general view, it becomes apparent that the attempt to implant a language in a new ecology can lead, logically speaking, to only two results: either rejection or adoption/adaptation. In other words, as for a graft, the implanting of a language can succeed or fail, but in this latter case, in Manessy's persuasive image, adoption implies a certain number of modifications, adaptations and 'subversions'. What we see, in fact, is a modification of the functions of French in Africa: it is at first a colonial language and then a language of African powers, but it is also an interethnic or interstate vehicular language; it slowly becomes in certain circumstances the language(s) of one's identity. Thus, in the conflict between exogenous norm (that of standard French) and endogenous norms (those of local variants of French), the local form can connote a desire to gain a firm foothold in African social realities. Auguste Moussirou-Mouyama, for instance, has emphasized how, in the opposition press in Gabon, the use of the endogenous norms shows a desire to 'speak properly', and that the way this kind of language is used by humorists and certain theatre actors allows people, symbolically, to 'wring the neck of the official norm'.[76]

African argots and the ecolinguistic niche: the example of Bukavu

A whole series of facts indicates this latter function, in particular the appearance, in different countries, of argots in which it is sometimes the French lexicon that dominates and sometimes a lexicon that has emerged from one or several African languages. Thus, in the Ivory Coast, there develops the *Nouchi* which I mentioned in chapter 1; and thus, too, there arises an argot specific to Burkina Faso, Senegal, Mali, Congo Kinshasa (*Indoubil*, based on French, English and an African language that varies from town to town: Lingala in Kinshasa, Swahili in Bukavu), etc.

I would like to explore this last example more fully, since it is probably the one that has been described in most detail. Didier Goyvaerts, who has studied the case of Indoubil in Bukavu (Congo Kinshasa), concludes that 'it is a means of identification for a group of a particular age which, as such, reinforces group solidarity'),[77] and he adds that Indoubil, like the types of vehicular language spoken in towns, overcomes the effects of ethnic division. These two terms (argot, vehicular language) do not designate the same phenomenon: *argot presupposes the existence of a common language, which it transforms, or languages that it mixes up together, while a vehicular language compensates for the absence of a common language.* But it is impossible to describe the form and function of the French of Africa (or of French in Africa, or the varieties of French in Africa) without considering it in its relations with the other languages and other linguistic forms that coexist in the same linguistic niche. In other terms, in a given niche, the many different linguistic practices that arise in different populations are all interrelated.

I have often described the linguistic situations in Africa in terms of a three-way opposition among mass languages, vehicular language, and official language (cf., for example, Calvet, *Language Wars*). In this tripartite division, which thus distinguishes between the languages of everyday management, the management languages of exchanges between different communities and the languages of state management, the communicative function plays a central role, as a kind of nerve centre. Languages of the great axes of communication (roads and tracks for Diola, for instance, the railway in the case of Munukutuba, the river in the case of Lingala, the coasts and ports in the case of Swahili, initially speaking – and, on another continent, in the case of Malay), these vehicular languages are also, especially these days, the languages of towns and cities. They thus have several different functions. They ensure communication between speakers with different mother tongues (and this is why they are vehicular languages); they are also simultaneously languages of integration into the town and they can finally play a pacifying, neutralizing role, in this context where ethnic oppositions are very strong, sometimes masked and sometimes violently manifested. Given the strong tendency to urbanization found in Africa today, it is thus in the ecolinguistic niche of an African town that we must try to understand the functions of French and of the African vernaculars and vehicular languages, as well as those of the different argots or secret languages that are found there.

Bukavu is, from this point of view, a typical example. In this town, which in 1985 had a population numbering 240,000 inhabitants, and is the capital of the province of Kivu (ex-Zaire), we indeed find between forty and fifty languages, three of which are vehicular languages: Swahili, French and Indoubil. The first two are exogenous forms that have adapted: French was imported by Belgian colonization; Swahili came from the east, Tanzania (cf. Whiteley, *Swahili*; Calvet, *Les Langues véhiculaires*). As for Indoubil, it is a relexification of the vehicular language of Swahili by different languages of the niche (Lingala, French – what in chapter 1 I called endogenous relexification) and sometimes by English (which I called exogenous relexification). These three forms are the least marked ethnically, or, if you prefer, the most consensual. And yet they are socially marked: Swahili is, according to Goyvaerts, the vehicular language of the oldest people and of formal situations, French that of educated people in every situation, and Indoubil the language of the young, especially in informal contexts.

The lexicon of Indoubil thus comprises Swahili or foreign words to which a completely different meaning is given, as well as neologisms, constructed for example by taking the first syllable of a French word and adding the first syllable of the Swahili word that has the same meaning.[78] It is thus incomprehensible to non-initiates and could therefore be considered a secret language or a form of argot. According to

Goyvaerts, however, this cryptic function is not predominant; rather, Indoubil creates a sense of identity (serving as a code for young urban people) and is also a neutralizer (it transcends ethnic differences and oppositions). There are, in addition, two other 'special' languages in Bukavu, Kinyume and Kibalele. Kinyume is a generic term designating a process that, as in French 'verlan' or back slang, consists in reversing the order of syllables. This linguistic game is essentially used by young girls, for playful or cryptic purposes, both in towns and in villages, and on the basis of absolutely any local language. Kibalele, on the other hand, is a secret code used for cryptic purposes in an urban milieu. Formally, it consists of the inversion of syllables (as in Kinyume) and in the addition of a final 'l' together with the vowel of the first syllable. Thus the Swahili word *soko* ('market') produces *kosolo*, the French form 'chez nous', 'in our home', produces *nushele* (whence another name for Kibalele, *Kinushele*, 'the language spoken in our home'), the Lingala word *lobi* ('tomorrow') produces *bilolo*, etc.

In order to analyse the functions of the different languages present the author begins with the idea that in Bukavu there is a coexistence between social classes and ethnicity, with social class determining, for instance, the district in which a person lives, the bar where he goes to drink his beer, and ethnicity determining with whom he will drink that beer and what language he will use.[79] In this equilibrium between different tensions, Kibalele and Indoubil are not in his view simply secret languages but also ethnically neutral and socially marked means of communication. Thus the languages swing, as it were, between what Goyvaerts calls 'accommodation' and 'distinction', as in an oscillating movement. And Goyvaerts thus arranges the different coexisting languages in a semi-circular diagram (like that created by the swing of a pendulum), whose right extreme is the place of *distinction* (Kibalele is deliberately cryptic), and that on the left the place of *accommodation* (which can be understood as adaptation to the milieu). From the point of view of communicability, the centre is the place of *unification* (as the use of Swahili corresponds to a desire to open up communication to the greatest number) and the extremes are the place of *alienation* (the use of a tribal language or of Kibalele corresponds to a desire to restrict communication to the circle of members of a group). The different coexisting languages are thus arranged, in his view, as in diagram 3.1.

The further we go from the centre, the more 'marked' and restrictive are the languages ('alienation'), the further right we go the more

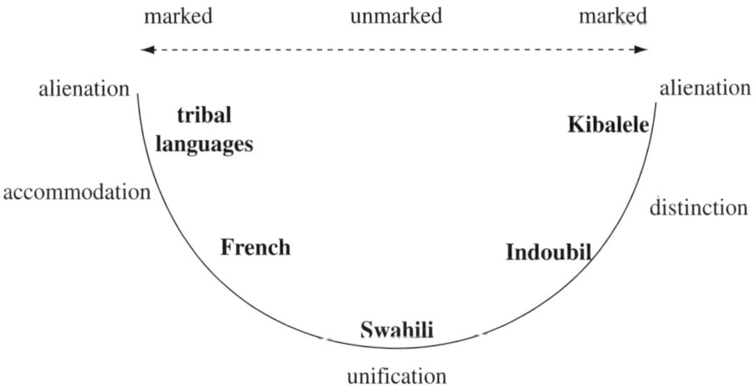

Diagram 3.1 Goyvaerts' semi-circular representation
Source: Didier Goyvaerts, 'Kibalele: form and function of a secret language in Bukavu (Zaire)'.

cryptic ('distinction'), the further left the more they are mass languages ('accommodation'). This schema, which has the advantage of attempting to analyse the functions of all the languages that coexist in Bukavu – and of showing that the choice of a language indicates where the speaker is situated and to which group he belongs – is, however, not generalizable since the different terms do not appear in all the situations. The case of Bukavu is in fact extremely idiosyncratic insofar as Indoubil is a relexification of Swahili, whereas the argots I mentioned earlier are more often than not relexifications of French. Furthermore, in the countries of French-speaking Africa it is wrong to speak of French as if it were a unified, standardized form. Together with standard French, as taught at schools and universities, what we find is both a local French (that has been baptized French of Africa) and, sometimes, a relexified French (the 'argots'). Finally, the ethnic languages (those which Goyvaerts calls 'tribal') are sometimes relexified, as in the case of Kibalele. So, in order to generalize it, we should be able to modify the schema as shown in diagram 3.2.

Local French and African vehicular language(s) tend to fulfil the same function of unification, while standard French and relexified French tend, respectively, to accommodation and distinction, just like ethnic languages and their potential relexified forms. The five varieties of languages present in this schema are thus not given concrete form in every situation; rather, they have to be conceived as tendencies.

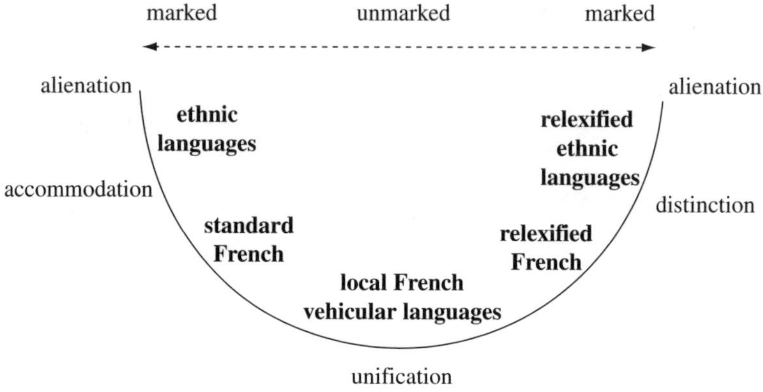

Diagram 3.2

Thus we have a tendency to unification as concretized in one or more vehicular languages (languages of African origin in Brazzaville or Dakar, and local French in Abidjan); a tendency to use mass languages, which is given concrete form in the use of ethnic languages; and a tendency towards the cryptic, which finds concrete form in various 'argots'. These functional varieties are closely related to one another, and any modification of the one will have an impact on the function of the others. Depending on the characteristics of a given ecolinguistic niche, they may be the product of the relexification of French (as in the case of Nouchi) or of a local language (as in the case of Indoubil). This is why the appearance of playful or cryptic forms – of 'argots' – cannot be separated from the analysis of other forms.

Justifiably deciding that, in the conflict between language as static and language as evolving, argot is on the side of evolution, Gisèle Prignitz concluded a study on argot in Burkina Faso with these words: 'And what if African usage were one day to save French?'[80] What she meant by this remark was the idea that vernacular African neologisms could act as a counterweight to anglicisms, but she seemed at the same time to ignore the fact that evolution is not always linear and does not always proceed from state A to state B; also, it can, in different situations, lead to different states B´, B´´, B´´´, etc., as symbolized in diagram 3.3.

My hypothesis is that we can see in these cryptic, playful or quite simply contextual adaptations of the imported language the product of

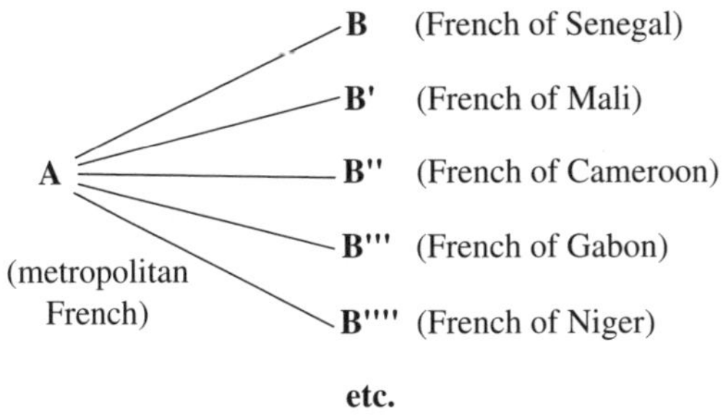

Diagram 3.3

an appropriation, of the shift from the function of a vehicular language to an identity-bestowing function that is accompanied by the formal modifications appropriate to each context and to each situation.

Conclusions: acclimatization and acclimatation

If the modifications of the French verbal system spring, as we have seen, from internal self-regulation, then vehicular language, the French of Marseilles or the varieties of French of Africa constitute examples of ecological self-regulation, of the reaction of one or more languages to the surrounding milieu. From the ecolinguistic point of view, these data can be analysed in terms of *acclimatization* and *acclimatation*. In ecology, the term *acclimatization* is used to designate the fact that a species displaced from one milieu *can survive in another*, and the term *acclimatation* is used when this species can also reproduce itself in this new milieu. Acclimatization thus constitutes a response to an external stimulus which leads to a transitory adaptation: the species adapts momentarily to the milieu in order to survive. Acclimatation implies an evolution of certain characteristics of the species which enables it to reproduce in its new milieu. I will be proposing that the same is true of languages. For instance, during the colonial period, Dutch experienced a period of short-lived acclimatization in Indonesia (Indonesia is now independent and Dutch is no longer spoken there). Latin constitutes a good example of acclimatation to different milieux on the part of a language that came from Rome – the result of which is today visible in the set of Romance languages.

French may be in the process of acclimatizing itself in Africa, fulfilling an identity-bestowing function and, to answer the question from which I started out, taking on specific forms that will eventually announce the emergence of a new generation of autonomous languages. For appropriating a language and using it for the purpose of indicating one's identity imply its adaptation. Foued Laroussi has emphasized that 'in order to really become an identity-bestowing form, not only in the Maghreb but throughout French-speaking Africa, French must adapt and transform itself'.[81] The African situations I have just been discussing are a good example of this. But the specific feature of these situations stems from the fact that, together with the endogenous norms coming into existence, there is a persistent exogenous norm, standard French, from which vernacular French becomes independent. 'The independence of a vernacular which is supposed to coexist with the language from which it has emerged (and not to succeed it) results from its appropriation by a social group that is seceding', wrote Manessy.[82] I would prefer to speak of social secession producing linguistic secession, or of parallel secessions. But it is impossible to know whether this new generation of languages will really come into being, in other words whether we really have acclimatization or acclimatation here, since this raises the problem of the transmission of linguistic situations, which I will be examining in chapter 5.

This leaves one last question: what adjective should we use to describe this potential 'new generation of languages'? Should we speak of Indo-European languages, Romance languages, French languages or, even, of types of 'new French' in the same way Mufwene speaks of 'new Englishes'?[83] In my introduction, I pointed out that the metaphor of 'families of languages', the idea that there are 'mother languages' and 'sister languages', had hampered research by overstressing linear descent over a possible 'coproduction'. We here have a good example of this: where the implantation of French in Africa would actually result in its acclimatation, the different products of this process would be simultaneously 'French' and 'African languages'. We still have not reached that point, of course, but the taxonomic choice of classifying them as 'French' languages, or 'Franco-African', or 'Europeo-African', etc., would require both an arbitrary decree that ignored historical realities (it is more often than not a linguist who names languages) and a theoretical problem to which I will return in chapter 5 when I discuss creoles.

— 4 —

Linguistic Representations and Change

In a novel by Stanislas Lem, *His Master's Voice*, one of the characters recounts his memories of a mass execution committed by German troops in a Polish town. He describes a young man, about to be shot, who suddenly flings himself on a soldier yelling that he isn't Jewish. But he says it in Yiddish. . . . This anecdote can be read on different levels. We can, for instance, simply interpret it in the terms of a contrast between denotation and connotation: the contents of the words uttered by the young Jew denote that he is not Jewish, whereas its form (Yiddish) connotes the contrary. There are a great number of more or less funny stories in which a person is betrayed by his or her language. The most famous is the one about the two German spies who were parachuted into England during the war. They go into a pub where they order, in perfect English, two Martinis:

> 'Barman, please, two Martinis.'
> 'Yes, dry?' replies the barman.
> '*Nein, zwei*,' replies one of the Germans.

A fateful error, to be sure. . . . There's another story, that of a customer who goes into a Jewish restaurant in New York. A Japanese maître d'hotel welcomes him in Yiddish, seats him at his table and takes his order, all in Yiddish. Then the manager comes over to say hello to the customer, an old friend of his.

> 'Say, your maître d' speaks Yiddish very well for a Japanese guy!'
> 'Sshh! Keep it quiet,' comes the reply, 'he thinks he's learning English.'

These stories can be analysed in different ways. On the logical level, for instance, nothing prevents you from declaring that you are not Jewish in Yiddish, or that you are not English in English. The only illogical behaviour would be to declare in perfect English that you can't speak English. . . . But the fact remains that, when faced with certain linguistic practices, we feel authorized to draw certain deductions: he speaks Yiddish, so he is Jewish. While this hypothesis is statistically plausible, the fact remains that it can be erroneous: a Japanese person can express himself or herself in Yiddish without being Jewish. But the first anecdote lends itself to other interpretations. We imagine, no doubt, that by speaking Yiddish the young man has betrayed himself. This is also evident – but less so – in the case of the German spy who hears the English 'dry' as the German *drei*, 'three', and instinctively corrects it: *nein, zwei* ('no, two'). The young man may be impelled by an unconscious death wish that leads him to use Yiddish to say 'I am Jewish' even when he seems to be affirming the opposite. He may also not know that he is speaking Yiddish. I don't mean that he is ignorant of the name of his language, which is not very important, but that he is unaware that it is perceived as emblematic of Jewishness. And it is, of course, this *perception* of Yiddish that is at the centre of our interpretations. For there is, at the other end of the chain of communication, the German soldier who hears him saying, in Yiddish, 'I am not Jewish'; he too can draw different conclusions from this, or indeed not understand what the young man is saying. Let's stick to the most probable hypothesis: the young man speaks only Yiddish, he wants to deny the fact that he is a Jew, and the German soldier understands what he is saying, perceives that he is saying it in Yiddish and draws the conclusion that he is indeed a Jew. Here we come up against a very particular dimension of linguistic communication, the fact that next to the use of codes, i.e. linguistic practices, we also have ideas about those codes, presuppositions and stereotypes, which partly constitute the subject of this chapter, namely representations.

We are now entering new territory: linguistics did indeed, some years ago, add to the study of practices and forms the study of a hitherto neglected, indeed glossed-over domain that we could define loosely as what speakers say and think about the languages they speak (or the way they speak them) and the languages spoken by others (or the way others speak those languages). This definition, deliberately rather coarse-grained, thus refers to all the representations of the object described by the linguist that need to be integrated into the description of that object and those practices, both because they are part of them and because, as we shall be seeing, they have an impact on their evolution.

In this 'new territory', two notions have long predominated: first that of stereotypes and attitudes on the one hand, and then that of linguistic insecurity, which one can find everywhere from the start of the 1990s onwards: articles, books, research programmes and conferences devoted to these topics have flourished, as have the – often contradictory and sometimes confused – definitions of the phenomena. This is why, to begin with, I would like to return to the sources of these notions and follow their trajectory through the linguistic literature. It is thus an epistemological approach that the reader will find below. I will then try to investigate, in the light of the theory, certain linguistic situations, so as to suggest a new theoretical framework.

Linguistic insecurity and representations: a historical approach

Right at the start of the 1960s, Wallace Lambert, who was studying Franco-English bilingualism in Montreal, established the methodology known as that of 'matched guise'.[1] In an attempt to bring out the 'attitudes' of English-speakers and French-speakers towards English and French, he used bilingual speakers, each of them recording two texts (one in French, the other in English). These recordings, presented as originating with different people, were then played to 'judges' who, on a scale going from 'very little' to 'a great deal', had to evaluate the speakers as regards height, physical attractiveness, leadership qualities, sense of humour, intelligence, religious feelings, self-confidence, reliability, cheerfulness, kindness, ambition, sociability, character and likeability. They were told the object of the exercise was to discover whether people could be judged on the basis of their voices.

The results of the experiment were extremely interesting. On the one hand, these 'judges' did not realize that the pairs of recordings were produced by the same person. On the other hand, the English-speaking judges gave a favourable judgement to the English speakers on seven points (height, physical attractiveness, intelligence, reliability, kindness, ambition and character) and only gave a favourable judgement to the French-speakers for sense of humour. The French-speaking judges, however, evaluated the English-speakers more favourably than the French-speakers on most characteristics, and preferred the French-speakers to the English-speakers in only two respects: kindness and religious feelings. In other words, the judges were not in fact evaluating voices, as they had been invited to, but languages, on the basis of the ideas they entertained about those languages and their relations to them. From this point of view, it was interesting to note that the French-speakers were evaluated more favourably by the English-speaking than by the French-speaking judges.

A few years later, W. Cheyne[2] used a similar technique to analyse reactions to people's accents: drama students had been recorded using an English accent and a Scottish accent at the same time, and the judges, from Glasgow and London, had to evaluate them from the point of view of personality and professional status, using scales inspired by those Lambert had devised. The results were just as interesting: English and Scottish judges evaluated the English accent more favourably for values relevant to competence, but the Scots evaluated the Scottish accent more favourably when it came to generosity, likeability and humour. Ever since then, studies inspired by Lambert have become more and more numerous. To take a non-European example, a survey carried out in Canton (China) with the technique of matched guise, using Cantonese and non-Cantonese students who were required to 'judge' the speakers who spoke good Putonghua (Mandarin) or spoke it with a strong Cantonese accent,[3] produced similar results. All the 'judges' agreed that a good knowledge of Putonghua was necessary if you hoped to get on in society, but the Cantonese 'judges', in particular the men, also showed a liking for Putonghua when it was strongly marked by a Cantonese accent.

So in the three cases there appeared the same tendency for the speakers of a dominated language or form (French-speakers, Scots, Cantonese) to conform in their judgements to the stereotypes of the speakers of the dominant form, but simultaneously to show a certain attachment to their linguistic form. In other words, what we have here, if we read between the lines, is the emergence of what would later be called linguistic insecurity (in the case of the French-speakers of Montreal or the Scots of Glasgow) and identity-based solidarities (in the judgements that the Glaswegians expressed on the Scottish accent or that the Cantonese expressed on 'Cantonized' Putonghua, for example).

But in the last two surveys (W. Cheyne and Ivan Kalman, Zhong Yong; Xiao Hong) the accent (of London or Glasgow, Beijing or Canton) was manifest in only one language (English and Putonghua). A more recent survey, carried out in South Africa, has demonstrated that it was also extremely important when it was manifested in another language. Vivian de Klerk and Barbara Bosch[4] have used the technique of matched guise with three trilingual speakers (Afrikaans, English, Xhosa), each of them reading a text in the three languages. The nine recordings obtained were then being submitted to 298 judges, most of them monolingual.[5] Overall, the results of this survey showed that:

1 English, whatever accent it is spoken with, is judged more favourably than Xhosa or Afrikaans. We should here emphasize that the speakers of Xhosa and Afrikaans had a more positive image of English than did English-speakers themselves.
2 However, an English accent and a Xhosa accent (in the three languages) were judged more favourably than the Afrikaans accent.

And, concerning the jobs which the judges were more specifically asked to attribute to the masked speakers, those with an English accent were deemed to have a profession of higher status (professor, businessman, minister, lawyer, etc.), and those with an Afrikaans or Xhosa accent a more middle-status profession (technician, civil servant, bureaucrat, etc.). Commenting on these results, the authors emphasize that they fly in the face of a received opinion which supposes that the language of power has, in people's stereotypical view, a positive status, and they explain this contradiction by the fact that South African power, held since 1948 by white Afrikaners, was rejected by all, while English generally enjoys a positive image in Africa. The most important thing here is the way that, as in Cheyne's survey discussed above, the *signifier* that provokes the stereotypical reactions is not simply a language but, in two out of three cases, an accent. So Klerk and Bosch emphasize that 'discrimination against people may well be linked to social and educational disadvantage',[6] and draw from this conclusions concerning linguistic policies and the teaching of different languages in a multilingual situation. But these surveys, and many others, show us the importance of linguistic stereotypes in social life and of the links between these stereotypes and the sociopolitical situation.

The methodology of these surveys, carried out in the context of social psychology, was later borrowed and adapted more widely by linguistics for the analysis of insecurity, in the first instance, and then, more broadly, for the analysis of linguistic representations. It is this introduction of a new area of study into the field of the sciences of language that I will now examine.

The sources of the notion: Einar Haugen and William Labov

There is a little-known and rarely cited article by Einar Haugen, 'Schizoglossia and the linguistic norm',[7] which was originally a paper presented at a conference on bilingualism. In this Haugen describes, with a nice touch of humour, the symptoms of an illness suffered by a speaker exposed to more than one variety of his language: pain in the diaphragm and vocal cords, general insecurity, an interest in the form rather than the substance of languages. And, in extreme cases, he continued, the 'schizoglossic' could become a professional linguist, just as schizophrenics become psychoanalysts, so as to study in others the symptoms of their own malady.

This illness, which is endemic to the United States, according to Haugen, is the product of a conflict between the norms there prevalent. And it is true that the English language lives in a normative universe, which explains for instance Bernard Shaw's play, *Pygmalion*, and the musical derived from it, *My Fair Lady*: there is no hope for anyone who cannot pronounce their aspirate /h/ correctly, and contempt is shown for those who do not respect the pronunciation that is considered to be a source of social prestige. The difficulties encountered by translators who attempt to convey in different languages the differences between the English of Professor Higgins and that of Eliza Doolittle are, from this point of view, characteristic. So Haugen used the notion of *insecurity* in reference to situations in which there coexisted different norms, different forms of the same language, but it was William Labov who developed it in several texts that were collected in *Sociolinguistic Patterns* (first published in 1973) and translated into French in 1976.

He indicates in particular how he calculates an ILI (Index of Linguistic Insecurity):

> The subjects were presented with 18 words which have socially significant variants in pronunciation: *vase*, *aunt*, *escalator*, etc., and were asked to select the form they thought was correct. . . . They were then asked to indicate which form they usually used themselves. The total number of cases in which these two choices differed was taken as the Index of Linguistic Insecurity (ILI). By this measure, the local middle class showed much the greatest degree of linguistic insecurity.[8]

Table 4.1

	Socioeconomic classes			
	0–2	3–5	6–8	9
ILI	**44%**	**50%**	16%	20%
1–2	25	21	16	**70**
3–7	12	25	**58**	10
8–13	19	04	10	–

Source: Data from William Labov, *Sociolinguistic Patterns*, p. 133.

He then presents a table showing the 'Distribution of index of linguistic insecurity scores by socioeconomic class'[9] (I have emphasized four figures in table 4.1).

It might seem surprising that Labov in his commentary essentially insists on the linguistic insecurity of the lower bourgeoisie and does not emphasize the linguistic security of informers from the sub-proletariat, the working class and the middle and upper bourgeoisie. It is clearly the lower bourgeoisie that interests him:

> Lower-middle-class speakers have the greatest tendency towards linguistic insecurity. (p. 117)
>
> This linguistic insecurity is shown by the very wide range of stylistic variation used by lower-middle-class speakers. (p. 117)
>
> The great fluctuation in stylistic variation shown by the lower middle class, their hypersensitivity to stigmatized features which they themselves use, and the inaccurate perception of their own speech, all point to a high degree of linguistic insecurity for these speakers. (p. 132)

In fact, it is not linguistic insecurity that is important, in his view – it is indeed secondary: what matters is the subsequent hypercorrectness and the role it plays in linguistic change.

The notion of linguistic insecurity was thus a relation between a judgement of normativity (correct usage in the speaker's view) and a self-evaluation (personal usage in the speaker's view) and, to repeat my earlier point, it was of little importance for Labov, being but a marginal fallout of his approach which consisted of seeking an explanation for linguistic change in social stratification. We will see that this point of view – a resolutely intra-linguistic one (Labov was working on one single language, studying English in Martha's Vineyard or New York) – has been hitherto maintained in the majority of studies that have been marked by his influence and use the notion of linguistic insecurity.

The three norms: Alain Rey

Labov's texts were translated into French only in 1976, but already in 1972, in a path-breaking article, Alain Rey had examined the notion of norm, distinguishing between subjective norm, objective norm and prescriptive norm.[10] The areas covered by the notion of norm, he wrote, 'are conceptualized in a confused and functionally ambiguous manner – by which I mean that ambiguity makes these concepts function – by ideology'.[11] The word 'norm', after all, has two different meanings in French, designating on the one hand the idea of a mean, a frequency (and corresponding in this sense to the adjective 'normal') and on the other hand that of submission to a value judgement, a rule (thus corresponding to the adjective 'normative').

William Labov had published little before that time.[12] Rey however, in 1972, saw in his publications an

> exemplary body of work, linking as it does the description and objective analysis of variants to the social situation of the speakers among whom they are observed and the criteria of evaluation (metalinguistic judgements) of those speakers. This last point, an essential one, allows us to combine the study of objective norms with that of evaluative norm, the basis of the prescriptive norm, and to relate the normal to the evaluative.[13]

In other terms, as opposed to what was claimed by the majority of linguists, it became possible to describe 'the attitudes of speakers to the usages of their language'. These evaluative attitudes are the social basis of normative attitudes, and the norm common to these speakers constitutes the cement of the linguistic community.

As Rey wrote:

> Only a linguistics of the objective norm, of the variations and types that underlie varying usages, and a systematic study of metalinguistic attitudes in a community that uses the same linguistic system (language or dialect, depending on the definition of the system) will be able to act as

> a firm foundation for the study of subjective norms, value judgements on language and the retroactive impact of these judgements on usage – a study that could constitute a social science akin to theories of value.[14]

Here his view was broader and deeper than that of Labov, the only difference – a significant one – being that he had no fieldwork to draw on. So at that time Rey distinguished between:

- the objective norm, internal to the system, which description brings out;
- the subjective norm, found in the metalinguistic attitudes and expressions of the speakers;
- the prescriptive norm, i.e. the normative intervention on usage ('you should speak like this, not like that'), constituting a pseudo-system.

On the other hand, he did not mention linguistic insecurity, a notion which, as I have said, appeared in a few passages of Labov's *Sociolinguistics*.

The heirs

For a long time this notion of linguistic insecurity would be absent from the French works devoted to the nascent science of sociolinguistics. J.-B. Marcellesi and B. Gardin, for instance, who found little place in their book for Labov, discuss linguistic insecurity in a few brief lines: 'A great number of New Yorkers live in a state of latent linguistic insecurity: they do not produce the forms that they acknowledge as constituting the norm: their behaviour is in contradiction with the norms that they do acknowledge'.[15]

The same is true of most sociolinguistic texts in French until the end of the 1970s. In 1982 Pierre Bourdieu presented what Labov called 'linguistic insecurity' in a slightly different way – in terms of 'linguistic market' and 'symbolic domination' – and emphasized 'all the corrections, whether ad hoc or permanent, to which dominated speakers, as they strive for correctness, consciously or unconsciously, subject the stigmatized aspects of their pronunciation, their diction (involving various forms of euphemism) and their syntax'.[16] But this approach hardly modified things, and merely set this notion within the author's conceptual framework.

Rey's three norms (objective, subjective, prescriptive) would, for their part, enjoy a fine career in the works of Nicole Gueunier, Genouvrier and Khomsi (1978), and especially Houdebine (1982, 1985) who would introduce a psychoanalytic flavour into this mainly sociolinguistic scheme. As is often the case, scientific advances entailed certain losses. Thus Labov, a student of Weinreich, forgot the multilingual dimension of his work, and Houdebine, starting out from Rey and Labov, in turn lost sight of (or relegated to the background) the social dimension of the problem. It is true that the necessary inclusion of the subject in the linguistic approach is complex, in the sense that it implies two dimensions, the individual dimension and the collective dimension, just as the necessary inclusion of the social community implies the analysis of intralinguistic phenomena (the 'structure' of the languages in question) and interlinguistic phenomena (the relations between languages).

Houdebine's suggestion – *l'imaginaire linguistique* – would be the object of successive definitions characterized by an increasing number of sub-categories within Rey's three norms, the result being subsumed into the notion of the '*imaginaire*' and the ever clearer deployment of Lacanian language. Thus *l'imaginaire linguistique* subsumes two sets of norms, *objectified norms* and *subjectified norms* (Rey had described these norms in 1972 as 'objective' and 'subjective'). The former are in turn divided into *systemic norms* and *statistical norms*. As for subjectified norms, they are divided into *communicational norms, fictive norms, prescriptive norms* and *evaluative norms*, which are finally divided into *self-evaluation* and *group evaluation*. Arguing for a 'dynamic synchrony',[17] Houdebine rightly considers synchrony as a methodological abstraction and suggests envisaging it as 'a coexistence of varied usages whose unequal weight in synchrony influences its evolution differently'.[18] In her view, we need to examine the language's weak points (fluctuations, neutralizations), since they are most affected by attitudes that 'play in one direction or another, as a brake or an accelerator, a conservation or an innovation'.[19] But as she did not at that time give a very precise definition of the terms she was using, it was difficult to see what difference she was drawing between linguistic attitude, linguistic representation and *l'imaginaire linguistique*. On the other hand, she proposed drawing a difference between dynamic synchrony and diachrony: from the first point of view, there is a coexistence between variants during the time of communication, whereas from the second point of view there is no coexistence of variants but a chain, a linear succession in time. This distinction, the main effect of which was to preserve the opposition between diachrony and synchrony, so as not to question one of the basic dichotomies of Saussure and his followers, could not however enlighten us about the different notions with which we are here concerned.

In her thesis, written under Houdebine's supervision, Cécile Canut in 1995 gave this definition of *l'imaginaire linguistique*: 'A set of subjective evaluative norms characterizing the representations of subjects on languages and language-based practices, and made manifest through epilinguistic discourses. It explains the personal relation that the subject has with his or her language.' So it appears that *epilinguistic discourses* are the signifier of *l'imaginaire linguistique*, which would make of this latter a part (or the equivalent) of people's attitudes. As for the 'subjective evaluative norms', these are the ones that can be brought out 'by the description of speakers' attitudes and more directly of their epilinguistic attitudes'.[20]

In a more recent text Houdebine gives us another definition of this same notion:

> *L'Imaginaire linguistique* (IL) is thus defined as the relation between the subject and *lalangue* (Lacan [i.e. Lacan's term for the desire-imbued materiality of language]) and between the subject and La Langue (Saussure [i.e. Saussure's term for the structure of language that subtends its individual actualizations]). It can be and is expressed in evaluative comments on usages or languages (the monolingual or plurilingual aspect of linguistic evaluations).[21]

And a year later, she repeats this passage almost word for word: '*L'imaginaire linguistique* is defined as the relation between the subject and *lalangue* (Lacan) and between the subject and La Langue (Saussure); it is expressed through its evaluative comments on usages or languages (the monolingual or plurilingual aspect of linguistic evaluations').[22]

And the same *imaginaire linguistique* is also defined by Cécile Canut as synonymous with representations: 'The study of speakers' representations (or the study of *l'imaginaire linguistique*)'.[23] In the same text, Houdebine in fact gives it something of a catch-all – or, if you prefer, ecumenical – meaning: 'This notion subsumes what is conventionally designated as linguistic awareness or ideology or opinions or even feelings; all terms which are problematic insofar as they are notions that have not been defined, at least not properly.'[24] But the set of notions that have 'not been defined, at least not properly' does not necessarily yield a well-defined notion, especially since the phrases then start to pile up: *statistical norms, systemic, objective, communicational, evaluative, fictive norms, ideal language and language ideal*, all on the basis of the Freudian notions of *ideal ego* and *ego ideal*, *evaluative instability, instability of attitude*. . . . And *l'imaginaire linguistique*, defined in 1996 by Houdebine as a 'notion', becomes in 1997, in the words of the same author, a 'theory': 'On a broader basis, one which justifies us talking of a theory, the study of *l'imaginaire linguistique* . . . presupposes that we relate subjective and objective norms'.[25]

These hesitations are, in fact, quite widespread in the literature on these themes, and we can only agree with Dominique Lafontaine, for instance, when he emphasizes that 'the term linguistic *attitude* is used indiscriminately, without any real difference in meaning, together with *representation*, *subjective norm*, *subjective evaluation*, *judgement* and *opinion* to designate any epilinguistic phenomenon relating to language'.[26] He points out on the same page that the term has a narrower meaning in the social psychology of language, designating 'the way in which subjects evaluate either languages, varieties or linguistic variables or, more often, speakers expressing themselves in particular languages or linguistic varieties'.

In the same work Nicole Gueunier emphasizes that 'the notion of linguistic representation has for a long time been confused with that of attitude', distinguishing between them shortly afterwards in the following terms: 'If linguistic representations and attitudes have in common the epilinguistic feature that differentiates them from linguistic practices and metalinguistic analyses, they are theoretically distinguished by the less active character (i.e. less aimed at a particular kind of behaviour) of the representations, a character more discursive and figurative.'[27] And Marie-Louise Moreau explains that the subjective norms (or evaluations) 'are to be found in the field of attitudes and representations' and 'consist in attaching these affective or moral aesthetic values to the relevant forms'.[28]

Faced with this terminological confusion, which hardly helps theory, I will try to simplify matters by setting out from two main categories: *practices* and *representations*. On the side of practices, we of course find what speakers produce, the way they speak, but also the way they come to 'accommodations' in order to communicate, the way they adapt their practices to the situations of communication, for example the practices and expectations of their interlocutor. On the side of representations is the way speakers think of their practices, how they situate themselves in relation to other speakers and other practices, how they situate their language in relation to the other languages that exist with it: in short, everything related to *epilinguistics*. We will see that these representations determine:

- judgements on languages and the ways in which they are spoken, judgements which are often widespread in the shape of stereotypes;
- attitudes to languages and accents, i.e., in fact, attitudes to the speakers that stereotypes distinguish;
- linguistic behaviour that tends to bring the speaker's language into line with his or her judgements and attitudes – this is the way that representations act on practices, and change the 'language' ['*langue*'].

These representations may affect just a few limited points, or even a single word. Rosaleen Howard-Malverde[29] reports for example that, while speaking with a monolingual Bolivian woman in Quechua, she happened to use the word *pacha-mama* (in Quechua, the earth goddess). The woman corrected her: 'Pachamama is a Spanish word, in Quechua we say *wirhina*', which is doubly untrue. There is nothing Spanish about *pachamama*, and this term is used throughout the linguistic territory of Quechua, while *wirhina* is borrowed from the Spanish *virgen*, 'virgin'. But representations more often than not affect the language as a whole and can, among other things, reveal a sense of security or insecurity in different domains (a subject to which I will be returning later), having as they do a retroactive effect on usages and being capable of modifying them. In this sense, the analysis of representations, which methodologically has to proceed synchronically, necessarily involves the change and evolution of linguistic forms, and is also tied up with diachrony.

The notion of linguistic insecurity thus came into existence, as we have seen, in monolingual contexts, or at least in analyses that considered the group or the community under consideration as monolingual. But linguistic situations are very rarely monolingual and it is important to reflect on the relations between insecurity and multilingualism: can linguistic insecurity, linked in the aforementioned works to the *form* of the language, also be linked to its *function*? In other words, does not feeling self-confident in another language also produce strategies of which the monolingual person is deprived? This is a whole new field for research, and the situation in different African countries, for example, provides us with a particularly rich area to explore. After this brief historical overview, I will now examine these theoretical problems more closely.

Some theoretical problems: a first approach

Security and insecurity: form and status

In a study of linguistic insecurity among Belgian French-speakers, Michel Francard suggests that 'linguistic insecurity is the manifestation of an unsuccessful quest for legitimacy'.[30] In his view, insecurity as it appears in French-speaking Belgium has four facets:

- linguistic subjection to France;
- a depreciation of linguistic forms felt to be non-legitimate;
- a use, nonetheless, of these disparaged forms on 'restricted linguistic markets' (which can be accompanied by the mockery of those who 'froggify', i.e. mimic the French);
- A pessimistic vision of the future of French.[31]

Behind all this appears a central idea: it is school that reinforces insecurity, since it transmits a standard form of the language; and behind this central idea is an implicit definition of insecurity, considered as the result of a conflict between the legitimate language and a non-legitimate or disparaged form of this same language. But this conception of linguistic insecurity is very limiting (it springs in fact from Belgium), leaving aside at least two problems:

- The (very frequent) situations in which insecurity results from the relations between languages that are not akin (for instance, in Africa, between African languages, the – European – official languages and sometimes Arabic). In these cases, we cannot reason in terms of the legitimate form and the disparaged form of the same language.

- The fact that very often the insecurity does not result (at least not solely) from the form of the language (in comparison with its legitimate form) but from its type or status (for instance, when a speaker imagines that he or she does not speak a language but rather a dialect or patois).

Now, Michel Francard as well as William Labov seem to conceive of linguistic insecurity only in situations of *intralinguistic* variations (by which I mean variations within one and the same language, relations between what are considered as variants within the same language), locating it in the opposition between 'own use' and 'correctness'.[32] But insecurity can also result from relations that I will call *interlinguistic*, between different languages, and it is then the product of multilingualism. In other words, insecurity can just as well result from a comparison between the way one speaks and the legitimate way of speaking (and then we have a problem of linguistic form in the context of one and the same language) as from the status granted to this way of speaking and interiorized by the speaker (and then we have a problem of linguistic status resulting from comparison with the status of another language). This position, which I have presented in a study devoted to a creole-speaking situation in Louisiana[33] to which I will return in the last chapter of the present work, had led me to produce the diagram of Model 1 shown, in which the continuum extending from less security to more in relation to the form or status of the language gives us four cardinal situations.

Model 1
(Security/Insecurity)

		Formal security –	*Formal security* +
Security of status	–	**1** Insecurity of form and status	**2** Security of form and insecurity of status
	+	**3** Insecurity of form and security of status	**4** Security of form and status

I will return to these four cases later, as we shall be seeing that at least one more parameter needs to be added to this table.

Evaluative security/insecurity

As I have said, it might be possible to stick to a dichotomy distinguishing between *practices* as the linguist perceives and describes them, and, on the other hand, *representations* (what speakers say and think about their practices and those of others). We should immediately add that the linguist too has representations and that his methodology and viewpoint, furthermore, can transform and skew what he is describing. Thus a dictionary not strictly established on the basis of a corpus would risk giving us the representations of its compiler rather than the reality of linguistic practice: the examples must forge sense and use, not the other way around (but that's another story, one that falls into the domain of epistemology). So representations are constituted by the set of images, ideological positions and beliefs of speakers on the subject of the languages under consideration and on linguistic practices, both their own and those of others. They are partly based on the speaker's self-evaluation of his or her own practices, which raises the problem of knowing to what extent the speaker really knows what he speaks – in other words, how he evaluates himself.

This problem has been tackled by Cécile Canut and Boniface Keita in connection with a region of Mali in which a linguistic continuum (which extends from a form called 'Malinke' to a form called 'Bambara') is complicated by a social mobility that entails an evolution in representations and practices.[34] Canut has examined things in greater detail in her thesis, and so I will be basing my comments on her text. She begins by distinguishing, among *linguistic attitudes*, between *awareness/non-awareness* (the awareness possessed by the speaker of his or her linguistic environment), *resistance/adherence* (acceptance or not of the dominant language) and *security/insecurity*. For this latter couple, she puts forward eight notions:

1 *the linguistic complex* (which in her view comes close to Robert Laffont's *linguistic guilt*);
2 *evaluative linguistic stability*, when the speaker claims to speak A and does speak A;
3 *evaluative linguistic instability*, when the speaker claims to speak A and speaks B;
4 *linguistic stability,* when the speaker speaks the same language as his or her group;

5 *linguistic instability*, when the speaker does not speak the same language as the group;
6 *evaluative linguistic security*, when the speaker claims to speak A, does speak A and thinks that one should speak A, or claims to speak A, speaks B and thinks that one should speak A;
7 *evaluative linguistic insecurity*, when the speaker claims to speak A, does speak A, but thinks one should speak B, or claims to speak B, speaks A and thinks one should speak A;
8 *total evaluative linguistic security*, when the speaker claims to speak A or B, does speak A or B but thinks that one should speak C.[35]

The way Canut presents things constitutes an obvious advance on previous definitions of linguistic insecurity, but she sometimes seems to me to classify under the same heading (evaluative linguistic security, for example) situations that are actually different (the speaker claims to speak A, speaks A and thinks that one should speak A, the speaker claims to speak A, speaks B and thinks one should speak A).

We thus find ourselves faced with three issues:

1 Linguistic practices: what people speak and the way they speak it (which the linguist can observe and describe).
2 The self-evaluation of these practices: what speakers think or say they do (which the investigator can discover via questionnaires and/or interviews).
3 The representations of these practices: what speakers would like to do or think one should do.

The combination between practices and self-evaluation thus produces, according to Canut, two different cases (evaluative stability/instability) whereas there are in fact four, since in addition the representations concerning these practices come into play. Let us consider for example a situation in which there coexist two languages, French and a creole. If we combine the practices of the speakers (what they speak) and their self-evaluation (what they say or think they speak), we theoretically have four possibilities, as in the diagram.

For Canut, 1 and 4 are equivalent situations (evaluative stability), but they would be so only if the speaker granted the same value to French and creole, which is far from being the case. To include this dimension, we in fact need to combine the self-evaluation of linguistic

	Speaks French	Speaks creole
Claims to speak French	1	2
Claims to speak creole	3	4

practices with the representations that the speakers have of these practices, which gives us the result shown in the diagram of Model 2.

Model 2
(Representations/Evaluations)

	Representations	
	Positive	Negative
Good	1 Evaluative and representative security	2 Evaluative security and representative insecurity
	Evaluation	
Bad	3 Evaluative insecurity and representative insecurity	4 Evaluative and representative security

1 *Evaluative and representative security* The speakers speak what they say they speak and have a good image of what they speak. This case corresponds to the first part of what Canut calls 'evaluative linguistic security' (the speakers speak A, claim to speak A and think that one should speak A).

2 *Evaluative security and representative insecurity* The speakers know what they speak but think they should speak something else. For example, 'I speak creole, but I'd like to speak French' or 'but you have to speak French to get on'. This case corresponds to the first part of what Canut calls 'evaluative linguistic insecurity' (speakers speak A, claim to speak A but think one should speak B).

3 *Evaluative insecurity and representative security* The speakers do not know what they speak but think they speak the language they should speak. This case corresponds to the second part of what Canut calls 'evaluative linguistic security' (speakers speak B, claim to speak A and think one should speak A).

4 *Evaluative and representative insecurity* The speakers do not know what they speak and would like to speak something else. This

case corresponds partly to what Canut calls 'total evaluative linguistic insecurity' (speakers speak B, claim to speak A and think that one should speak C).

A few suggestions

Throughout the previous passage I have been discussing evaluative insecurity without questioning this notion. But it raises a certain number of problems. The first is, of course, the word itself; it is difficult to get rid of it since it has been widely used since William Labov and has acquired, as it were, a right of residence. But its connotations are very limiting, which in turn entails other problems. In Model 1 presented above, we were including two things: what speakers think about their way of speaking (security/insecurity of form) and the value they grant to what they speak (security/insecurity of status). In other words, we were merely combining data coming from the speakers themselves, leaving aside another problem, that of the relevance of the evaluation that speakers have of their practice. If a language can indeed, in comparison with another language or another form of the same language, produce in the person speaking it either security or insecurity, we can ask ourselves how much this speaker really knows what he speaks, in other words how he evaluates himself. But this point raises huge problems, since it presupposes that someone (as it happens, the linguist) decides that the speaker is evaluating himself or herself correctly or incorrectly. I have discussed this problem elsewhere,[36] and I will come back to it in the last chapter of this book, so I will mention it here just briefly.

There are numerous situations in which the speaker and the linguist disagree about the names of languages: the Croats, for instance, say they speak Croat and not Serb, whereas the linguist sees only one language, namely Serbo-Croat. Just as the phoneme does not exist, being merely a class of sounds, language too does not exist, being simply a set of practices and representations, and the problem here referred to (one or two languages?) is thus the problem of knowing to which 'language' we are to attribute this or that speech act. From this point of view, the *naming* of the language, the fact of giving it a name, is already an evaluative choice, a representation, for the speaker as well as for the linguist. Now the judgement of the linguist and the representations of speakers do not necessarily correspond: once again, is it Serb, Croat or Serbo-Croat?[37] Should we then appeal to the authority of the linguist, who is supposedly right, as against the representations of the speaker? I have some hesitation in going down that road, and that is why I feel it is preferable to stick to the discussion of the data coming from the speakers themselves – as indeed did Labov, who contented himself with combining two things: the forms considered by the speakers as correct and those they thought they were using.

It might be objected that the scientist can be considered as more objective or more competent than the average speaker, and that popular 'beliefs' concerning language are hardly any more serious than the superstitions associated with walking under ladders, or with cats or the moon . . . This reputation for objectivity and competence is, however, thrown into considerable doubt by the previous errings of linguistics: colonial discourse, for example, distinguishing between languages (European) and dialects (African), often drew its arguments from 'scientific' sources.[38] And things are still complicated, even today. We can note first of all that self-evaluation may bear on a phoneme (the speaker claims for instance to be pronouncing /g/ but in fact pronounces /k/) or on a language (the speaker claims to speak Bambara but in fact speaks Malinke) and these two extreme cases raise the problem, in their very different forms, of the scientist as someone whose knowledge is power. In the first instance, we may think that the ear of the describer is more reliable than that of the speaker, and that the former can thus better distinguish between a /k/ and a /g/. In the second case, we can also conclude that the linguist has a precise definition of languages and can thus locate the points that differentiate between Bambara and Malinke (vowel system, syntactic elements, lexicon, etc.). But none of this in any way changes the fact that, while the speaker does indeed have representations of his or her language, those of the linguist are not negligible either. We need for instance merely to reread Meillet's work on languages in Europe[39] to realize that this man – without doubt a great scholar – had adopted positions that stemmed more from his representations than from science, in particular in the case of Hungarian.[40] We also often find among the specialists of this or that language certain evaluative choices of which they are doubtless unaware but which weigh heavily in the balance when they start to busy themselves with linguistic plans. I have no intention of putting the linguist's representations on the same level as the speaker's, but simply of emphasizing that:

- The former exist, and scientific objectivity, though of course desirable, is only a goal which one can aim at but never completely achieve.
- The latter, even if they can be refuted by a scientific discourse, have an impact on practices and situations. Linguists were perhaps correct fifty years ago when they proclaimed that Hindi and Urdu were one and the same language, just as they are perhaps correct today to consider Serbo-Croat as one single language. The fact remains that the representations of speakers have acted (conjointly with political, social and ideological factors) on situations, and that Urdu and Hindi are diverging more and more, just as Serb and Croat will perhaps continue to diverge. In other words, we are not here in a 'folk linguistics' that treats of beliefs about languages, something that certain people call an 'epilinguistic discourse', but we *are* at the centre of linguistics, seeking one of the factors of change.

So I propose, for the sake of simplicity, to distinguish between linguistic representations and practices, and I will now go into more detail on this topic. Representations concern at least three domains: the form of languages (how people speak, how one should speak), the status of languages (what one should speak, the 'legitimate' language) and their function as markers of identity (what characterizes the community).

To begin with, I will be combining these data in three ways, which will enable me to calculate three rates:

1 *The rate of security of status* (from 0 to 100 per cent): the relation between the number of speakers claiming to speak A and the number of those among them who think one should speak A.
2 *The rate of security of identity* (from 0 to 100 per cent): the relation between the number of speakers claiming to speak A and the number of those among them who think that A is characteristic of their community.
3 *The rate of security of form* (from 0 to 100 per cent): the relation between the number of speakers claiming to speak in such-and-such a way and the number of those among them who think that one should speak in such-and-such a way.

In these three points, the rate of 'security' (of status, identity and form) is the result of a combination of the evaluation and the representations of the speaker, without any judgement on the part of the linguist: basically, it is a matter of making the speaker examine his or her own practice in the light of his or her own declarations.

All of this might seem nothing more than a purely theoretical game, but these definitions are fundamental since they lie at the heart of the problems of a description of situations and their evaluation. How do these few suggestions advance matters? We began by supposing that linguistic situations produce security/insecurity, which constitutes the motor of linguistic change: linguistic practices are affected by the speaker's relation to his or her language. Then I tried to distinguish between different kinds of insecurity: *insecurity of status* (the relation between the number of speakers claiming to speak A and the number of those among them who think one should speak A) and *insecurity of identity* (the relation between the number of speakers claiming to speak A and the number of those among them who think that A is characteristic of the community) – these two types being situated in the context of an interlinguistic approach; and *insecurity of form* (the relation between the number of speakers claiming to speak in such-and-such a way and the number of those among them who think that one should speak in such-and-such a way). Only the third of these corresponds, without any major changes, to Labov's definition. The first two introduce a hitherto neglected dimension, no longer that of form (the 'items' discussed by Labov), but that of language conceived of as

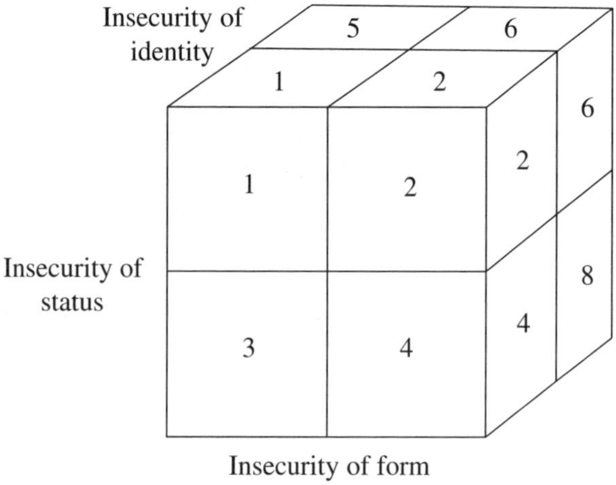

Diagram 4.1

Table 4.2

Security	Identity	Status	Form
1	–	–	–
2	–	–	+
3	–	+	–
4	–	+	+
5	+	–	–
6	+	–	+
7	+	+	–
8	+	+	+

an entity characteristic of a community or a social norm. If we combine these three kinds of insecurity, we obtain eight situations that we can visualize in diagram 4.1 or else as a table.

The eight situations thus identified can be characterized in the following fashion.

1 *Insecurity of status, form and identity* These are the situations in which the speakers think they speak 'badly' a form which is 'not a language' and which is not characteristic of the community to which they think they belong or wish to belong. This would be the case of an Indian of Ecuador who thinks he has not mastered Kichua, which he considers to be a dialect (or more exactly: the dominant discourse he has interiorized impels him to consider it as a dialect), who would in addition like to belong to the Spanish-speaking community.

2 *Security of form, insecurity of status and identity* These are situations in which speakers think they can speak well a linguistic form that they consider nonetheless to be not legitimate from the point of view of status, and not characteristic of the community to which they think they belong or wish to belong. This would be the case of a Catalan speaker who considers his language as 'illegitimate', thinks he speaks it correctly, but would like to belong to the Spanish-speaking community.

3 *Security of status, insecurity of form and identity* The speakers of a language of legitimate status consider that they speak a non-legitimate form of it, one which is not characteristic of the community to which

they think they belong or wish to belong. This is the case of a Spanish migrant who thinks he speaks this language badly and desires to integrate himself into the French-speaking community.

4 *Security of status and form, insecurity of identity* The speakers are convinced they speak well a language whose status is uncontested but which is not characteristic of the community to which they think they belong or wish to belong. For example, the speakers of the 'Oxbridge' form of English can, in the United States, find themselves in a doubly secure situation: they are sure of their language in terms of *status* and sure of the way they speak it from the *formal* viewpoint, but they are in a situation of insecurity of *identity* insofar as the form used by the local community is different.

5 *Security of identity, insecurity of form and status* The speakers consider that they speak a linguistic form shared by the community to which they think they belong or wish to belong, but at the same time they consider that this form is not legitimate and that they speak it badly. This for instance would be the case of a Moroccan migrant in France who thinks he speaks badly a 'dialect' form that other migrants also speak.

6 *Security of identity and form, insecurity of status* The speakers think they speak well the language of their community, but they regard it as 'not a language'. This would be the case of a Galician who considers that he speaks well the language of his community but regards that form as less prestigious than Castilian or Portuguese.

7 *Security of identity and status, insecurity of form* The speakers think they speak badly the language of their community, a language that they consider as prestigious. This would be the case of a Breton who thinks that Breton, the language of his community, is prestigious, but considers that he speaks it badly.

8 *Security of form, status and identity* The speakers think they speak well a language that they consider as at once prestigious and characteristic of their community. This would be the case of the Oxbridge speaker referred to in 4 above but living in England. This situation of maximum security is characteristic of linguistic power, of absolute legitimacy.

As for insecurity of *value* or *stability*, it is worth repeating that these notions necessarily imply that the linguist knows what the speakers speak better than they do themselves, which is a way of reducing the linguistic representations of speakers to approximations that count for relatively little in comparison with the linguist's knowledge. My own view of the matter – and this is the crux of the whole debate – is that representations (those of speakers of linguists) are also constructions, a way of acting on situations, and that they should thus be included in the description of the latter. To illustrate this problem, let us take a simple example, that of a speaker on Saint-Barthélemy who claims to speak patois (or a Croat who claims to speak Croat) but who, in the linguist's opinion, speaks French (or Serbo-Croat). Should we draw the conclusion that they are in a situation of insecurity of value, or should we conclude that they have a conception of French which includes patois (or a conception of Croat that sees it as different from Serb), and that this conception can eventually lead to patois and French becoming melded together (or Serb and Croat becoming different)? This question is important from both the theoretical and the practical angle, and discussion on this point is, of course, open. But we should not systematically adjudicate on conflicts between the representations of speakers and those of the linguist by decreeing that the speakers are in a situation of insecurity or instability of value simply because the linguist is always deemed to be right.

Some problems of description

I indicated above that linguistic insecurity (or security) should not be considered as a binary value (+ or −) since we are here dealing with continuous values, which need to be presented in percentage terms: there is no security or insecurity as such, there is 20 per cent, 30 per cent, 60 per cent or 80 per cent security. But we first need to look more closely at the very notion of *security* or *insecurity*, which is not innate but, of course, acquired, produced by sociolinguistic situations. From this point of view, we need to distinguish between *security/insecurity* (which are part and parcel of the representations of the speaker) and *reassurance/lack of reassurance* (which are part and parcel of the discourse of the other, of the influence of the sociolinguistic environment of the speaker). And this reassurance (or lack of reassurance) concerns the three types of security (or insecurity) that I have just identified. To illustrate this notion, let us take a few cases of lack of reassurance.

1 *Lack of reassurance regarding form*: the discourse of the other, social correction, feedback intimate to the speaker that he 'speaks badly'. This kind of figure is frequent and easy to observe.
2 *Lack of reassurance regarding status*: social discourse, the dominant ideology intimate to the speaker that what he speaks is of less value than other linguistic forms available – that he speaks, for instance, a dialect or a patois, and not a language.
3 *Lack of reassurance regarding identity*: the group, the community intimate to the speaker that he does not speak the same form as his peers, that he is not recognized as one of their number because of what he speaks or the way he speaks it.

In all three cases, we see that lack of reassurance is one of the forms of 'the war between languages'. This distinction between insecurity and lack of reassurance thus enables us to introduce into the analysis of representations the problem of their production, of their mode of emergence. It reminds us that representations are produced. This is clear as regards lack of reassurance regarding status: the speaker does not invent all by himself the idea that he does not speak a language but a dialect or a patois; he inherits this negative view, as it is transmitted for instance in the colonial discourse that I described a while ago in *Linguistique et colonialisme*. But the same is true in the case of insecurity of form. It is the normative discourse, that of the society, the group, or the schoolteacher, which produces it. As for insecurity of status, its mode of emergence is more complex, since it depends simultaneously on the speaker's choice of identity (when the speaker would like to belong, or thinks he already does belong, to a given group), on the idea that the individual has of the language of this group and on the group's reactions to the individual and his language.

These phenomena of reassurance/lack of reassurance are not static, they produce certain linguistic forms, and have an impact on situations. A good example of this is the linguistic behaviour of the children of migrants, for instance the *Beurs*, children born in France to parents of Maghrebi origin. Their social and cultural situation (social 'divide', racist rejection, failure at school, the awareness of speaking both their parents' language and that of their host country badly) puts them in category number 1 (insecurity of status, form and identity) twice over, with regard to both Arabic and French. In this case, given the way they find themselves living in the gap between different cultures,[41] they create a language and a culture that will give them a sense of identity: verlan, rap, graffiti, etc. The lack of reassurance that they experience leads them, in their quest for identity, to produce a new form of the dominant code thanks to which they tend towards case 8 described above: security of form (since they are masters of the norm), status and identity (they consider that they are speaking their own language, not that of the 'Gauls'). It is, of course, also the case of black Americans, who, with the help of politically correct ideas, increasingly tend to consider as a language different from English what was not so long ago called 'Black English', later baptized 'African American English' and today called, by certain people, 'Ebonics'.

The Songhays and their neighbours

The Songhay people live on the two banks of the River Niger, in a zone that reaches approximately from Mopti in Mali to Niamey in Niger, by way of Timbuctoo and Gao, and this geographical situation means that their immediate neighbours are the Tamasheqs in the north and the Bambaras in the south, and they have frequent relations on all sides with the Fula. We will be seeing how, in this particular environment, social factors produce representations that we can perceive both in the way that human beings and languages are named and in the judgements and stereotypes that are applied to these men and these languages.

In a dissertation on the linguistic situation of the Songhays of Mali,[42] Amidou Maïga has analysed the representations that the Songhays have of their neighbours. Thus the Songhays designate the Tamasheqs by the term *surgoboro*, which they also use for the Moors,[43] and this name, a pejorative one (*boro* means 'man' in Songhay; *surgu* could be the Bambara word *suruku*, 'hyena'), summarizes sufficiently well the image they have of the Tamasheqs: they are cruel pillagers, pitiless, hard-hearted, 'hyena-men'. This image, a product of past history, is amplified by recent history: for several years, a violent armed conflict in Mali has been setting the Tamasheqs against the state, and the nationalism of the official modes of discourse and the media has constructed for them an extremely negative image that the Songhays have apparently adopted. So while the Tamasheq is a *surgoboro*, a hyena-man, his language is called *bella ciini*, 'language of the Bellas', and not *surgu ciini* as we might expect. Now the Bellas, the slaves of the Tamasheqs, constitute a despised social category, and this name, *bella ciini*, adds an additional touch to the way the Songhays view their neighbours. The Tamasheqs are, in their eyes, 'wicked', their language is 'insipid', 'heavy': the situation is perfectly encapsulated in declarations such as:

- I don't like the Tamasheq language. God preserve us from it.
- The Tamasheqs . . . May they stay far from us.

A Fula, on the other hand, is perceived as deceitful, wily: 'He knows the right way perfectly well, but he still asks you for it as he passes by', as a proverb puts it. But he is also perceived, writes Maïga, as physically handsome, noble and a good believer. His language is at once poetic ('the Fulani language is intelligence, it comes out of one's head'), noble, beautiful and rich, but it is also a language of beggars and chatterboxes. So the use of Fulani is ambiguous, a matter of mistrust and admiration: it stands out against the use of both Tamasheq and Bambara.

The reason is that the image of Bambara is made of successive superimpositions that are just as negative as one another: heathen, animistic (this is the image it acquired before colonization), auxiliary to the colonial and military administration (this is the image that dates from the colonial period), and, finally, these days, as an imperialist danger that could swallow up the other cultures, in particular Songhay culture. On the linguistic level, they are considered as *meeberaw* ('those who have changed language'), like former Songhays who have changed their language. This language is 'hot', 'bad', and symbolizes brutality. In addition, the Bambaras are seen as people who refuse to speak anything other than their language. And the representations obviously culminate in aesthetic judgements:

- Bambara is heavy, you have to have thick lips and a very flat tongue to speak Bambara well. The Bambaras speak forcefully. They are like Germans, they cannot speak gently.
- When the Bambaras talk, you get the impression that they turned up late when the different languages were handed out. It's a mixture, it causes surprise, the language is heavy in one's mouth.

- The Bambaras, to judge from the way they speak, sound like sheep and goats; they reply to greetings by /nba/ for men and /nse/ for women. *etc.*

This does not prevent certain speakers finding this language useful and functional.

So we can see that there is neither contradiction nor even separation but, on the contrary, convergence between social representations (the image the Songhays have of their neighbours) and linguistic representations. In fact, judgements on languages are judgements on human beings and are produced by social situations. The Songhays feel threatened by the Bambaras (who control the state apparatus, so that the language, the language of communication, is well on the way to becoming general in Mali) and by their immediate Tamasheq neighbours (whom official discourse presents as underground resistance fighters and terrorists), but not by the Fula, and so they can permit themselves to judge their language more or less positively while the language of the Bambaras and that of the Tamasheqs both have, as we have seen, a completely different image.

These stereotypes are nothing new and they have probably always accompanied contacts between different peoples. Tullio de Mauro has noted a certain number of them, going back to a distant period:

> Already Charles V, apparently, habitually said that 'if he wanted to talk to men, he spoke French, if he wanted to speak to his horse, he spoke German, and . . . if he wanted to speak to God he spoke Spanish'. This, of course, is the Franco-Spanish version of the anecdote; for the Italians, it is French that is the effeminate language and Italian is naturally 'the language of men'. German is also slandered in another proverb going back to the seventeenth century: the German yells, the Englishman weeps, the Frenchman sings, the Italian plays out a farce and the Spaniard talks.[44]

And this last example is particularly significant since it obviously mixes men and languages: if the German yells, the reason is that he is speaking German. . . . And if German is 'slandered', as de Mauro puts it, the reason is that it is perceived negatively, for reasons that are, of course, historical. In these different cases, as in the example of the Songhays, we thus see that social factors produce representations, bearing simultaneously on human beings and on their languages. We shall now see how, by way of representations, social factors can also produce linguistic forms, essentially by hypercorrection.

From village to town: the example of Malinke-Bambara

In chapter 2 I examined, in the context of the gravitational model, the practices of speakers,[45] and their use of languages seen as a constellation centered around Bambara. I will now, in the same field, study the representations and the effects of these practices and these representations on the form and evolution of languages. The study by Canut and Keita[46] is a good opportunity for doing so. The area studied lies between Bamako and Kayes, in the Mandingo zone, and the survey was carried out in two villages, Bendugu and Sagabari, a middle-sized town, Kita, and the capital, Bamako, all of which constitute a linguistic continuum: at either extreme, Bamako and Sagabari, there are two different forms, Bambara and Malinke, but the situation is more ambiguous in Bendugu and Kita, where we see languages alternating and getting mixed up at one and the same time. In this area, where social mobility (most often from one generation to the next but also within one generation) is significant (migration from the village to the medium-sized town, then to the capital), there is an almost total lack of mutual understanding, but also an evolution of representations and practices. The authors, who ask whether 'the linguistic continuum that exists between the Malinke village and the capital . . . is mirrored by a continuum on the level of attitudes',[47] begin by presenting the dialectal situation with three entries, Malinke, the mixed dialect of Kita, and Bambara, insisting as they do so on the differences between these three forms: phonological, lexical and morphological differences. I in turn will present their data rather differently, showing that phonological fluctuation can explain most of the other variations.

The vowel system This can be shown schematically as follows, with the brackets representing the vowels subject to variation:

i			u
	(e)	(o)	
	a		

The variable (e) corresponds to two variants, /e/ and /ɛ/, the variable (o) corresponds to the difference in degree of openness; all these vowel phonemes also exist in the nasal form and present, at one of the poles of the continuum (Bamako), an opposition in length.[48]

The consonant system As regards the consonants, I will merely indicate the main variables and their corresponding variants, insofar as they will enable us to understand the dialect variations:

- the variable (c) corresponding to the variants /c/ and /k/, with the palatal being used in Bamako and the occlusive in the three other places in the survey;
- the variable (f) corresponding to the variants /f/ (Bamako, Kita) and /h/ (Bendugu, Sagabari);
- the variable (r) as intervocalic corresponding to the variants /r/ (Bamako, Kita), /d/ (Bendugu) and /t/ (Sagabari);
- the variable (k) corresponding to the variants /k/ (Bamako, Kita) and /x/ (Kita, Sagabari, Bendugu).

The lexical and morphological variants These phonetic variants enable us to explain most of the differences between the Mandingo dialects. Here are a few examples:

- Sagabari *hutu*, Bendugu *hudu* and Bamako *foro*, 'field', explained simultaneously by the variable (f) and the variable (r).
- Sagabari and Bendugu *hato*, Kita *hato/fato*, Bamako *fato*, 'mad', are explained by the variable (f).
- Kita, Sagabari and Bendugu *a xa nyi*, Kita, Bamako *a ka nyi*, 'that's good', are explained by the variable (k).
- Sagabari *alu tagata*, Bendugu *alu tagada*, Bamoko *u tagara*, 'they have gone', are explained by the variable (r). (*etc.*)

In fact, one need only leaf through the dictionary compiled by Delafosse[49] to garner dozens of lexical variants of this type, and only a few differences remain, some of which, such as the third-person plural pronoun (*alu/u*) are still variants and the rare other examples are items of vocabulary that are different in origin.

Representations This is what the linguist can describe, hence concluding that there is just one language at stake: there is no great difference between this situation and that of Parisian French vis-à-vis the

French of Marseilles for instance. But speakers distinguish in this zone between four dialects, to which they give different names: *bakokan* ('the dialect from behind the river') for Sagabari, *kitakan* for Kita, *bendugukan* for Bendugu and *bamokokan* for Bamako. They are aware of the differences that I have just set out, especially since whenever the 'provincials' go to their capital, their dialect rouses laughter, especially the most peripheral form, that of Sagabari:

- 'We laugh at the Malinkes when they leave their milieu.'
- 'The kind of Malinke language that makes me laugh is that spoken in Sagabari.'
- 'We laugh at the Malinke spoken in Sagabari, as it's too heavy.' (*etc.*)[50]

The problem migrants face, when they go to the towns, is thus that of masking their provincial origins, replacing for example *alu* by *u*, /h/ by /f/, etc., sometimes with hypercorrections that betray them just as much as their original pronunciation: 'To escape their geo-social status, the Malinkes transform their dialect, and this sometimes leads to hypercorrections (the replacing of every /h/ by /f/ for instance, which makes them say "young boy", /foron/, a non-existent term in Bambara, for /horon/, "noble").'[51]

After giving a lengthy account of the results of their survey on representations, the authors conclude that the linguistic continuum that goes from the village to the town is mirrored by a continuum in attitudes: the closer one comes to the town, the greater value one attributes to Bambara and the more one identifies with it. I will add, for my part, that what is exemplary in this situation is the fact that social factors give birth to linguistic results, that ecolinguistic conditions produce, via representations, certain practices and thus certain forms. The linguistic practices of the speakers of Sagabari or Bendugu when they are in Bamako are simultaneously the product of the action on Malinke of its gravitation around Bambara (a tendency to produce Bamaku variants found among the young migrants) and the product of strategies of dissimulation (an attempt to mask their origins and to assimilate) or strategies of integration.

Thus the Bambara constellation is traversed and shaped by linguistic representations and the insecurity they generate, the practices (languages used, the form of these languages) change under the action of these representations, and we could go up to the next level by studying the way in which, in the French constellation, Bambara, here a peripheral language, is in its turn transformed. The dialectic between these two points of view, practices and representations, is thus the driving force of change. The presentation I first adopted, in terms of constellations and galaxy, might lead one to imagine that things are static, but this dialectic shows that movement is always present.

Conclusions

I pointed out at the start of this chapter that only relatively recently had people started to take account of representations in the study of linguistic data. There was one obvious reason for this: everything that was part of the epilinguistic discourse, of what speakers think and say about linguistic practices, was considered as non-scientific. Pierre Bourdieu had brought this out very clearly when he wrote:

> Nothing is less innocent than the question, which divides the scientific world, of knowing whether one has to include in the system of pertinent criteria not only the so-called 'objective' categories (such as ancestry, territory, language, religion, economic activity, etc.), but also the so-called 'subjective' properties (such as the feeling of belonging), i.e. the *representations* through which social agents imagine the divisions of reality and which contribute to the reality of the divisions. When, as their education and their specific interests incline them, researchers try to set themselves up as judges of all judgements and as critics of all criteria, they prevent themselves from grasping the specific logic of a struggle.[52]

The gradual inclusion of these representations, and the subsequent terminological inflation to which this inclusion led, has to a certain extent put us in the opposite situation: nobody today denies their importance, and we have seen how significant it is if we are to understand change. But I have tried to show at the same time that scientists went into this study weighed down by their own representations, and this parameter should henceforth be at the centre of our epistemological representations.

In the swarm of new terms that have arisen, we have seen that it was possible to simplify things without losing in precision, by positing that linguistic representations produce *security/insecurity*, the motor of linguistic change, a *security/insecurity* that can be classified under one of three categories: *security/insecurity of status, of identity* and *of form*. In doing this, I refused to take into account the problems of security of evaluation, so as not to set the judgements or the classifications of speakers against those of the linguist, and thus combining only the data that come from speakers themselves. And a few quick examples (that of the Songhays or that of Malinke/Bambara) have demonstrated what this approach could yield. I will be returning to it at greater length in chapter 6, when I look at five case studies.

Let us finish with a French example, simple and illuminating. A recent study has shown that, despite a widespread conviction in Le Havre that its inhabitants have a particular accent, the pronunciation there is no different from that of working-class Parisian French. In addition, when they participated in a survey of the kind mentioned at the start of this chapter ('matched guise'), 'judges' from Le Havre as well as from elsewhere found themselves unable to recognize local speakers. On the other hand, they often gave an example – always the same one – of this 'accent': the fact that inhabitants of Le Havre often say 'dè' (a local form of 'dis!', 'say!'). So what we have here is a linguistic myth and we could leave it at that, concluding that, in spite of epilinguistic discourses, the Le Havre accent does not exist, that we are here up against representations. But the authors attempt to go further by asking the following question: 'Have the inhabitants of Le Havre felt an unconscious need to make up an accent for themselves, as a passport to an identity? Were they tempted to associate this accent with what is left of their identity, namely the sea and the port?'[53] And this hypothesis sheds a new light on the collected data. For example, every time that they refer to this 'accent', the people questioned quote the dialect spoken by dockers or workers. 'The myth of the Le Havre accent and the myth of the docker's accent are linked, and certainly play a part in the legitimacy that is sought by the inhabitants', the authors write.[54] We here have a typical demonstration of the desire for an identity: we exist autonomously, we are inhabitants of Le Havre, and the proof lies in our accent. The fact that this 'accent' is not readily perceptible to the ear, unlike the accent of Marseilles for example, changes nothing in this quest for difference. And the fact that the linguistic difference affirmed is more social (dockers, workers) than geographical shows that behind this demand for linguistic specificity there lies a nostalgia for what constituted the specific character of the town and the port: the naval dockyards are dying, the memory of the liner SS *France* is still vivid, etc.

This leaves the question of whether these representations produce practices, whether the inhabitants of Le Havre, when they wish to mark their identity, use for instance the 'dè' mentioned above in any statistically significant way, as this is the sole characteristic on which all the informers are in agreement. The survey carried out by Hauchecorne and Ball does not tackle this point, but all my hypotheses imply that, in situations of convivial, identity-based communication in mass languages, it is probable that this form and the lexical elements that constitute the sole really specific quality of the dialect of Le Havre have, as it happens, increased. We have seen that when Malinkes want to mask their origins, they try to talk like the Bambaras, even if they sometimes produce, by hypercorrection, non-existent forms (/foron/ for /horon/). Here we have the opposite type of behaviour, made of *ostentation* instead of *dissimulation*. But these two types of behaviour are evidence of the same phenomenon, namely the importance of representations and their effect on practices and linguistic change.

— 5 —

Transmission and Change

There is a relatively risk-free way of giving weather forecasts, one which consists of announcing that the weather will be tomorrow approximately the same as today: it is true that, statistically, there is little chance of your being wrong. But, even though this means that you have an acceptable chance of being right, you thereby deprive yourself of understanding the major subterranean movements that create change. The same is true of languages and linguistic situations: they seem to be unchanging and you can announce that tomorrow they will be the same as they are today. But a predictive science should be able to detect, behind the apparent stability, the disequilibrium that creates change. For if the history of languages shows us *one* thing, it is that change and instability are a constant, and theory must be able to take on board this instability and this change. 'It is characteristic of a language that is following its natural course to change; when it remains immobile, or more or less so, the reason is that something abnormal is happening.'[1] This passage, attributed (like everything in the *Course on General Linguistics*) to Ferdinand de Saussure, is, as far as the form of languages is concerned, unquestionable. In chapter 3 we saw how the internal and external regulation of languages and linguistic situations played a part in their evolution. But there is another factor of regulation and evolution that I shall be analysing in this chapter: the transmission of languages and linguistic situations.

Whatever the degree of contempt and racism found in the colonial discourse on languages, something which I have analysed elsewhere, I have always considered that the 'hussars of the Republic', the secular and republican schoolteachers who endeavoured to force the speakers of peripheral languages to swallow their 'coarse idioms', before going off to do exactly the same thing in the colonies in Africa, were sustained by a noble idea. Paradoxically, they believed that they were thereby accelerating their pupils' march towards culture and civilization, and enabling them to make a great leap forwards in history.

There was in fact, in their approach, a Darwinism reinforced by a certain humanism: the Darwinism consisted in the extent to which the idea of an evolution of societies and languages led people to consider that western societies and inflected languages (ours, of course) were the *ne plus ultra* of evolution; the humanism in the extent to which certain happy possessors of these languages and these cultures were ready to share them with those 'savages' that nascent anthropology was inventing for itself. Jules Ferry had been a perfect illustration of this Janus-faced West, both colonialist and colonizing, and Claude Lévi-Strauss in turn gave us, in *Tristes Tropiques*, the Rousseauist version of the same story: the objects of anthropology were *good* savages, but savages all the same. . . . This vision originally rested on the metaphor that presented societies as living organisms whose evolution was determined by the selection of species, 'the survival of the fittest', and this metaphor was present in linguistics right from the start. To convince ourselves of this fact, we need only remember the titles of a few books such as *The Life and Growth of Language* (W. Whitney, 1867), *Ordenes Liv* ('The Life of Words', K. Nyrop, 1867), *La Vie des Mots* (also 'The Life of Words', A. Darmesteter, second edition, 1918), or else emphasize the importance in everyday life of metaphors such as 'living' and 'dead' languages.[2]

My point of view here is going to be different: I will not be discussing the 'life of languages' but the life of people (and I am deliberately using this term, 'people', which is both banal and everyday) – of people who, in their everyday social practices, manage their communicational needs. For *action on languages* constitutes *an answer* to problems of social communication, an answer that is in part determined by *collective representations* which constitute an *intervention* on the form and functions of languages. It is in this sense that I talked in terms of a *homeostat*: it is not a matter of conserving, but of adapting and *regulating*. We have seen that the main limiting factor of languages was the number of their speakers. This varies in two ways: by natural increase in the population of speakers (on condition, of course, that this increase is accompanied by the transmission of the parents' language to their children) and by the acquisition of second languages, which can be transformed into vehicular languages. In this process, certain languages are doomed to die, to make way for others which appear and develop. In other words, the transmission of languages and linguistic situations does not produce an identical reproduction of what was already there to begin with, since *transmission is not the same as conservation*, and a certain number of factors intervene in these movements:

1 the transmission of the language within the family cell, which depends in its turn on the environment, on the relations between language and family and the language(s) of the milieu, and on the networks of communication;
2 the linguistic representations, i.e. the image that speakers have of their language, its usefulness, its future, etc.;
3 the firmness of gravitational relations;
4 external interventions, in particular interventions on the part of the state, carried out via its linguistic policies.

And this raises a question: *at what moment does an ecolinguistic niche cease to be itself?* In other words, at what moment do these permanent movements completely transform a situation? We can decide that an ecolinguistic niche is modified when languages change, when the relations between languages change and when the relations between languages and the milieu change. But this reply is much too general to be useful, and here too I will try to go into more detail in specific concrete situations.

The transmission of first languages and the myth of the mother tongue

In chapter 2 I introduced a presentation of the acquisition of languages that distinguished between the mode of acquisition and its direction: the *programmed learning* of a language, or the *spontaneous learning*, informal in nature, turned towards a *horizontal bilingualism* or a *vertical bilingualism*. I was here referring to the acquisition of second languages, and things are different in the case of first languages: the problem of horizontality or verticality does not arise, and learning is here first spontaneous and then programmed. This learning is generally considered as taking place within the family, and the traditional way of referring to the first language (*mother tongue, langue maternelle, Muttersprache, lingua materna*, etc.) is characteristic of this representation: children are seen as inheriting the language of their mother. But that is false in many cases, as will be shown by the following few examples.

The 'mother tongue' is not always that of the mother

Children, in fact, do not always inherit their parents' language, and the African situations, in which it is not rare that, within a couple, the man and the woman do not have the same first language, provide us with a good example of this.

Thus, in Senegal, a survey has brought out the way the children of linguistically mixed couples most often inherited Wolof, the dominant language, whether this was the father's language, the mother's, or the first language of neither of the parents. In Bamako (Mali), the children of mixed couples likewise inherit Bambara, also the dominant language in that milieu, while in Niamey (Niger), it is the two dominant languages, Hausa and Zarma, that impose themselves in the same conditions.[3] Another survey, this time in Koutiala, in the south of Mali, reveals the same phenomenon. Out of 188 of those surveyed who declared that Bambara was their first language, this was:

- the father's language in 31 cases,
- the mother's in 35 cases,
- that of both parents in 48 cases,
- that of neither parent in 74 cases.

To put it another way, the first language of those surveyed is the father's in 17.48 per cent of cases, the mother's in 13.64 per cent of cases, that of both parents in 41.95 per cent of cases and another language in 26.92 per cent of cases.[4]

In all these examples, the language which can occasionally replace that of the parents as first language is thus that which dominates in the ecolinguistic niche – Wolof in Dakar, Bambara in Bamako or Koutiala, Hausa or Zarma in Niamey: in other words, an African language in each case, an endogenous dominant language with the function of a vehicular language, one that is powerful enough to impose itself even within families.

In Libreville (Gabon) the situation is slightly different but produces a similar result.[5] The absence of an African vehicular language here confers on French a status that it enjoys nowhere else in Africa. In market places, for instance, French predominates over Fang and Punu, whereas all the surveys carried out in the market places of other African capitals show that it is practically absent from them: it is thus an exogenous language that fulfils the function of a vehicular language, a function that is performed elsewhere by an African language. Now, in mixed couples, this exogenous language plays the same role as the dominant endogenous language in the situations mentioned above: here, the children of mixed couples inherit in 43 per cent of cases the language of their mother, in 16 per cent that of their father, in 9 per cent of cases both parental languages and in 32 per cent of cases, French. The children of linguistically homogeneous couples inherit the language of their parents in 82 per cent of cases and French in 18 per cent. It is clear that French benefits from the existence of mixed couples, and imposes itself to a significant degree when the couple is linguistically homogenous. In other words, in Libreville it is the dominant language in the milieu and plays the same role as African vehicular languages elsewhere: its intrusion in the system of transmission is part of the change in the overall situation.

These few examples thus show us that there is no automatic transmission of the 'mother' tongue, or even the 'father' tongue, and the dominant language in the milieu sometimes penetrates right into and imposes itself on the family cell. The same phenomenon comes about in Bamako, Niamey and Libreville (i.e. a poor transmission of the parents' language), and this is evidence of the fragility of certain family languages, a phenomenon which, however, presents variations (the language of replacement is endogenous in Niamey, Dakar or Bamako and exogenous in Libreville), illustrating differences between the eco-linguistic niches concerned.

Another problem is that of knowing the extent to which speakers in the situation of migration transmit their languages to their children, and a survey carried out by the Institut National de la Statistique et des Études Économiques (INSEE), the French national institute of statistics and economic studies, together with the Institut National d'Études Démographiques (INED), the French national institute of demographic studies, provides us with some interesting details on this issue. Starting with two questions ('in which language or dialect did your parents usually talk to you when you were children?' and 'what language or dialect do you usually speak to your children?'), the survey brings out the fact that only a third of those people surveyed whose parents did not speak French do not in turn speak French to their children: Spanish would thus in two generations have lost 80 per cent of its speakers in migrant families, African languages 75 per cent, Arabic 50 per cent, etc.[6] More recently, a study carried out by Fabienne Leconte[7] on the second generation of African migrants in the region of Rouen (where there is the greatest number of African migrants outside the Paris region) gives us additional information on the same point. In families from the Congo, for instance, children address their parents in French in 80 per cent of cases, while their mothers speak to them in Lingala (18 per cent), in French (32 per cent), in both languages (14 per cent) or in a mixture of the two (36 per cent). We find the same situation, with different percentages, in other groups. Senegalese children speak to their parents in French (56 per cent of cases), Wolof (33 per cent), or a mixture of the two languages in the case of the Wolofs, with Pulaar and Soninké resisting the competition more effectively. These are average figures, since the situation varies depending on the parents' degree of competence in French. Indeed, Fabienne Leconte shows that the use of this language is in direct proportion to their schooling: the longer they have stayed on at school, the more they address their children in French.

The notion of 'mother tongue' is thus a mixture of myth and ideology. The family is not necessarily the place where languages are transmitted, and sometimes we observe breaks in transmission, often translated by a change of language, with children acquiring as first language the one that dominates in the milieu. This phenomenon is not encountered only in Africa: it concerns all multilingual situations and most of the situations of migration. Thus, in the abundant literature devoted to language maintenance and language shift in the United States, we read that the tendency is towards change. There are, however, notable exceptions, such as Chinese. The inhabitants of Chinese origin living on American soil numbered 1.64 million in 1990. Among them, 66.8 per cent were foreign born, but the descendants of some families who moved there two centuries ago still speak 'Chinese', i.e. one or other of the Han languages, 'dialects' as they are called in China. Originally, Cantonese and Toishan were especially widely spoken in these communities, English being the vehicular language used in contacts between Chinese who spoke different languages. Today, with the arrival of new migrants from Taiwan or mainland China, it is Putong Hua (or Guo yu, as it is called in Taiwan; Mandarin in the West) which is spreading as a vehicular language.[8] These communities live mainly in the big cities, gathered together in 'Chinatowns' which show a clear tendency to increase in size (in New York and San Francisco) and to multiply (in Chicago, Houston, etc.). 'The Chinese in the United States have created "cities" within cities and communities within communities', writes Xia,[9] and this situation, in which marriages within communities are frequent, shows that where Chinese populations are gathered together they can better maintain their specific character. Each 'Chinatown' in fact constitutes a little ecolinguistic niche and, in the same way, the Spanish-speaking populations from Cuba or Mexico that have come together in California or Florida have maintained their language for similar reasons. But numerous other migrants have abandoned it in order to adopt English: this is the case of the Italians, the Poles, the French, etc.

But this shift is not shown uniquely by the abandonment of the parents' language to the profit of the language of the milieu; it can also impact on the latter and transform it, as the following case study shows.

The case of the Spanish of Buenos Aires

In South America, Spanish has undergone an evolution that has led both to local differences, in particular in the domain of the lexicon, which can vary from one country to another, and to a more unified form in the phonetic and morphological domain. The main characteristics of this Atlantic Spanish, which have often been analysed as being the product of the influence of Andalusian (only partly true),[10] are the following:

- 'yeismo', i.e. the shift from /ly/ to /j/, /z/ or /dz/ in words such as *calle, lluvia, llano*, etc;
- 'seseo', i.e. the disappearance of the opposition between /θ/ and /s/ (*ciento* and *siento*, for instance, are both pronounced the same way);
- the aspiration of the final -s (a typical formula of the Spanish of Argentina is for example *ma o meno* for *mas o menos*, 'more or less');
- a system of personal pronouns and conjugations that is different from the standard Spanish system: where the Spaniards say, for example, *tu tienes, vosotros teneis* ('you (sing.) have', 'you (pl.) have'), the Argentines say *vos tenes, ustedes tienen*. Furthermore, in the Spanish of Argentina, there is a vocative form, *che*, the form which gave Che

> Guevara his nickname. In the middle of the nineteenth century, a constant fluctuation was observed between these Iberian and local forms, which then evolved towards the present Argentine system.[11]

These features, which can in part be found in other Spanish-speaking countries of South America, were already evident in the seventeenth century in the dialect of Buenos Aires in Argentina. According to Angel Rosenblat, Latin-American Spanish was even fixed in the sixteenth century, based on Castilian as it was spoken by the middle and upper classes of society who constituted the first conquerors.

> It is clear that after the sixteenth century, especially given the migratory movement of the nineteenth and twentieth centuries, the lowest sectors of the population flocked to an already domesticated continent. But they were incorporated, with some new contributions of their own, into a Hispano-American society that had already been consolidated, as far as its linguistic basis was concerned, in the sixteenth century.[12]

The reader may be wondering what all these considerations are doing in a chapter devoted to the transmission of languages and linguistic situations. The fact is that the language of Buenos Aires, the *porteño* dialect, which was subject to the general evolution of South American Spanish, has also been marked more recently by the non-transmission of a language of migration, namely Italian. The demographic growth of the city between 1810 and 1887 was slow to begin with (40,000 inhabitants in 1810; 51,000 in 1820; 62,000 in 1836; 85,000 in 1852) and

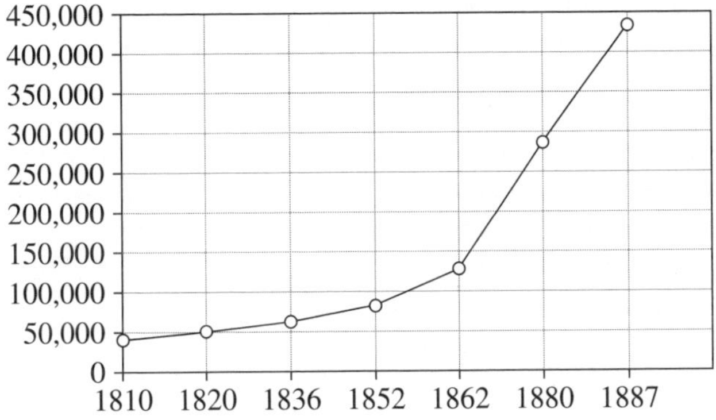

Figure 5.1 Population growth in Buenos Aires, 1810–1887

then suddenly accelerated in the second half of the century (128,000 inhabitants in 1862; 286,000 in 1880; 433,000 in 1887).[13]

This curve (figure 5.1) demonstrates that we are not dealing here with a natural increase but with a phenomenon of migration essentially due to the contribution of migrants from Europe, a migration that would only increase – the population went on to reach 2,254,000 in 1930. These migrants who came seeking their fortunes on the banks of the Rio de la Plata constituted over half the population, a demographic situation that would have important repercussions on the language spoken in the city. Thus, according to the 1887 census, there were 47.4 per cent Argentines, 32.1 per cent Italians, 9.1 per cent Spanish, 4.6 per cent French, 6.9 per cent other foreigners.

But the indication of the nationality of the inhabitants does not give us any exact information about their language. To begin with the 'Argentines' did not necessarily have Spanish as their first language: they could be the children of migrants, and they might have inherited their parents' language. The Italians were, at the time, most often the speakers of dialects and not of standard Italian. The Spanish were mainly Galicians, and the French might speak Basque, Gascon, etc. So if we add to the percentage of Italians the children of Italians born in Argentina who learned their parents' language, we can conclude that over half the population spoke 'Italian'[14] and that three linguistic forms dominated the city: Spanish, Italian dialects, and to a lesser degree French. How was this situation of urban multilingualism going to evolve? What languages would be transmitted from generation to generation, between migrants and their children? As far as the Italians are concerned, Maria Beatriz Fontanella de Weinberg[15] distinguishes three typical situations between which the population was equally shared:

1. The loss of any active knowledge of the language among migrants, and thus among their descendants: this was especially the case among the men (women are linguistically more conservative) who arrived in Argentina while still children or youths.
2. The continued use of the language among migrants, but a passive knowledge among some of their children: the parents speak Italian, the children reply in Spanish.
3. The continued use of the language among migrants, and transmission to their children: this was most often the case with migrants who had arrived in Argentina as adults and whose children were born at

> a time when Italian was the language of the hearth. In certain families, the older children learned Italian, but not the younger ones. In other words, the change of language can intervene within a single generation.[16]

So on the one hand we had a Spanish-speaking population, and on the other a population of Italian origin that spoke, depending on its social standing, different dialects and/or standard Italian, and it was in this group as a whole that 'Cocoliche' would appear.

Let's take time to retrace the origin of this word. Common names that spring from proper names are not rare. There is the example in French of the word *poubelle*, 'dustbin', which immortalizes the name of the prefect Poubelle. Certain of these names come from works of literature – such as *pipelette* ('concierge'), the patronymic of a couple of porters in *The Mysteries of Paris* by Eugène Sue – and this is true of *Cocoliche*. Apparently it was the actor José Podestà who, adapting the feuilleton *Juan Moreira* for the theatre at the start of the twentieth century, introduced a character inspired by a member of the company, Cocoliccio, who spoke a mixture of Calabrian and Porteño (the dialect of Buenos Aires).[17] This character enjoyed considerable success and was taken up in several other popular pieces, giving birth to the expression *hablar cocoliche*, 'to speak Cocoliche', i.e. to speak the language of immigrants.

Beatriz Lavandera defines this form as follows: 'Cocoliche is the name given by monolingual native Spanish-speakers in Argentina and Uruguay to the variety of Spanish used by Italian migrants in their interactions with the members of the local population.'[18] Giovanni Meo Zilio who, in the middle of the 1950s, published several articles on this form, defined it in turn as 'the linguistic results of the encounter between Italian and Spanish in the Rio de la Plata',[19] or as 'the mixed language of the Italians of the Rio de la Plata'.[20] In fact, the term Cocoliche, which these days merely refers to a rather extravagant way of dressing, at the start of the twentieth century designated the Spanish of foreigners, and more especially of Italians. A dictionary of Argentine idioms published at the start of the twentieth century defined it as a '*castellano chapurreado y macarronico que hablan los extranjeros ignorantes, en especial los italianos*' ('a broken and macaronic Castilian spoken by ignorant foreigners, especially Italians').[21] This, of course, is a representation, in the sense I have given this notion, but in spite of the racism with which it is imbued, this definition gives us quite a good idea of what this linguistic form actually was. Indeed, 'Cocoliche' appears as the product of a learning situation, 'an underdeveloped variety, more supple than Spanish' in the sense that even the speakers who speak it fluently 'do not use many of the possibilities of the Spanish of B A'.[22] So it would seem to be the Spanish of Italians, an incomplete and reduced Spanish: 'We can say that Cocoliche is a reduced variety of Spanish, in the sense that it is lacking many of the forms used in particular to express semantic and stylistic nuances'.[23] And Lavandera concluded with three observations:

1 The use of variants based on the Italian dialect does not transmit any social or stylistic meaning to the Argentine listener: he interprets it as a poor knowledge of Spanish and sometimes finds it difficult to understand.
2 The Spanish component of the Italian speakers' repertoire does not include the sociolinguistic variables of Buenos Aires.
3 Hence it is impossible to isolate variants of the type formal/ informal.[24]

Maria Beatriz Fontanella de Weinberg is, on this same point, both much more precise and less normative. Cocoliche is, in her view, first and foremost a continuum: 'This term covers a field that extends from an Italian with Spanish interference to a Spanish with Italian interference, by way of mixed forms that it is impossible to attribute to either of these languages and that constitute a linguistic continuum whose two poles are Spanish and Italian.'[25] Meo Zilio likewise insists on the fact that we are not dealing with a third language, a vehicular language, but a fluid form that 'tends to grow ever closer to Spanish' and to get further away from Italian. This 'fluid' form, varying from one speaker to another but also from one district to the next and marked as it was by different Italian dialects,[26] was thus the product of a situation of learning or appropriation, the linguistic trace of a *passage*. Such a continuum is of course possible only between two languages that are akin, and Fontanella de Weinberg adds that 'Cocoliche' appears among Italians who speak different dialects and do not know the standard form:

> The importance of a low cultural level in the emergence and use of 'Cocoliche' is corroborated by the fact that what we have here is a

> phenomenon that is practically absent among Italians of a higher level, among whom, while we do find logical interferences in the two systems, both of the systems remain clearly distinct.

So we here seem to have a continuum with a dual purpose, turned simultaneously toward communication with Spanish-speakers and toward communication between the speakers of Italian dialects. To this can be added a socio-professional dimension. Men dominated the more Hispanicized varieties, and their professional activities determined the breadth of the varieties used. But this continuum simultaneously constituted a moment in the acquisition of Spanish and the non-transmission of Italian forms, a transitory form turned towards the acquisition of Spanish in one or two generations:

> The generalized multilingualism of Buenos Aires during the period from 1880 to 1930 led in the majority of cases to a rapid change of language, with the result that the grandchildren of immigrants, even, indeed, their own children – especially in the case of Italians – became Spanish monoglots.[27]

Furthermore, Fontanella de Weinberg emphasizes that a certain number of factors accelerated this change of language:

- the urbanization and industrialization of Argentina;
- the massive character of immigration, which prevented immigrants from remaining separate from the rest of the community as a whole;
- the possibilities of social and educational ascent, in particular the existence of a free and effective school system, at both primary and secondary levels, favouring linguistic assimilation;
- the fact that Italians are in the majority among immigrants, and that there is a significant dialectal variation in their ways of speech and a linguistic proximity to Spanish. To this can be added a religious community and cultural similarities.

(The second point may appear paradoxical but it is fundamental. The dimensions of a minority group determine its linguistic loyalty and there is a critical mass beyond which a linguistic ghetto becomes impossible, especially when society offers numerous possibilities of integration. Thus Christine Deprez has pointed out that, in France, a very reduced community such as the Armenian community kept up its language better than a bigger community, such as the Arabic community:[28] so the paradox is merely apparent.)

This transitory character of Cocoliche, this 'inter-language' aspect, is confirmed by Giovanni Meo Zilio: 'Its degree and its extension change over time in each speaker: certain forms tend to disappear, new forms appear, but we can say overall that – again in each speaker – [Cocoliche] tends to draw ever closer to Spanish and to get further away from Italian.'[29] Fontanella de Weinberg is even clearer in her final text, completed just a few days before her death. Argentina, she explains, has been the second biggest country of destination for migrants worldwide, after the United States but ahead of Canada, Brazil and Australia: between 1895 and 1930 there were around 25 per cent migrants. The small isolated groups (such as the German-speakers from the Volga, the non-urbanized Danes or the Welsh) have preserved their languages right up to the present day. But the Italian speakers, for the reasons I have set out, would lose their dialects, and it was this non-transmission that marked the local variety of Spanish.

It is worth adding that Cocoliche as an interlect is not a linear continuum but a sort of spectrum in which Spanish is a single pole, while the other poles are constituted by different dialectal varieties. Fontanella de Weinberg proposes the representation in diagram 5.1.

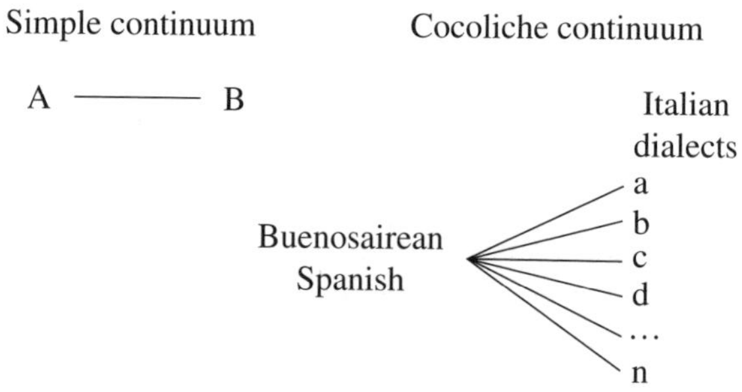

Diagram 5.1 Simple continuum and Cocoliche continuum
Source: M. B. Fontanella de Weinberg, 'Contacto lingüistico: lenguas immigratorias'.

She adds:

> It is noteworthy that, while the active usage of Cocoliche was limited to Italian immigrants, a passive knowledge of it was significantly widespread in the linguistic community of Buenos Aires, with the vast majority of

speakers being able to understand it. In the case of Spanish speakers, this understanding concerned the zones of the spectrum that were closest to the Spanish pole, and the Cocoliche speakers tried to draw closer to these varieties when they spoke with persons of non-Italian origin.[30]

This coexistence between Spanish and different Italian dialects initially had a fallout on those two sets of language. Giovanni Meo Zilio, who in the 1950s described this process *from the point of view of Italian*, nonetheless insisted on the fact that, in tandem with the modifications of Italian, this coexistence could be seen also in the influence of Italian on Spanish. What we have been calling Cocoliche was thus an amorphous and ever-changing intermediary form, used *simultaneously* between Italians and Spaniards and between Italian dialect speakers; it constituted the product of a movement that radically changed a certain ecolinguistic situation, with the massive introduction of Italian dialect forms into Spanish, and Spanish forms into Italian – a radical change that found a transitory expression in the emergence of an interlanguage but that would later lead to the constitution of Porteño Spanish, via several intermediate steps:

1 There were numerous direct loans from Italian into the lexicon of Buenos Aires (*chau, pibe, nono, cucha, capo, chimento, toscano, tratativa*, etc.).
2 At the end of the nineteenth century there appeared a certain kind of argot called Lunfardo, whose vocabulary was only 50 per cent Spanish in origin, an argot that would gradually penetrate the vernacular, in particular through tango. We find for example, in the first line of *Mi noche triste* by Pascual Contursi (1917), as performed by Carolos Gardel, a lexicon that 'reveals an innovative linguistic attitude', 'a non-official discourse in poetry':[31]

   Percanta que me amuraste
   en lo mejor de mi vida
   dejándome el alma herida
   y espinas en el corazón.[32]

   Indeed, we see in the first line two terms that are unknown to Spanish: *percanta* ('woman', 'lover') and *amurar*, ('to abandon'), and there are numerous examples of this type in Lunfardo and, to a lesser degree, in Porteño Spanish.

3 Modifications in the phonological system of Spanish, such as the appearance of the sound 'sh', initially in loan words and especially those taken from French (champagne, chef, chic, charmant, chauvinismo, etc.) and English. The phoneme occurs first in the language of the upper classes, then passes over into the everyday Spanish of Buenos Aires, in words such as *short* (for 'shorts'), *pasha*, *flash*, *misho* ('poor' in Lunfardo), etc., and sometimes alternates with /ch/ in words such as *chalet*, *chope* (draught beer), *chef*, etc. In addition there is a tendency to pronounce the /j/ as /ch/, to muffle it, which leads to the confusion between *pillado* ('caught'), and *pishado* ('pissed'), etc.

We can thus see that, in the tense coexistence between Spanish and Italian dialects in Buenos Aires, the non-transmission of the latter does not constitute a merely statistical fact and does not simply show that Spanish was imposed. The modifications introduced into the ecolinguistic niche and the way that Italian speakers 'manage' multilingualism have actually played a part, via interlinguistic forms (Cocoliche), in the transformation of the vernacular of Buenos Aires. The non-transmission of the Italian dialects has here been a factor of change in the other form found in the niche, leading to Spanish as it is spoken today. And this example thus shows us how a language can vanish while leaving its imprint on the one that takes over: 'Porteño' is, of course, a kind of Spanish, but a Spanish that has preserved the trace of the different dialects and languages that it has replaced in the linguistic practices of individual families over two or three generations.

And the story does not end there. Buenos Aires is even today taking in new migrants from Korea, Paraguay, Peru, etc., and Korean, Quechua, Garani, etc. are all present in the ecolinguistic niche and will doubtless leave their mark in future on the form taken by Porteño.

The case of creoles: upheaval in the ecolinguistic niche and linguistic change

The term *creole* is a typical heteronym, i.e. a name given to a language by those describing it: neither the speakers of 'creoles' nor those who rubbed shoulders with them originally used this term, preferring to speak of 'patois', of 'negro patois', of 'jargon' or 'corrupt French',[33] and even today, in Réunion or Guadeloupe, certain people claim they speak 'patois'. The word originally referred to whites born 'in the intertropical colonies', in the West Indies and in America, and it was only slowly and belatedly, through the simplification of forms such as 'creole patois', or 'creole dialects', that it assumed its current meaning. But once this meaning was established and generalized, we inherited a first artefact: a set of languages of different lexical origins (French, English, Portuguese, Dutch, etc.), all of them subsumed under the same label. And this term entered a wider set, a sort of clandestine typology, barely if at all theorized, in which there coexist *language, dialect, patois, pidgin, creole, jargon, argot or slang, vehicular language*, etc.

If we try to introduce a little order into this swarm of different labels, we find a generic term, *langue*, around which there gravitate *dialects*, a sometimes pejorative term (dialect is a 'sub-language' in the eyes of common sense), and sometimes purely descriptive (dialect is a form – geographical or social – of language). *Language* thus gradually became established as a scientific entity (as described by the linguist) and a geopolitical notion (once the United States was established, they had their own language), which explains a current tendency to derive the names of languages from those of countries and citizens: in older states (in France there live French people who speak French, in Italy Italians who speak Italian, etc.) but also in more recent states (Malay was rebaptized in Indonesia as Bahasa Indonesia). To this hard core, language, and its bastard offspring, dialects and patois, we need to add the shameful products either of the appropriation or transformation by the people of standard languages (jargons, argots), or of mixtures (pidgins, sabirs, creoles, vehicular language). Creoles, originally considered as bastard forms, are now well on the way to becoming recognized, not as legitimate children but as legitimized natural children. This is where the difficulties begin, since there forms, functions and history all get mixed up together without anyone being able to arrange them in a hierarchy. It would be reassuring to be able to conclude at this point that the science of linguistics has established precise and unambiguous concepts which the representations of speakers then come along and mess up; reassuring but false, since all these terms – language, dialect, patois, pidgin, creole, etc. – which do not constitute a unified terminology are used on a daily basis by the discourse of linguistics.

The legitimation of creoles begins with the hypothesis of the pidgin-creole cycle, with the idea that a creole is a pidgin that has become the 'mother tongue' of a community. There is something very revealing about this: in an ideological continuum that extends from jargon to language, a classification is carried out on the basis of a criterion (the mother tongue) whose roots lie in German Romanticism, which gives a strong positive evaluation to communicative practices without taking into account all of their functions and all their conditions of emergence. At the end of the day, it is the myth of mother's milk that dominates; and this is, of course, a matter neither of theory nor of any explanation, but simply of representations. And this short-sighted analysis leads to a strange historical dead-end. On the one side it gives us 'languages' and, on the other, mixed, incomplete forms that are still emerging. Hence the frenzied extension of the word *creole* to a whole series of vehicular languages which are not considered as languages in their own right; and a parallel tendency to name these forms 'pidgin/creole', as if to avoid taking a position in the debate on the pidgin-creole cycle while continuing to consider them as similar to the forms born on plantations, in the melting-pot of slaves speaking different languages and trying to appropriate the language of the boss.

What creoles are not

The negative form of this subtitle is a way of expressing my opposition to the quite widespread tendency to consider as 'creoles' all the forms of languages that are used more or less as vehicular languages, in particular in Africa. A good example of this tendency is constituted by the descriptions of the Arabic of Juba and of Ki-Nubi, Arabic vehicular languages (which in certain cases have become vernaculars) in South Sudan, Uganda and Kenya. The history of the Arabic of Juba and Ki-Nubi is presented in similar terms by Kees Versteegh and Catherine Miller.[34] The two languages, it seems, originated in 'Bimbashi Arabic', an 'Arabic pidgin' (Miller) or 'a pidginized version of Arabic' (Versteegh) used at the end of the nineteenth century as a mode of communication between Egyptian soldiers and non-Arabic-speaking recruits, when the Anglo-Egyptian army embarked on its pacification of South Sudan. Later on these recruits, for the most part originating in Nubia, followed the British Army to Uganda and Kenya and continued to speak this form of Arabic that came from Bimbashi Arabic, was baptized Ki-Nubi ('the language of the Nubians') and is still spoken around Kampala and Nairobi. In parallel, Bimbashi Arabic continued to be used as a 'trade jargon' in the region of Juba, in the south of Sudan, where numerous interethnic marriages made of it a mother tongue, and thus a creole,[35] a vehicular language in the rural areas and a first language in the towns.[36] Mauro Tosco presents us with more or less the same picture of the situation, considering as he does the Arabic of Juba as 'a stabilized pidgin for most speakers . . . and a creole for a minority',[37] and Jonathan Owens[38] classifies both Ki-Nubi and the Arabic of Juba as pidgins/creoles. In all four cases (Versteegh, Miller, Tosco, Owens) we are within the framework of the classical theory of the 'pidgin-creole cycle': a creole is a former pidgin that has become the mother tongue of a community, and here the 'minority' for which the Arabic of Juba has become a creole is that part of the population which speaks it as their first language; for the others it remained a pidgin.

Now, the descriptions of the situation of this Arabic of Juba presented by Versteegh or Miller show that what we have here is a vehicular language that has become the vernacular for part of the population. There is nothing rare about this process. It occurs these days with, for instance, Wolof in Dakar (urban Wolof seems to be a pidgin for some people, a creole for others) and with Munukutuba in Brazzaville and Pointe Noire. Munukutuba is a creole in the towns, a pidgin along the railway line where it fulfils the function of a vehicular language, just as the French of Abidjan is a pidgin or a creole, depending on the situation. Likewise, William Samarin has in several publications presented Sango (spoken in Central Africa), Kituba and Lingala (spoken in both the Congos) as pidgins and/or as creoles.[39] And we could cite several other cases of this tendency to consider as creoles practically all forms of vehicular language that spring from a more or less mixed origin and have become vernaculars. By thus imposing on linguistic situations the interpretive grid of the pidgin-creole cycle, all the languages in the world could be considered as creoles, which would not be of much use to theory and would be singularly lacking in rigour: we have nothing to gain by adapting the term *creole* to so many different uses.

One day people will probably cease to speak of the creole of Haiti and will talk instead of Haitian, just as the creole of Mauritius will become Mauritian, etc. But as this time still seems far distant, it is important to be precise in the terms we use. If there had been linguists at that – distant – period when English was formed, perhaps this form would have been baptized 'pidgin', then 'creole'; but nobody these days denies English the status of a language.

So what is a creole? It is not my purpose to provide a definitive solution to this debate, which has lasted a good long while, but rather to analyse in the light of linguistic ecology certain situations, essentially those which result from the importing of slaves to the plantations in the Indian Ocean or the Caribbean Sea. In my view it is reasonable to reserve the word 'creole' to designate the autonomous forms that sprang from the languages of the colonizers, in conditions that I will be discussing more fully, and to consider the Arabic of Juba, Munukutuba or Sango as vehicular languages that have in certain cases become the vernaculars. At least, that is the position that is adopted here.

What creoles perhaps are

For many years creoles were considered as pidgins that had become the first language of servile populations. This point of view, generally abandoned nowadays,[40] was particularly debatable since the terms in question, pidgin and creole – used to name forms that had often been described poorly if at all – were themselves ill-defined and adapted to too many different senses. I propose to define a pidgin as *the response of social practice to the absence of a common language* in situations where the need to communicate becomes compelling: a pidgin fulfils the function of a vehicular language limited to certain domains. Let's take one example. In 1658, in his *Histoire naturelle et morale des îles Antilles de l'Amérique*, Rochefort dedicated a chapter to 'Remarks on the language of the Caribbean Islanders'. He points out that as well as their own language they 'have formed another (language) which is a mongrel form mixed with several foreign words, through the commerce they have developed with the Europeans. In especial they have borrowed several Spanish words, since these were the first Christians they encountered.'[41] What he is here describing is typically the emergence of a pidgin, i.e. a form with limited uses that is employed between groups which, for other functions, each have their own language. And he continues:

> When they are conversing or negotiating with the Christians, they use their corrupt language. Apart from that they can jabber away quite pleasantly when they wish to speak in some foreign language. As when

> they say *Compère gouverneur*, [Friend Governor], using this word *compère* in general to all those who are their friends or allies. Thus they would say quite openly, if the opportunity for it arose, *Compère Roy*, [Friend King]. Thus it is a compliment on their part when they say to us French, with their merry faces, *Ah si toy bon pour Caraïbe, moy bon pour France* [Ah, if you good for Caribbean, I good for France].

Thus, in Rochefort's view, there are two different forms, a 'corrupt language' for speaking to Christians, and a 'pleasant jabber' when they wish to speak 'in some foreign language'; and while the first is, as I have said, closer to pidginization, the second is more like an informal acquisition of French.

Pidgins should thus be classified in the set of vehicular languages, a typology of which we should here draw up, distinguishing for instance between the vernaculars that are used as vehicular languages (English, French, etc.), the languages created to fulfil the function of a vehicular language (Munukutuba or Bimbashi Arabic for example), which sometimes become vernaculars (as is the case with the two previous examples, respectively in the south of the Congo and in Juba, Sudan) and approximate forms, the pidgins whose use was limited to a few contacts where they serve as vehicular languages. This typology by no means exhausts the problems, of course. We still need, for instance, to study the formal impact of the way a language becomes a vehicular language (or a vernacular) but it can serve our purposes for the time being.

After pidgins come creoles. I will start from the principle that *there is no reason to distinguish between a creole and a language*. One can of course argue that the difference between them is diachronic, that the way creoles appear enables us to differentiate between them, etc. But what is specific about creoles is quite simply their youth, which means that we know their history (or think we know it) better than we know that of older languages. In fact, we need to combine the pairing young/old with another pairing, orality/writing. There are 'old' languages about which we have significant written documentation (this is the case with French, for example), and the existence of this documentation compensates for the oldness of the language; and then there are others about which we know little because we have practically no written sources (this is the case of Quechua, in the Andes, for example). But nothing distinguishes the *functioning* of a creole from that of another language, and it seems that this term has nowadays an ideological usage comparable to the way the term *dialect* was once used; indeed, the difference is not a scientific one, but a social one, and the term *creole* tends to designate quite simply something that one does not wish to call a language. Once again, creoles are contact languages (but this is the case with many other languages, the most famous being English) whose relative youth enables us to reflect more fully on their conditions of emergence.

But this does not necessarily mean that all the forms that get to be called creoles are distinct from the languages from which they spring, and this brings us up against another theoretical problem, which goes far beyond the boundaries of the creole question: *At what point does a language cease to be itself so as to become another language, or to break up into two different languages?* To this question some people reply: when the speakers no longer understand one another. But the criterion of mutual understanding cannot be used, for two reasons.

1 *From the synchronic point of view*, there are situations in which languages are considered as different because their speakers want them to be different. This was the case with Hindi and Urdu in India, and these days it is the case with Croat and Serb in the former Yugoslavia (I will be returning to this case in chapter 6). Nobody questions the fact that the Serbs and the Croats are mutually comprehensible, but Serbs and Croats now claim to speak different languages, Serb and Croat. Of course, linguists can always claim to be right *in spite of* the linguistic representations of speakers (and, from one point of view, this is quite true), but the fact remains that these representations can be factors of differentiation and result in the linguist being wrong in the long term: forms that people insist are different end up by actually being different.

2 *From the diachronic point of view*, the difference between certain linguistic forms is quite simply a phenomenon of evolution, and what is called *popular* or *vernacular language* is often an 'advanced' language that is separating off from the more fixed standard language. If we take for example the data provided by Catherine Miller[42] on the Arabic of Khartoum and that of Juba:

	Khartoum	Juba
1	naas balad	al-nasi ta béle ('the people of the country')
2	beeti	jua tai ('my house')
3	chuftak	ana ainu eta ('I've seen you')

4	chuftani	eta ainu ana ('you have seen me')
5		uo **ra**kabu laam ('she has cooked the meat')
6		ra**ka**bu ta laam ('the cooking of the meat')
7		laam raka**bu** ('the meat has been cooked') *etc.*

We see in 1 and 2 the shift in Juba Arabic to an analytical construction to express the genitive, in 3 and 4 the shift in Juba Arabic to invariable verbal forms, in 5, 6 and 7 the use of the tonic accent, in particular in words of three syllables, to distinguish the verb from the substantive and the passive, etc.; and all this closely resembles a self-regulated phenomenon of dialectal evolution. When one and the same language spreads over a huge area, it is possible that different 'advanced' forms will result from it. At each of the points in the area these may be sufficiently close to the standard to make mutual understanding between themselves and the standard form possible, but at the same time these may be less and less understandable to one another. This may appear paradoxical, but there are numerous examples to be found. A Bolivian peasant who speaks 'Spanish' cannot necessarily understand a Spanish peasant who also speaks Spanish; a Moroccan peasant who speaks Arabic cannot understand a Lebanese peasant but, in each of these countries, there may be mutual understanding between the speakers of the standard and the vernacular [popular] forms of the language.[43] Likewise, the French seem to be able to understand one another, as do the Quebecois, but a farmer from the south-west of France and a fisherman from the Magdalen Islands, in Quebec, will probably find it difficult to communicate.

The same is true for creoles. There is sometimes mutual understanding between a speaker of standard French and a creole speaker, sometimes not. The reason is that this situation is affected by history, determined by the social situation and linguistic representations; these forms evolve, and they can initially evolve in two directions: fission (separation) or fusion (de-creolization). These two opposite possibilities are thus not merely the product of internal forces, which means they are quite unpredictable: nobody can say if the 'creole' of Réunion, for instance, will in a century's time be a regional form of French or a language independent of French belonging to a new generation of Indo-European languages, a 'French language', in the same way that we now say that French is a 'Romance language'; the evolution will depend on external factors such as representations, linguistic policies, etc.

This problem of the genesis of creoles has over the past twenty years led to lively theoretical debates, and various different hypotheses confront one another. While there is a practically universal agreement that the language of power, the 'superstrate' or 'lexifying language', gives creole a major proportion of its vocabulary, opinions and theories then diverge, and they can now be classified into three major groups.

1 The *substratist* theory The morphology and syntax of creoles are mainly provided by the languages of the substrate, i.e., as regards the creoles of the West Indies, by African languages. Creoles would thus be African languages in their syntax, their morphology and their semantics, while only the lexicon was borrowed by European languages. Taken to its logical conclusion, this theory has given birth to the theory of relexification: a team of researchers working with Claire Lefebvre in Quebec[44] argues that Haitian is Fon (the language spoken in Benin), of which only the phonic form is French.

2 The *universalist* theory The influence of the languages of the substrate is not decisive, and creoles show a 'bioprogramme', a sort of innate linguistic organization that lies at the origin of all languages, though history and evolution have to some degree erased it or blunted it. This bioprogramme would re-emerge both when children acquire their first language and in the formation of creoles. This position, held by Derek Bickerton,[45] had its moment of glory in the 1980s, but it now seems to have lost a great number of its defenders.

3 The *Eurogeneticist* or *superstratist* theory Creoles are derived from European 'mother languages', in the form spoken by the whites who sailed for the islands. This leaves us to explain how and why they became different from the European languages. The fullest reply to this question is the one which defines creoles as 'approximations of approximations'. This position, illustrated by the work of Robert Chaudenson, insists on the socio-historical conditions of appearance of creoles (the number and origin of slaves, relations between slaves and masters) and distinguishes between two phases, the society of dwellers and the plantation society. In the first phase, which corresponds to the time when the colonizers settled, there are few slaves

(four or five per family of colonizers), they live and work alongside the whites whose language they quickly pick up – or, at least, enough of it to be able to communicate easily. In the second phase, which corresponds to the agro-industrial development of the plantations, the slaves are necessarily much more numerous, and the new arrivals, placed under the command of creole slaves, will have as their point of departure the form of the whites' language which the whites themselves speak. This second-order approximation would thus be the explanatory model for the emergence of creoles.

The distinguishing feature of the first two positions (relexification and bioprogramme) is that they fall within the same theoretical framework, that of generative grammar – or at least they do not contradict it. In my introductory remarks I noted, in reference to a work by Steven Pinker, the Chomskyan theory called 'principles and parameters', which saw in the languages of the world nothing but surface variants of one and the same innate grammar. All of them illustrate the same 'principles' and are distinguished only by the action of 'parameters'; at a certain level of abstraction, people would thus all speak the same language. But this analysis lessens the interest of any approach to creoles in terms of relexification. To try to demonstrate, for instance, that Haitian creoles and Fon are one and the same language is in fact quite futile if we view all languages as being actualizations of the same principles. The idea of bioprogramme, on the other hand, whose compatibility with the 'principles and parameters' theory is easy to see, comes up against the same problems: the unavoidable fact that the world's languages are different and are organized in extremely varied ways which it is difficult to reduce to a single model. The third position, that illustrated by Robert Chaudenson, is for its part the only one that tries to take into account historical and social facts. After all, there is no point in postulating the influence on this or that form of creole of this or that language spoken by slaves if we cannot demonstrate beforehand that, in their majority, these slaves came from a zone in which this language was spoken, and it is difficult to wish to reconstruct the appearance of creoles without closely studying its demographic and social conditions. Now the first two hypotheses have the remarkable characteristic of continuing to consider languages as *objects*, without taking into account the speakers and their situations.

But these three hypotheses on the origin of creoles, however different they may be, nonetheless have one characteristic in common: the problem of creolization is always approached in terms of the appearance of a linguistic form. Now, whether creole is considered as a new form (a new language) or as the evolution of a previous form, its appearance is necessarily correlative with a disappearance and/or a transformation. This is why the case of creoles is here being discussed in a chapter devoted to the transmission of languages and situations; it constitutes a particular case of that. Linguistics has often used the model of communication, with a sender (S) and a receiver (R) between which there can be sent a message thanks to the existence of a common code, and feedback, which means that the sender can verify that the message has indeed been received by the receiver:

S——-message——- >R
common code

This model also makes it possible to represent the process whereby codes are acquired: the learner is then sender and receiver in turn, insofar as he receives information on his social environment (his parents, the group, society) and sends out phrases, while the social body is a sender (of both codes and representation), but code and message are here melded together. In fact, acquisition consists in extracting codes from messages, via successive hypotheses, which feedback from the social body confirms or disconfirms. Thus the child constructs phrases by applying rules that it extracts, by hypothesis, from what it receives, and it is corrected (picked up) by the environment when its rules are inadequate, i.e. when they do not permit it to produce phrases that are accepted by that environment. A young child learning French as its first language will thus tend to consider that all verbs are governed like those of the first group (*parler*, 'to speak', *manger*, 'to eat', *chanter*, 'to sing'), which will lead it to two types of behaviour which the environment will repress:

- inventing verbs of the first group that do not exist in French, such as **boiver* instead of *boire*, 'to drink', **rier* instead of *rire*, 'to laugh', etc,
- applying to other verbs transformations that are not acceptable outside the first group.

Thus, on the model

> _Je mange_, 'I eat' > _Il faut que je mange_, 'I must eat'
> _Je parle_, 'I speak' > _Il faut que je parle_, 'I must speak'
> _Je chante_, 'I sing' > _Il faut que je chante_, 'I must sing', etc.

the child will produce statements such as

> _Je sais_, 'I know' > *_Il faut que je sais_, for 'I must know'
> _Je viens_, 'I come' > *_Il faut que je viens_, for 'I must come'
> _Je prends_, 'I take' > *_Il faut que je prends_, for 'I must take'. (_etc._)

Versions that will generally eventually be corrected by the environment.

This model functions to a satisfactory degree in the case of first-language acquisition, especially when it is spoken simultaneously in the family and in the social environment. The learner is then in constant contact with 'legitimate speakers' of his language, with those who determine the norm; he is subjected to constant corrections from the social milieu. Things are different when the language is used between speakers who do not have this normative feedback available to them, and the case of creoles as well as that of colonial languages acquired outside the educational framework (English and French in Africa, for instance) are exemplary in this respect, but they are barely different from other cases such as that of 'marginal' types of French (spoken in North America for instance).

It is thus clear that the 'creole laboratory'[46] does not necessarily show us the birth of a new language but, rather, an accelerating evolution under the influence of an ecolinguistic upheaval. If, in particular areas of the world, linguistic forms have managed to change very quickly, this is because the ecolinguistic equilibrium has been dramatically disturbed. So we need to measure this disturbance while taking into account a great number of parameters, including the displacement of populations (which populations, from whence did they come, what languages did they speak?); the absence of vehicular language between slaves; the modes of acquisition of the language of power that was available in the linguistic environment; the absence of a 'legitimate' speaker to correct hypotheses about the code; the embryonic bits of code that were extracted from messages; the forms of social organization, etc.

My hypothesis, then, is that the 'genesis' of creoles brings into play two correlative processes, the non-transmission of the slaves' languages, on the one hand, and the 'wild', informal appropriation of another language present in the ecolinguistic niche, on the other, and that we need to analyse this as a fact of acquisition. There is nothing revolutionary about this position,[47] and it follows directly on from that of Chaudenson (summarized above), but it enables us to analyse creolization within the same framework as that used in chapter 3 for the varieties of French spoken in Africa: *acclimatization* and/or *acclimatation*. We have seen that there was *acclimatization* when a species displaced from one milieu to another could survive in it, and *acclimatation* when this species could, in addition, reproduce itself there. Acclimatization is thus a transitory adaptation, while acclimatation is to some extent a putting down of roots. From this point of view, creoles are obviously involved in acclimatation: they can now be transmitted from generation to generation. The ecolinguistic conditions in which the slaves found themselves (plurality of languages, absence of mutual understanding, the absence of any vehicular language apart from the European language of their masters, etc.) led them to respond to the problem of communication with which they were confronted by the acquisition of the language available in the environment – French, English, Portuguese, etc. But, in the absence of direct contact with those who laid down the legitimate norm of this language and left to their own devices, the slaves, on the one hand, took the language to its logical conclusion (like a child saying, incorrectly, **il faut que je sais* on the model of *je mange* > *il faut que je mange*) without being corrected and, on the other hand, interpreted the statements to which they were exposed on the basis of acquired habits, their phonology (the sounds absent from African languages are also quite often absent from creoles) and their semantic universe – just as the Gauls or the Iberians interpreted Latin on the basis of other acquired habits (the dialectal fragmentation of Romania is partly explicable by different substrates). We have fallen into the habit of classifying French among the Romance languages because the power relations favoured Latin, which transformed itself under the influence of local languages. In the islands in the Caribbean, the power relations also favoured the European languages, which thus became modified under the influence of the languages of slaves. In other words, in the evolutionary possibilities of these languages, the substrate (which is here a multilingual substrate) favoured one direction rather than another.

The ecolinguistic system of the islands in the Caribbean or the Indian Ocean was thus overturned by the arrival of the first colonizers and by the importing of European languages. The acclimatizing of French, Spanish and English led initially to the disappearance of the local languages (when there were any). Then the importing of a great number of African slaves to work on the sugar-cane plantations led to a new homeostatic reaction: their languages did not acclimatize, since the sociolinguistic conditions did not allow it (significant multilingualism, reduced linguistic communities, the existence of an already acclimatized European language, the numerical superiority of the whites in the first period), but they did modify the language of the colonizers and give birth to creoles. In this development, there are thus two 'parents', a European language on the one side and African languages on the other, just as there are two 'parents' in the emergence of French, Latin and the Germanic language. Then the problem of knowing whether the new language stems from the father or the mother is both a false problem (it proceeds from both parents) and a problem of nuance, of balance. A child inherits its parents' genes in variable proportions and what we face here is a problem in the genetics of populations.

In my introduction I mentioned the numerous metaphors that have been used in linguistics, and yet I have chosen in this book to use the ecological metaphor. But while a metaphor may simply provide a thematic link, it can also be a problematic. In the first case, we say what we would have said differently or what we have already said in a different way in the light of the metaphor, a procedure which can be brilliant but unproductive. In the second case, we seek through the metaphor a new problematic for what is actually true of languages, and this is what I am going to attempt with the ecological metaphor. So I am now going to take a short but necessary detour via ecogenetics. What we are facing here is the problem of the selection of linguistic traits in the interaction between the characters of a language and its milieu. In ecogenetics this selection is considered to arise from the fact that, when we have a couple of *alleles* **A** and **B** (i.e. a couple of *allelomorphic* elements,[48] elements with the same function but different effects), the probability of the *genotypes* (the characters inherited) **AA**, **AB** and **BB** playing a part in the formation of the following generation is not the same and varies with the selective action of the milieu. Thus black ladybirds with red spots and orange ladybirds with black spots do not stand the cold equally well, and are divided up differently in the autumn and spring generations.

If we try to apply this to 'creologenetic' situations, we have to take into consideration the fact that when we have two linguistic alleles (i.e. two elements having the same function but different effects), their participation in change will vary as a function of the selective action of the milieu and reactions to the milieu. Reactions to the milieu are shown in linguistic practices and initially take the form of individual responses that can converge and end up by producing collective modifications. Let's take a simple example. In Haitian, the definite article is a postpositive form *la*: *tabl-la* ('the table'), *piebwa-la* ('the tree'), etc. It is difficult to deny that this form comes from French, from expressions such as *cette table-là*, 'that table' or *la table-là*, with similar meaning. But this raises two problems: why is it *là* which remained as the postpositive article and not the prepositive forms *le, la* or *les*, and which form of French lies at the origin of this evolution? The central question, the great unknown factor, is here the *terminus a quo*, the linguistic forms which the slaves tried to appropriate, i.e. the French of the colonizers (or, in other situations, the English of the colonizers, the Dutch of the colonizers, etc.). It could not, of course, be the 'standard' French of the period but of popular and/or regional forms of the seventeenth century, doubtless already modified. On this limited point (the definite, indefinite and demonstrative determiners of the substantive) Robert Chaudenson has compared the different creoles with a French lexical basis, the rural Quebec dialect, the popular French of Montreal and the French of Missouri.[49] His conclusion is that the weakening of the definite article entailed in these three last forms the appearance of a postpositive *–la* (*le . . . la, c'te . . . la*) and in most of the different creoles the preservation of this single *–la* is enough for the definite, and a *–sala* for the demonstrative.

This analysis would tend to consider the North American forms of French as intermediary between the *terminus a quo* and the creoles, but constituting, like them, a way of managing the situation. 'Appropriation, change and creolization consist, in different conditions and following different modes, in seeking "inheritance solutions", i.e. they consist in reorganizing in and through the assimilation and use of linguistic systems.'[50] The fact remains that evolution towards the ultimate form demonstrated in creoles, the postpositive *–la*, can both be put down to the movement postulated by Chaudenson and also show the role of African languages. And the ecolinguistic approach here enables us to formulate this hypothesis more precisely. In the process of acquisition of French by slaves speaking different languages, there were, in my view, a couple of alleles constituted by the French form (*la, les . . .*) *. . . là* (for example *le livre-là, ce livre-là, la table-là*, etc.) and by the different ways in which the determiner is marked in the different African languages found in the plantations (for example, a tonal modification of the final, as in Bambara, or a postpositive element as in Fon). The forms that appeared in the varieties of French of North America, *le* (*la, les, ce, ces*) *. . . là* were felt to be redundant and susceptible to simplification. It was then that certain factors in the milieu (the languages found, the number of people speaking them, etc.) played a part in the selection of the prepositive or postpositive form of French. This does not mean that Haitian, for example, is an African language, but simply that ecolinguistic conditions favoured the evolution of French (elsewhere of English, Portuguese, etc.) in a certain direction. The succession of the forms described by Chaudenson, from prepositive *le* or *ce* to postpositive *–là* via *le . . . la* or *c'te . . . la*, in which the forms of North America seem to occupy an intermediary position, is thus not the result of a programmed evolution, inherent in French from the start, but the fruit of varied influences, amongst which certain traits of the slaves' languages played the role of catalyst. In different ecolinguistic niches, the same language was thus able to evolve in a different way.

If we now turn to the following examples (taken from Chaudenson, *Les créoles*), the translation into four different creoles of the French phrase *je ne sais pas où il est*, 'I don't know where he is', gives:

1 m'pa kone (ki) koté li yé (Haitian),
2 moin pa sav ola i ye (Guadeloupean),
3 mi koné pa ousa i lé (Reunionese),
4 mo pa koné kot li été (Mauritian).

We see that all the elements of these phrases come from French, but that the verb used is not the same (*sav/koné*, *savoir/connaître* [two standard French verbs meaning 'to know a fact' and 'to know by acquaintance', respectively], with the latter predominating over the former; that the locative form is also different (*koté, kot*, from *côté*, 'side', *ola, ousa*, from *où, où là, où ça*, 'where', etc.); that negation comes before the verb (in 1, 2, 4) or after it (in 3); that the personal pronoun has again come from the emphatic French form (*moi*) but is actualized in different ways (*moin*, *mi*, *mo* . . .), etc.

As far as the verbs *connaître* and *savoir* are concerned, we find the same type of alternation in the different varieties of French in Africa: *connaître* is sometimes used with the meaning of *savoir* and vice versa.[51] The two verbs have, in standard French, meanings that are very close and are distinguished above all by their constructions (for example, *savoir* can be followed by an infinitive, which is not the case with *connaître*). Now in Africa we find uses of *connaître* followed by an infinitive (*vous connaissez parler l'anglais* for 'you can speak English', *je connais faire la cuisine* for 'I know how to cook'), and it can be considered that these *alleomorphic* verbs have been selected in different creoles (*connaître* here, *savoir* there) under the influence of the language of substrates; in this case, what we have is a case of African *semantax* (Manessy) manifesting itself in different forms of creolized French.

If so, how are we most sensibly to analyse these data? Here, as in politics for instance, it is always easier to set out and try to impose an extremist viewpoint (Haitian creole *is French* or Haitian creole *is Fon*) than to set out a moderate point of view (a certain creole is the fruit of evolution, self-regulation, a European language under the more or less significant influence, depending on the case, of different languages of the substrate). And yet it is this position that seems to correspond best to the linguistic data. It is undeniable that creoles were established on the basis of European languages: all hypotheses agree on the existence of these 'lexificatory languages'; they simply diverge on the question of their relative significance. We could say that they restructured those languages while preserving the same basic materials. And this word *materials* suggests a comparison that might be illuminating. It often happens that one building is torn down so that another can be built using the same *materials*. But one may simply make a few modifications (for instance restoring an old farm to turn it into a second home) or else build something completely different (for instance tearing down an old church and using the stones to make a jetty, or tearing down a Greek temple to build a stable). In both cases the materials remain the same, but they are not used in the same way. There is relative continuity when an old farm becomes a second home; a total break when a church's stones are used to build a jetty, or those of a Greek temple are converted into a stable.

Do the relations between creoles and lexifying languages lie on the side of continuity or break? A radical break is here unimaginable: a language cannot be taken to pieces and then rebuilt, like a church from which you then build a jetty, for the simple reason that communication necessarily continued all the time you were carrying out the work of restructuring; of course the restructuring occurred, but communication never ceased. This is a formidable lesson for the whole of linguistics: the European languages picked up by slaves changed under the pressure of different ecological conditions even as they continued to be used. So it is impossible and futile to want to choose in any absolute sense between the hypothesis of the substrate and that of the superstrate: in each case we need to try and reconstruct the ecology in which this or that creole was formed, to reconstruct the languages that coexist, their statistics, their functions – in other words, to try and reconstitute the particular ecological niche in which a particular language gave birth to another particular language.

We can thus see that this situation is totally different from those which saw the appearance of the pidgins: a pidgin implies the existence of at least two groups, each of which speaks its language and gives itself, for the purposes of communication, a third, mixed form that is reduced to quite limited functions. This is absolutely not the case with creolization, a situation in which one of the groups is deprived of its languages and is obliged to borrow (and to transform) the language of the other group. Creoles would thus be the result of the acclimatization of a European language to ecolinguistic niches that are varied but are all characterized by an upheaval in the environment that entails the impossibility of transmitting servile languages and the obligation to 'cobble together' a solution on the basis of the colonizers' language.

However, as we have just seen in regard to *connaître* and *savoir*, this cobbling together does not inevitably lead to the same result. Salikoko Mufwene for instance has compared two 'creoles', those of Mauritius and Haiti, from a limited syntactic point of view, that of the functions and forms of the reflexive. His conclusions are undeniable: 'creole dialects cannot be defined by their structural features . . . they do not constitute a morphosyntactic typological class. . . . There is no single creole solution to the problems of communication. The two creoles have found different solutions to the same problem.'[52] This means, more broadly, that the forms we baptize 'creole' are the result – different in each case (creole speakers in Haiti, Guiana or Mauritius cannot understand each other, quite simply because they do not speak the same language) – of an acclimatization, in a given ecological niche, of a European language; and it permits us at the same time to understand why creoles are not found in certain situations where everything would have inclined us to believe that creolization should have occurred. This is the case with the immense Spanish-speaking territory that resulted from the colonial Spanish empire, in particular with islands such as Cuba or San Domingo. This last example is particularly interesting since a creole of French origin is spoken in one part of the island (Haiti) and Spanish in the Dominican part. Chaudenson's analysis in terms of a society of *habitation* and then of *implantation* here provides a convincing answer. Cuba was occupied by the Spanish from the start of the sixteenth century, but nearly two centuries later, in 1792, there were still more whites than blacks on the island (76,180 blacks, 96,440 whites), and it was only between 1790 and 1830 that the massive importing of slaves would take the percentage of blacks to 80 per cent of the total population. The situation was comparable to that of San Domingo: 'In both cases,' writes Chaudenson, 'the centuries-long preservation of the society of habitation led the black communities to a total linguistic Hispanicization; there ensued, in the following phase, a generalization of Spanish without creolization.'[53] More recently, without referring to Chaudenson, John McWhorter has come to the same conclusions.[54] For him, the rarity of Spanish creoles is explicable by three factors:

- The Spanish did not cultivate sugar cane until after a century of agriculture based on small plantations (in Cuba, for instance).
- They often settled where there were already Portuguese creoles (this is true of Curaçao, false in Cuba or Haiti).
- They did not have any settlements in West Africa where a pidgin might have developed.

The two authors thus agree on the first point, one which in my view is quite central as it determines the situations we are concerned with most clearly: the ecolinguistic niche of Cuba (or San Domingo) was different from that in Guadeloupe, where the relation between the numbers of whites and blacks quickly evolved in favour of the latter, creating the conditions necessary for creolization. The parameters *European language + island + African slaves* are thus not sufficient to characterize a 'creologenous' ecolinguistic niche – we need to add a demographic factor to them, one which, here, seems to have a defining role to play and which itself stems from economic and social change.

As the title of this section suggests, creoles are thus perhaps the result of an evolution of European languages in different ecolinguistic niches under the influence of different factors, in particular that of the semantax and of the phonology of certain substrate languages. This evolution happens to every language, in every place and time, but the data at our disposal allow us, in the case of creoles, to witness this evolution almost 'live', and in this way creolistics has a great deal to offer linguistics.

The transmission of gravitational systems

'The weather will be tomorrow approximately the same as today.' This relatively risk-free way of forecasting the weather is sometimes invalidated by sudden weather changes: a blue sky can suddenly cloud over and a storm can all too quickly replace a fine period. The same is true, as we have seen, for linguistic situations, which, in spite of received ideas, can sometimes evolve really quickly under the pressure of social modifications, changes in milieu or direct human interventions. We saw in the first chapter that the evolution of ecolinguistic situations was neither totally predictable nor totally random and that, for instance, an apparently minor fact (the taming of the horse by 'Indo-Europeans') had played an important role in the linguistic history of Europe, just as a butterfly beating its wings could, thanks to the Lorenz effect, unleash a hurricane on the other side of the planet. More generally speaking, these factors of change can be of different types and intervene in different ways, in either an *in vivo* or an *in vitro* manner.

1 The migration of a group that speaks a dominated language can entail the change of dominant language, and a shift from a central language to another one. Thus the Moroccan Berber-speakers who go to live in Spain find themselves in a new linguistic ecosystem, in which Spanish replaces Arabic as the central language, just like Algerian Berber-speakers who go to live in Flemish-speaking Belgium, where

Flemish replaces French as the central language.[55] The gravitational relations are thus entirely modified.

2 The *in vivo* growth in the number of speakers of a language, by natural increase in population or by migration – in particular in the case of migrations from country to town – is also an important factor of change: the country dwellers acquire the dominant vehicular language, their children often have it as their first language, and this shift increases the value of the language in question. But this increase needs to be analysed with care, and it should only be considered as a proportion of that of the general population. Thus, between 1930 and 1990 the number of speakers of Indian languages in Mexico rose from 2,251,780 to 5,282,347, which is a significant apparent increase. But in the same period of time the overall population of the country increased from 14 million to 70 million, which means that the proportion of speakers of Indian languages diminished, shrinking from 15 per cent to 7.2 per cent of the population. The natural increase of population is thus deceptive and could not curb a general movement towards a change of language – to Spanish.

3 The *in vitro* increase in the functions of a language, i.e. the creation of a linguistic demand on the part of society, can, if it entails any effect, lead to a modification in the relations between languages. The Central African Republic, for instance, has decided to make Sango the official language, on an equal footing with French. This decision, a purely theoretical one for the time being, will considerably change the Central African ecolinguistic niche if it is really implemented. We here have the case of the modification of an ecosystem by the linguistic policy of a state.

4 Action on the identity-bestowing function of languages also needs to be taken into account in the way that situations evolve. In France, for example, certain defenders of minority languages create an artificial demand, compensating for the fact that Occitan and Breton have become languages without social function by the affirmation of a militant linguistic demand. This means an intervention on the homeostatic couple language/society as I defined it in chapter 3, i.e. an attempt to modify the *linguistic needs of society* to make up for the absence of *social functions of the language*. But this deliberate intervention (which was quite recently demonstrated to be effective in Israel, and will perhaps be so again in the case of Croatia and Serbia in the future) is not enough: the social conditions for the emergence of

a new language or a new function must also be implemented. For instance, when in 1928 the PNI (Parti Nationaliste Indonésien) decided that Malay would be the national language of Indonesia, this deliberate and interventionist decision was purely symbolic and only came to be implemented after the country gained independence, twenty years later.

All these factors can thus modify an ecolinguistic niche. Indeed, the situations seem all the more stable the closer one is to them, but this stability becomes more relative when you take a certain distance. So, fifteen or so years ago any observer could have considered the island of Hong Kong to be characterized by English/Cantonese diglossia. But this affirmation, acceptable in rough-and-ready terms, was true only from a strictly synchronic point of view: the situation was being undermined and modified by factors of change. Before the island of Hong Kong was ceded to the British in 1842, its few inhabitants spoke different Chinese 'dialects' (in fact the languages of the Han group), Hakka, Min, Yué, etc. Under British rule, the island became a prosperous commercial harbour, lured more and more people from the continent, i.e. the province of Guangdong, whose language, Cantonese, became the vehicular language.[56] The situation thus changed on this first occasion, and it is undergoing a second change now that Hong Kong has been handed back to China and Putonghua has become the main language. The diglossia of English/Cantonese will no doubt eventually be replaced by a diglossia of Putonghua/Cantonese or a triglossia of Putonghua/English/Cantonese.

Thus there is a dialectic of individual, group and society. The individual, in isolation, has practically no power over the language. But the set of speakers as a whole is more than the sum of its parts. If individuals, considered in isolation, all have their proper linguistic representations, which determine and explain their practices, the set of them as a whole constitutes collective representations (which can be pulled in different directions simultaneously), which in their turn determine and explain the dominant practices. The example of Sagabari–Kita–Bamako mentioned in an earlier chapter is here very clear: individuals may wish not to speak any language other than Bakokan, and Bamakoese may find the language of Sagabari attractive, pleasant, etc. But in their majority, speakers consider that peripheral dialects, different from the Bambara of Bamako, seem 'old-fashioned', 'peasant-like', 'ridiculous', and the result of these representations is a change in practices which entails a change in the form of the language.

From the point of view of a state's *in vitro* intervention, the case of the former Zaire is interesting. This country, politically a member of the group of French-speaking nations and with a population of nearly 45 million in 1997, has often been presented as the largest French-speaking country of the future: the birthrate and the presumed progress in education gave this analysis a certain plausibility. The seizure of power by Laurent Kabila in 1997 changed this situation. Originally supported and financed by Uganda and Rwanda and, through them, by the United States, Kabila often, during the civil war, ostentatiously spoke in English when in public, thereby showing his desire to distance himself from the language of the former colonial power, Belgium. A few months later, during the Hanoi summit of French-speaking heads of state, Kabila announced that his country was going to leave the group of French-speaking countries (a decision that he was later to reverse). The country, in which some 200 ethnic languages have been catalogued, is in addition divided into four large geographical zones in which four great vehicular languages function: Swahili, Lingala, Kikongo and Ciluba. But these officially 'national' languages do not really have the same functions, and Lingala is, traditionally, the language of the army. Now Kabila's troops comprised in particular young men from East Africa where the couple English/Swahili fulfils more or less the same functions as the couple French/Lingala in ex-Zaire. The political action of Congolese power might thus modify linguistic ecology on different levels: that of vehicular languages (Swahili versus Lingala in the army) as well as that of the official language (English versus French and perhaps Portuguese, if we consider the political support given by Angola to Kabila). In other words, a linguistic niche, always subject to change, can in certain conditions see this change accelerate and the gravitational system become totally modified.

France experienced an upheaval of this kind at the start of the twentieth century, during the 1914–18 war. The regiments were in fact 'regional' to begin with, so that men from Occitan- or Breton-speaking areas could meet and continue to speak their languages – some of them did not know French. The huge number of victims would lead the military authorities to reconstitute the regiments and mix up the recruits so that they would be able to communicate only through the French that they learned (or improved their knowledge of, if they spoke it only badly or not at all). We can add to this the factor of representations: for Bretons, Basques, and Occitans, French was experienced as the language of the whole nation, and in the trenches they thus acquired both a language and a certain image of its function. On demobilization, recruits had considerably changed both from the point of view of their linguistic practices and from the point of view of their representations, and, once they returned home, they intervened in their respective ecolinguistic systems as so many factors of change, in particular in their linguistic policies within the family, in the non-transmission of their first languages to their children. The spread of education, followed by radio and television, and the centralizing intervention of the French state would do the rest, but in these few wartime years we have an example of yet another sudden change in an ecological niche that until then had been evolving but slowly.

Conclusion: evolution and revolution

In chapter 1 ('The influence of the horse on European languages'), I suggested that it was possible to view linguistic systems as chaotic systems whose evolution was neither totally predictable nor totally random but susceptible to being marked by an escalation of minor phenomena. We also saw that the human sciences formulated tendencies rather than laws. As far as the transmission of languages and linguistic situations is concerned, these tendencies are the product of a certain number of factors, some of which arise in social practices, *in vivo*, and others from the intervention of the state, *in vitro*. The couple languages/milieu is thus permanently regulated, and this regulation can sometimes accelerate in a brutal fashion.

In spite of what has just been said and in spite of what certain observations might lead us to expect, linguistic situations are sometimes transmitted even when everything seems to indicate that they should change. The permanent presence of Berber in Algeria and Morocco is a good example of this unexpected persistence. Another example is that of German speakers in Belgium. Peter Nelde, in a paper presenting an ecolinguistic approach to identity among bilinguals,[57] has tackled the problem of what he calls 'non-linear patterns of a bilingual identity'. He notes that, for 160 years, successive studies have regularly predicted the decline or disappearance of the minority language, German, in Belgium, because it was spoken by older generations (young people using French). This prediction was made in 1833, and repeated in 1897 and 1935, so that one might have expected that German would disappear – and yet it is still there. Nelde's explanation is simple: young people adopt the dominant language at school, then at work, but when they return, at the end of their lives, from the industrial zones to the villages and farms, they pick up their vernacular again. In addition to this, the geographical situation of these German speakers along the German frontier favours the preservation of the language. We might also say that the 'predictions' referred to by Nelde constituted so many photographs leading one to think that a language was dying out, whereas a film would have shown us the opposite.

And this example is extremely eloquent since it indicates that combining the percentage of speakers of a language and their class by age is not always significant. Indeed, it is the social function of German and French that explains the way speakers are divided (with the young speaking French and the old German). But as this function is maintained and *transmitted*, we find the same division generation after generation. In other words, in this particular niche, the relations between languages and milieu determine the different practices of speakers in accordance with their age. It is well known that, generally speaking, the younger generation use forms of the language that they then abandon once they have become adults. As this tendency is reproduced with each generation, the differences at any time T between 'young ways of speaking' and 'adult ways of speaking' are much more significant than those which, at a time T + X, will result from the linguistic action of young people on adult forms of speech. In other terms, the way young French people speak their language today will inevitably have repercussions on the French that they will speak when they are adult and transmit to the following generation. But these repercussions will not consist in the replacement of one form by another: self-regulation acts in a more subtle and nuanced form.

This slow evolution, which characterizes both languages and situations, can thus sometimes be brutally accelerated by a 'revolution', when the state intervenes in an authoritarian way, as in Turkey at the time of Atatürk.[58] These 'revolutions' which drastically change a linguistic landscape and reshape a niche are however more reversible than the results of an evolution. It was a revolution of this type that introduced European languages into Africa. Its effects seem to be enduring. Thus elites speak French in Morocco, even though the French protectorate there lasted for under half a century (1912–56). But this presence of French was historically speaking very brief if we compare it to for instance that of Berber.

An ecolinguistic system is thus in constant change under the pressure of a permanent *evolution*, the fruit of practices and representations, and this *evolution*, which simultaneously affects the form and the functions of languages, can suddenly accelerate under the effect of a *revolution*: systems are transmitted and change at the same time. It is possible to isolate and to describe the factors of change by internal analysis (the self-regulation of the linguistic system) and external analysis (the modifications in the ecolinguistic niche), but the difficulty of a prospective analysis stems from the unpredictability of this type of *revolution*.

— 6 —

Five Case Studies

The following studies use data of different origins. The first three (Arabic, Kituba and Serbo-Croat) are analyses based on work carried out by other people: they are, so to speak, surveys of already published work (even if, as far as the first case is concerned, I have lived and researched in Arabic-speaking countries for long periods; in the second case I have done research in Brazzaville, the capital of the Congo; and in the third, I have done some work in Zagreb, in Croatia). The two others rest on personal fieldwork carried out in Louisiana (Kraemer) and in the West Indies (Saint-Barthélemy). In all five cases, however, the aim is the same: to illustrate in greater detail the different theoretical positions that were presented in the previous chapters.

One name for several languages: Arabic schizoglossia

I referred at the start of chapter 4 to Einar Haugen's text on 'schizoglossia', the situation of a speaker who, exposed to more than one variety of his language, is not sure of what he must speak or write because there are several possible forms available. While Haugen visibly enjoyed dwelling on the amusing side of this situation, he was also raising a real problem, that of the relationship to the norm, which Americans had to face in the first years of the Republic (when the norm was the British norm), and which Noah Webster and Samuel Johnson discussed in vigorous terms (in their works they wanted to get rid of the British linguistic model and establish an American norm). On a more serious note, Haugen explained that when linguists claim that all linguistic forms are equal, they are adopting a generous-hearted but false position, and the only scientific position consists in recognizing the existence of a problem and studying it: 'It needs to be clearly understood that "scientific" is not necessarily identical with "tolerant". A plea for tolerance may be laudable from a moral or ethical point of view, but does not of itself follow from the premises of science.'

And he concluded with an allusion to Eliza in *Pygmalion* (or *My Fair Lady*): 'It would be nice if we could persuade polite society to accept Eliza Doolittle as she is, but in our heart of hearts most of us would prefer to associate with her after Dr Higgins has straightened out her aitches.'[1]

While Eliza Doolittle might well be, for English-speakers, the individual archetype of schizoglossia, the situation in Arabic countries provides us with a more interesting collective example, insofar as the norm there weighs more heavily and is more dogmatic than in most other situations. Dalila Morsly has pointed out that 'the linguistic question is one of the favourite themes in the everyday conversation of Algerians. Everyone feels empowered to speak about language, and they all set themselves up as legislators of language.'[2] This epilinguistic activity, which is not confined to Algerians but seems to concern a great number of Arabic-speakers, is interesting insofar as it is linked to the very situation of the Arabic language. The 'Arabic constellation' is in fact one of the most difficult to describe: the history of the language is complex; its status has varied and remains variable from situation to situation. As Catherine Miller puts it:

> Arabic, in all its forms and throughout its history, was at times a language spoken by a minority of conquerors and then acquired by significant numbers of native communities; at times it was a language spoken by a majority while remaining in contact with minority languages; at times a language of prestige, a religious and literary language that spread among literate bilingual Moslems on the shores of the Atlantic and Asia; at times a dominant language, rejected by culturally different groups; and sometimes a dialect or an isolated variety headed for extinction.[3]

Furthermore, the linguists who are specialized in these domains are forever oscillating between an approach in terms of levels, or strata, an approach in terms of continuum, and an approach in terms of diglossia or triglossia[4] or even quadriglossia or indeed multiglossia.[5] Together with this great swarm of *practices*, to which I will be returning, we need to add an avalanche of *representations*, which here weigh more heavily than in other situations. Between a language that is deemed to be unsurpassable in eloquence and perfection, the vehicle of God's language, the language of angels and paradise,[6] and the so-called dialectal, vulgar, corrupt forms, it seems impossible to think of linguistic situations in terms of change, in terms of history. The rareness of Arabic etymological studies, for instance, must surely be related to two unformulated prohibitions:

- the fear of finding, in the divine text, borrowed words which an etymological approach might reveal (and all specialists know how numerous they are);
- the fear of finding in the actual contents of the Koran borrowed sequences, for example influences from the oral tradition.

In both cases, in fact, the dogma of a divine and thus 'pure' text, one dictated to the Prophet, would be undermined. And all of this weighs on the Arabic sociolinguistic situation: if secularization, for instance, is not easy to envisage in Arab countries, this is also for reasons that have to do with language. From a certain point of view, Islamic thought needs a fixed, invariant Arabic, just as structural linguistics initially needed the concept of *langue* or language in Saussure's sense. Muslims live in *parole* and pretend to believe in *langue*, just as Saussure needed the concept of *langue* in order to build his theoretical edifice. Both groups are, or were, to different degrees afraid of *parole*, which for different reasons (of course) posed problems for them. In other words, in certain ways of speaking about Arabic-speaking situations, one has the impression that the realities have been carefully ironed out and that it is difficult to look at them dispassionately, without an upsurge of political, ideological or theological passions. And yet this is what I would like to do.[7]

The first linguistic reality comprises what people speak every day, the first language they acquire – let's say their 'mother tongue'. On this first level, we have *different kinds* of Arabic, which have been given different names. In French we speak of *dialectes* (the Tunisian, Algerian 'dialect', etc.), in English of *colloquial Arabic*, in Arabic of *'ammiya* ('vulgar', 'common'), *lahja* ('dialect', in fact 'accent'), *darija* (the 'current' language), etc. These forms of mass languages, linked to a particular territory and arising from the contacts between the Arabic of the conquerors[8] and Berber in the Maghreb, Coptic in Egypt, Turkish or Persian elsewhere, have tended to become 'nationalized' through urban intermingling and the influence of the capital, so that these days we speak of Egyptian Arabic (even if we are really talking about the Arabic of Cairo), Tunisian Arabic (even if this is mainly that of Tunis), etc. Within the framework of these entities there are of course local and regional specificities, the only ones that can be called dialectal in the proper sense of the word.

On a second level, we find a great hesitancy in the descriptions. Certain people speak of a 'median' or 'average' sort of Arabic (in English, *Modern Standard Arabic*, in Arabic *arabiyya wusta*), others of a *modern* Arabic, defined, depending on the case, as a lexically modernized classical form (together with an erosion of case endings), or as the language of the written and spoken news media, education, etc. The latter has a certain tendency to be marked by the first language, it is permanently being *transformed* by two contradictory and convergent tendencies, the influence of 'dialect' (in the form of interferences) and the move away from dialect (in the form of hypercorrections). Alan Kayes thus points to a tendency in Egypt to prefer in Modern Standard Arabic the negative form *lam* (for example, in *lam 'arahu*, 'I did not see him') to the form *ma* (*mâ ra'aytuhu*) to avoid proximity with the Cairo form *ma chuftûch*, with the same meaning.[9] It is avoidance procedures of this type, associated with their contrary, interferences (of which there are many examples), which tend to give to Modern Standard Arabic its various forms of 'local colour', to shift it slowly from the singular (Modern Standard Arabic) to the plural (Modern Standard Arabics). The ambiguity lies on the boundary between oral form and written form: 'standard' Arabic seems to lie on the side of *parole* or speech, a set of ill-defined practices intended to ensure communication between cultivated speakers in spite of dialectal differences, while 'modern' Arabic lies on the side of writing, the modernized form of what we find at a third (or fourth) level, classical Arabic, that of the Koran (*fusha*, sometimes called *fusha al turat*, 'patrimonial language'). This is all far from clear and could also be presented in terms of continuum, with the sole difference that synchrony and diachrony are constantly getting mixed up, and it is difficult to see if analysts are referring to the history of the language or its current situation, etc.

We can thus see that the way Ferguson presented the matter, in terms of *diglossia*, is far from explaining the complexity of the situation. What he did was to freeze around two poles, the 'high variety' (classical Arabic) and the 'low variety' (dialectal Arabic), a continuum in which ideology and linguistics have quite separately invented different languages, a continuum whose extremes are further apart in the Maghreb or Lebanon than they are in Jordan or Syria. We might say, to simplify things, that there is a solely *written* Arabic (classical Arabic, which is the language of nobody, but which certain people learn, a fixed, 'dead' language), an *oralized* written Arabic (Modern Standard Arabic, which tends to take on local forms and is also learnt) and *spoken Arabics* (the 'dialects', the only ones which one inherits from one's family; but also the whole amorphous category of 'Modern Standard Arabic') which are all different languages. But it is impossible to hierarchize these forms in terms of a constellation, since they are not implanted in their societies in the same way. Classical Arabic is a 'dead' language,[10] comparable to Latin in thirteenth- or fourteenth-century Europe, but a language that is heavily laden with representations, with, in rough and ready terms, three directions:

1. its filiation with the sacred texts, which means that it is considered as the 'language of God';
2. its relation with pan-Arabic ideology;
3. its relation with the ideology of the *umma*, the community of believers.

These representations all make it necessary for national Arabics to be rejected.

The definition and frontiers of this *umma* are not clear. To begin with, the term itself is ambiguous: sometimes it refers to the 'Arab nation' (but in that case they say *umma al-arabiya*) and sometimes (when used alone, or in the form *umma al-islamiya*) the community of believers. But these two groups are not identical. A majority of Muslims around the world are not Arabic-speakers; and if we add the Muslims of Indonesia to those of Pakistan, Turkey, Iran and black Africa, we have a figure of several hundreds of millions of Muslims who do not have Arabic as their first language and who, more often than not, have only a rudimentary knowledge of the classical language – if they have any knowledge of it at all. While, for certain ideologues, to be an Arab means to be a Muslim, to be a Muslim does not necessarily mean to be an Arab nor, of course, an Arabic-speaker. The same goes for those who have a certain ('dialectal') form of Arabic as their first language: the only knowledge they have of the *fusha* is at best a passive knowledge, as very few can write it and practically nobody speaks it. So there is a certain ambiguity in the relations between the *umma* on the one hand (which, as we have seen, *is not Arabic-speaking in the majority of cases*) and Arab nationalism on the other, which, for half a century, has pinned its hopes on the *fusha*, seen as the language of Arab unity, with language acting as the bond between the history of the Arab people and its religion and enjoying a very special status both on the juridical level (it is the only official language in most Arab countries) and on the symbolic level (it is the language of God, of eloquence, of paradise).

The general situation as just sketched out varies, of course, from one country to another. Mohamed Benrabah points out, for instance, that when a *common lexical basis* for the three countries of the Maghreb (Tunisia, Algeria, Morocco) was being worked out at the start of the 1970s – when it was the rule to seek terms that were part of the spoken usage of at least two of the three countries (the aim being to build up a vocabulary that would be used in school textbooks) – what tended to happen was that words were taken from classical Arabic or a Middle-Eastern dialect. Thus, in spite of the existence of *hut*, 'fish' – used in the three countries of the Maghreb – or of *china*, 'orange', it was *samaq* and *burtuqal* that were used, borrowed from the classical form.[11] The lexicon eventually had 4,800 words, of which only 3.5 per cent were of Maghrebi origin. Behind this classicizing creation of neologisms lay, of course, a negation of local specifities, what Benrabah called 'self-hatred', which was also demonstrated by a fascination for the Near East: in the history manuals used in Algerian schools, 'Roman remains are ignored, while 75 per cent of the text discusses the Middle East'.[12]

What we have here, in fact, is the product of a *schizoglossia* constitutive of Arabic linguistic situations. 'National' Arabics, in fact, meet with a different fate in different countries. Thus Egyptian Arabic (or rather the Arabic of Cairo), widespread beyond that country's borders thanks to cinema or song, enjoys a very special status, which can lead to a sort of subversion of the alphabet itself. For example, in Egyptian Arabic there is a /g/ where Maghrebi Arabics (and the classical form) have /j/ or /dj/: *gabal* instead of *jbel* for 'mountain', *gamal* instead of *jmel* for 'camel', etc., and Egyptians reading classical Arabic usually pronounce /j/ instead of /g/. In the graphic context, the letter 'jim' thus systematically transcribes the /g/ of Egyptian Arabic, so that when they have to write a /j/, in particular for foreign words, they use an invented letter, 'jim' with three subscript points. On the other hand, in Algeria, where many people have a satellite dish (in French, *parabole*) to pick up foreign television programmes, the national press publishes the programmes of the /barabul/, with a capital initial B in the Arabic version, whereas everyone pronounces it *parabul* and the /p/ in fact exists in Algerian Arabic.[13] The paradox is that, in the quest for Arabian identity, Egyptian Arabic has been promoted in Algeria, as it is spread by films, television, and song. This is a 'dialectal' Arabic, used in Algeria at every level of state business. We can see here a desire to bar Algerian Arabic from access to writing, to freeze the relation between the written and the spoken language, and as the discourse of representations insists on the importance of writing, we thus have the most anti-democratic situation imaginable: a people deemed to speak a vulgar dialect and refused access to knowledge in their own language. This is an example, and a significant one, of the way linguistic insecurity comes into being: the more power intervenes on language, the more it drives its speakers to fall ill. For degrees of schizoglossia are linked to degrees of normalization. A standardized language obviously implies the existence of forms other than the standard form, and it is this duality, or this plurality, which generates schizoglossia.

Up until now I have focused mainly on the situation in the Maghreb, but the situation in other Arab countries poses quite a different problem, that of the way the 'legitimate' language is imposed. This last adjective is a reference to the work of Pierre Bourdieu, who first set out his positions on this topic at a teachers' conference[14] – a circumstance of some significance. Bourdieu set out from the idea that 'communication in a situation of pedagogic authority presupposes legitimate emitters, legitimate receivers, a legitimate situation and a legitimate language',[15] i.e. teachers, pupils and pupils' parents recognizing one another mutually. And in reply to a question he went into greater detail to say:

> An institution, or an action, or a usage is legitimate when it is dominant but not recognized as such, in other words tacitly recognized. The language that teachers use, the language you use to speak to me . . . [A voice: you use it too . . .!] Of course I use it, but I never stop explaining that I use it! . . . the language that *we* use in this space is a dominant language unrecognized as such, and so tacitly recognized as legitimate.[16]

Five years later, in a work with the same name as the conference paper, he wrote:

> In order for one mode of expression among others (a particular language in the case of bilingualism, a particular use of language in the case of a society divided into classes) to impose itself as the only legitimate one, the linguistic market has to be unified and the different dialects (of class, region or ethnic group) have to be measured practically against the legitimate language or usage.[17]

This *legitimacy* and the symbolic domination that, for Bourdieu, is linked to it, thus in his view imply a state (a unified linguistic market) and the tacit recognition of a dominant language, a tacit but 'unrecognized' recognition, at different levels of a structure of pyramidal type. In other terms, the legitimate language (the official, standard language, etc.) is the language of the dominant class transformed into the state language. Now the situation in Arabic-speaking countries goes quite counter to this analysis. How does 'the production and reproduction of legitimate language' work there?[18] Niloofar Haeri has studied this question with regard to Egypt, where the linguistic situation is the one I sketched out above: the official language is 'classical' Arabic (*al-lugha al-'arabiya al-fusha*), the language of the Koran, while the first language of the inhabitants is 'dialectal' Arabic (*'ammiya*, also called *masri*, 'Egyptian'). The distinction I proposed in chapter 2 between spontaneous learning and a programmed learning of languages applies perfectly here: classical Arabic is not transmitted from one generation to the next, it has to be learnt at school, in a 'programmed' way, whereas the 'dialect' is transmitted and acquired in a 'spontaneous' fashion. Now, as Haeri emphasizes, the Egyptian ruling classes 'have received their education in a foreign language in Cairo, Alexandria, or other cities and towns. Many have attended private Catholic missionary schools in which the main languages of instruction are English, French, Italian, and so on'.[19] Contrary to what Bourdieu writes, she continues, the acquisition of symbolic capital and access to the labour market are not here linked to the official language but to a foreign language.

This situation is comparable with that in Maghrebi countries where it is not a knowledge of classical Arabic that guarantees symbolic capital but rather a knowledge of French and, to a lesser degree, of English:[20] elites in this region are French speaking and do not necessarily have a good knowledge of classical Arabic. In fact, in Egypt there is coexistence and conflict between the recognition of the *fusha* as an official language and the economic market on which this language has no value. As a result, there is a great ambiguity as regards the linguistic market. Graduates of the religious schools (in particular at the Al-Azhar University) enjoy a certain capital, but only on the restricted market of religion, and this reproduction of symbolic capital is not under state control. Haeri draws a parallel between this situation and the relations between the state and shari'a (Islamic law):

> Both are mentioned in the Egyptian constitution, one as the official language of the nation and the other as the basis for its legal system. However, even more problematic than the language situation, the state at times faces insurmountable contradictions in its dealings with legal suits and rulings that seem to conform to the sharï'a but not to its desired path toward privatization, Europeanization, and Americanization.[21]

This situation is not confined to Egypt, and Niloofar Haeri's analysis sheds an interesting light on the situation in the Maghreb. Confronted with popular and essentially oral forms, Arabic or Berber, written Arabic there enjoys a special symbolic status, which is clearly summarized by Gilbert Grandguillaume in these terms:

> To compare the Maghrebi situation with the situation in France, we have to acknowledge that, in the struggle of French against the different forms of 'patois', the dominant language has found support in the idea of 'upward social mobility' attached to the abandoning of one's regional language. There is no analogous phenomenon in the case of the dialects of the Maghreb: on the contrary, the shift to Arabic in the process of Arabicization is not felt as leading to a rise in class.[22]

I would add that it is, for certain people, experienced as sanctifying, which gives one a good idea of its status.

In Arabic-speaking countries as a whole, 'dialectal' Arabic is thus the dominant language of everyday communication, English and French predominate in much of the linguistic market place, Modern Standard Arabic has an indeterminate status, and classical Arabic, as an official language and as the language of religion, is legitimate only in a restricted market. To be sure, these examples show that Bourdieu is somewhat mechanistic in his view of the relations between official language and power, or at least that his analysis does not really apply to Arab-speaking situations. But they show us above all that the 'Arabic ecosystems' are characterized by an interaction between different contradictory forces: State, religion and dominant classes all have ambiguous relations with languages. What we see, then, is a strange ballet that, in a linguistic continuum that is all the more shifting because the territories in question are so vast, tends to blur the reality of the situation. 'Officially official' Arabic is what it is only for tactical reasons, and its historical stasis, explicable for ideological reasons (you cannot change God's language), prevents it from fulfilling the functions that an official language ought to fulfil (modernization, Europeanization, etc.). So there is a contradiction between the *linguistic needs of society* and the *social functions of language* (as discussed in chapter 3): the official language can, in its current form, fulfil only a small number of the demands of society (let's say, for simplicity's sake, that it fulfils only the Islamists' demands), and it is incapable of fulfilling another, stronger demand, that of modernization. The *valency* of classical Arabic is thus limited, and it is neither the power of the ruling classes nor the demands of the market that ensure its official function, but the complex, ambiguous relations between the State and Islamist ideology. In Algeria, for example, between the 1962 decision to make classical Arabic the official language and the decision to Arabicize the country completely, which was taken on 5 July 1998 – via the National Charter of 1976 and the law on Arabicization voted through in 1996 – the authorities declared that they wished to accelerate the process of Arabicization every time that they encountered problems with the Islamists, thereby foregrounding a symbolic but poorly prepared symbolic reform that each time was doomed to failure.[23] The *representations* (representations of the language – 'God's language' – and the speakers – deemed to be Muslims, members of the community of believers, of the Arab nation) are thus very powerful in this case, and tend to immobilize *in vitro* practices even as they ceaselessly continue to develop *in vivo*.

How can these situations develop? The self-regulation of the situation can occur in four different scenarios:

1 by adapting classical Arabic to social demands;
2 by promoting more strenuously Modern Standard Arabic (*'arabiyya wusta*), which could eventually rival classical Arabic in its official capacity;

3 by promoting dialectal Arabic and, in Algeria and Morocco, Berber, so that they can perform official functions;
4 by creating a bipartite functional system, or sharing legitimacy, between a symbolic language, that of religion, and a language of modernity.

The first scenario is unimaginable: unless there is a seizure of power by Islamists in one country or another, the *fusha* seems destined to remain frozen by its religious status. The second comes up against the fact that in the Maghreb, Modern Standard Arabic is not, any more than the *fusha*, the language of upward social mobility for elites, but it could become so. It would then impose itself easily, and in that case it would come with a significant regional variation, rendering written mutual comprehension difficult.[24] The third would be technically imaginable: if people were prepared to make the right arrangements – a matter of linguistic planning – the different 'dialects' could easily fulfil this function. But this solution would, like the previous one, come into conflict with another ideological tendency, that of Arabic unity, which can be demonstrated linguistically only by means of classical Arabic, the only form that is unified. As for the fourth scenario, it has come into operation on a *de facto* basis, but cannot be recognized *de jure*, since that would imply an eventual separation of religion and state which, for obvious political reasons, is unthinkable these days.

So the situation seems to be blocked, and the future development of Mahgrebi linguistic situations has a huge interest for everyone working on the problem of linguistic politics and the relations between languages and nations. But it is clear that the decisive factors in this development have to do with political, not linguistic, practices. States in the Maghreb currently most often practise what I have called a 'linguistic policy by default',[25] a somewhat blind hands-off policy, turning a blind eye in a way I am here describing from the linguistic point of view but which can easily be seen in many other areas of social life. And these examples show how a linguistic ecosystem, the relations between languages and their territory, is determined by numerous non-linguistic factors. I spoke above of a proliferation of *practices* and an avalanche of *representations*. We can now see more clearly how a continuum that is social (the different practices of Arabic in one and the same place) and geographical (dialectal variations) produced by the expansion of Arabic was divided by state boundaries within which, *in vivo*, practices tended towards a certain 'nationalization' of dialects (in particular via urbanization), whilst, *in vitro*, apparently opposed ideologies (Arabism, Islamism) tended to impose other forms whose coexistence with the previous form generated schizoglossia. But at the same time we can also see the contradictions between the approach of the Arabicizers, who tend to build up an objective typology of dialects and cannot reach agreement, and the representations of Arabic speakers, which function either in stylistic terms (*fusha*) or in social terms (*ammiya*, etc.). In other words, Arabic linguistic ecosystems are at once determined by borders (hence a tendency to 'nationalization'), by the relations between different languages (*fusha, wusta, ammiya* . . .) and by representations. In this sense, they are a prime source of examples for an ecolinguistic approach.

Several names for one language: the example of Kituba

When you consult any work presenting the set of all the world's languages, the authors frequently provide a great number of labels for what they consider as one and the same language. Thus, in a book on African languages published by the French research institute, the Centre National de la Recherche Scientifique (CNRS),[26] we find several examples of this plural glossonymy, and we can sketch out an embryonic typology for these cases. In certain cases, the many names simply reflect a dialectal situation: Songhay, Zarma and Dendi, for example, are in Mali and Niger regional forms of what is generally considered to be just one language. In other cases, they are the result of a conflict between the language's 'official' name (the name given it by the administration or linguists) and the name given it by its speakers, as is indicated in the following quotations by the term 'self-designation': 'Sura or Mwaghavul (self-designation)',[27] 'Buduma or Yidena/Yedina (self-designation)',[28] etc. In certain cases, a language bears a local name, that which its speakers give it, such as *Fulfulde*, a name in a colonial language, such as '*peul*' in French, and another in another colonial language, such as *Fulani* in English (the first is a borrowing from Wolof, the second a borrowing from Hausa) – these three different names, of course, bearing witness to the colonial period and to the fact that the

Fula lived in territories which were colonized by either France or Great Britain.

Things are sometimes complicated when dialectal variations, self-naming and naming by others are all mixed up. This is the case for Kotoko, for example: 'Kotoko is the Arabic name of a whole series of dialects: Shawe (Schoe), Makari and Ngala, Gulfei, Afade (Affadeh), Msir (Kuseri) and Klasmou (Klesem), Logone (Lagouané) and Jilbe'.[29] Finally, it sometimes happens that the same name, or similar names, designate both a first (or ethnic) language and its vehicular language form. Thus Kikongo, the first language in the two Congos and in Angola, has given rise to one (or more) form(s) of vehicular language that can be given different names: 'The Kongo dialectal form has engendered several vehicular languages: "literary" or "unified" Kikongo . . . Kikongo-Kileta or "the Kikongo of the government" . . . Monokotuba, Fiot',[30] we read in the same work, which goes on to say, 300 pages later: 'Kituba (also known as Kisodi, Kibulamati, Munukutuba, Fiote, Ikeleve, Kileta, commercial Kikongo, commercial Kikwango, etc.), springing from Kikongo, is used by perhaps two million persons as a second language.'[31] In other words, we find in the same book (though one written, admittedly, by several different authors), a vehicular language that has generally been baptized as Kikongo in the first case (by Pierre Alexandre) and Kituba in the second (by Ian Hancock) and which bears several other names. This latter situation, a complex one as is evident, can be a good example for us to analyse the relations between glossonymia and the environment.

In a more recent article devoted to the presentation of what he calls *Kituba*,[32] Salikoko Mufwene presents a list of the different names this language has received:[33] *Kikongo-Kituba, Kikongo ya lèta, Kilèta, Kikongo ya bula-matadi, Kibula-matadi, Mono kutuba, Ikélé vé, Kikwango, Kikongo*. The generic term chosen by the author is already a definite choice: the prefix *ki–*, which designates the class of instruments and in particular of languages, followed by the verb 'to speak' or 'to say' (*tuba*), producing *Kituba*, which thus connotes the idea of 'serving to communicate'. In fact, Mufwene distinguishes between *ethnic Kikongo*, in other words a language (which may or may not be a first language) that plays a role in bestowing identity (the language of the Bakongos), and *Kikongo-Kituba* or *Kituba*, a vehicular language springing from the previous one and presented by certain authors as a 'creole'. The analysis of these different names gives us an interesting insight into the historical and social environment of Kituba, for which I will initially follow the analysis of Mufwene:

- *Kituba*, whose meaning we have already seen, is a term used essentially by linguists.
- *Kikongo-Kituba*: the form *Kikongo*, 'Kongo language' or 'language of the Kongo people' (the *Bakongos*), is used by linguists to designate a set of dialects that their speakers have different names for. The association of the two terms is typically a name given by the other, the invention of those describing it.
- *Kikongo ya lèta*, 'the Kikongo of the state', thus named because it was used by the Belgian colonial administration, is a typically popular name.
- *Kilèta*, 'the language of the state', is a shortened form of the previous one.
- *Kikongo ya bula-matadi*, 'the Kikongo of the stone-breakers', is a reference to the construction (between 1891 and 1898) of a railway line between the port of Matadi and the capital of the Belgian Congo (Leopoldville, today Kinshasa), for which it was necessary to dynamite a good number of rocks.
- *Kibula-matadi*, 'the language of the stones', is a shortened form of the previous one.
- *Mono kutuba*, 'I speak, I say', is a name that seems to have appeared in the Congo in the 1930s, at the time of the construction of the railway line between the port of Pointe-Noire and the capital, Brazzaville.

(In the four last cases, *Kikongo ya lèta, Kikongo ya bula-matadi, Kibula-matadi* and *Mono kutuba*, we thus have a name that relates directly to a social practice, the construction of a railway line and the importing of a workforce from different parts of Africa (including West Africa), necessitating the use of a vehicular language created ad hoc from the local basis of a mass language.)

- *Kikwango*, 'language of Kwango', is a reference to the Christian missions from the region of Kwango-Kwilu where this vehicular language was used to catechize the populace.
- *Ikélé vé*, 'it's not true', was, according to Mufwene, used in the same zone 'as the neutral term without any metalinguistic function'.[34]

Thus we have, for the same linguistic form, a good ten or so names which, depending on the case, refer to geography (Kikwango), the functions of a vehicular language (Kituba, Mono kutuba) or official functions (Kikongo ya lèta), or the historical conditions of appearance of the language (Kibula-matadi). Some were born *in vivo* (Kikwango, Kilèta, Mono kutùba), i.e. they were created by their speakers, while others (Kituba, Kikongo) were born *in vitro*, i.e. they were created by linguists. Mufwene's remarks on this situation are twofold, marked simultaneously by the question of knowing whether we can consider 'Kituba' as a creole and by the desire to understand the emergence of vehicular languages from an ecological point of view. I will leave to one side the question of whether this language can be classified as a creole (I have some reserves about this classification, as I explained at length in the last chapter), but it is clear that different *in vivo* names, when they coexist geographically, are evidence of *representations* in which the thus-named languages are different.

More interesting are the links between the names of languages and their conditions of appearance, as glossonymia here rarely refers to a people (except in the case of Kikongo, which refers to the Bakongos) or to a state (Kileta refers to an entity, to the administration in general, and not to the *name* of a particular state). There are at least three hypotheses about the origin of the language:

1 Kituba could be a vehicular language which, in the view of H. Fehderau, was born in the sixteenth century from the contact of dialectal varieties of Kikongo in the region of Manyanga, a town on the River Congo downstream from Kinshasa.[35] These days, nobody seems to take this position seriously, in particular because it is not based on any historical proof. William Samarin notes for example that in 1816 an expedition sent to see whether any vehicular language existed along the River Congo found nothing of the kind.[36]
2 Kituba could be a vehicular language that appeared at the end of the nineteenth century in contacts between the Bakongos and the workforce imported by colonization from West and East Africa. This thesis, as presented by William Samarin,[37] thus implies that Kikongo was pidginized by Africans from elsewhere, which would explain why we find isolating forms in Kituba whereas Bantu languages are agglutinating.

3 Kituba could be the product of contacts between Bantu speakers and West Africans (in particular those who acted as interpreters for the whites). This hypothesis, formulated by S. Mufwene, makes the West Africans the catalysts of a process of creation of a vehicular language involving endogenous languages ('Kikongo' in its various forms), exogenous contributions (the languages of West Africans which, by interference, have left traces on Kituba) and, above all, a special sociolinguistic situation.

Kituba, which was a vehicular language right from the start, would thus be the product of an encounter between different groups not speaking the same language and not necessarily speaking the languages of the same group. Whether we are talking about new urban centres or railway lines, places of encounter, as the products of the colonial era, thus constituted an external intervention on an environment which from that time onwards was unable to draw on traditional means to manage a new situation that posed new problems of communication. There is nothing here that we did not know already: a great number of the vehicular languages in the world were born in these conditions; others appeared along the traditional channels of communication, trails, rivers, ports, etc.[38] What matters for us here is what this emergence teaches us about languages in general. Mufwene uses a fine formula, explaining that these new conditions have led to a new 'division of labour' between ethnic languages and Kituba: the former are used in the family, in private contexts, while the vehicular language is used in public life. Kituba becomes vernacular in the towns, while still being a vehicular language in the rural zones, and it is thus always the product of a negotiation between speakers, some of whom have it as a first or second language, while the others have only an approximate knowledge of it. 'It seems legitimate to characterize the spectrum of varieties of Kituba in the towns and the rural zones as a continuum extending from the urban norm of native speakers to the most deviant rural form', writes Mufwene,[39] adding that this continuum is not comparable to that constituted by creoles. Neither French nor Kikongo here play the role of an acrolect towards which linguistic forms would tend – which amounts to saying that Kituba has acquired its autonomy.

What are we to draw from this example and the debates to which it has given rise? The fact, to begin with, that a modification in the environment entailed a modification in the linguistic situation: whatever the role played by the immigrant workforce, the interpreters, the whites, the religious communities and the nascent urbanization in the emergence of Kituba, we here have a good example (one of several, it is true) of the relations between the milieu and linguistic change. Then there is the fact that a certain number of *practices*, which we can analyse as the response to an environmental change, are named by speakers and linguists in different ways, with a tendency towards fission in the first case and towards fusion in the second. In other words, where, *in vivo*, there is a clear tendency to differentiate between them by giving them different names (these languages are different because we – the speakers – have different names for them), *in vitro* there is a clear tendency to do the opposite (all these practices constitute a single language which we – linguists – call Kituba).

We here meet again the pairing presented in the introduction to this book, the distinction between *practices* and *representations*: the modifications in the situation engendered practices that gradually led to the emergence of 'Kituba', and the representations of 'Kituba' have thus led, inter alia, to the different names that it bears or has borne.

One, two or three languages? The example of Serbo-Croat

Since the publication of the *Grundzüge der Phonologie* of Nicolas Troubetzkoy (1939), there has been a classic problem in phonology that can be summed up in the question: 'One phoneme or two?' This question actually breaks down into two sub-questions:

- Are there two different phonemes or two variants of a same variable?
- Are there two successive phonemes (a group of phonemes) or a single phoneme?

In the first case we are talking of paradigmatic relations between two forms, only one of which is present; in the second case of syntagmatic relations between two co-present forms. But this functional approach to the problem can be complemented by another, which does not consider the phonological value of these forms (variants or phonemes) but their representative value. Thus we can analyse, from a strictly phonological point of view, the pronunciation in Alsace of certain French consonants (with the voiced consonants being devoiced), but we can also take an interest in the perception of this pronunciation on the part of both Parisian speakers (as a mark of Germanness, strangeness, ridiculousness, etc.) and Alsatian speakers (mark of identity, normality, conviviality, etc.). We can see that this double approach corresponds to the distinction widely drawn in this book between *practices* and *representations*: on the one side there is the way Alsatians pronounce the /v/ or the /g/ for instance, and on the other the way this pronunciation is perceived, the way people either flaunt it or try to hide it, etc. Now, in numerous situations, there appears a similar situation, not with regard to phonemes this time but with regard to languages. We will begin by describing one before turning to the relations between linguistic criteria and 'representative' criteria (i.e. those springing from representations) in the treatment of this problem and, more generally speaking, in the approach to languages.

In 1968, in a book edited by André Martinet, Joseph Verguin presented Serbo-Croat as the first language 'in the autonomous republics of Serbia, Montenegro, Bosnia-Herzegovina and Croatia. It also serves as a second language for the Slovene and Macedonian communities, and also for the non-Slav ethnic minorities of the country'.[40] And he distinguished between three dialects:

- Shtokavian in the centre and the east;
- Chakavian in the west and the islands;
- Kajkavian in the north.

He added: 'Serbs and Croats are divided by a sometimes tetchy nationalism more than by their language which, at least in literature, became unified in the form of Shtokavian. However, the Catholic Croats adopted the Latin script while the Orthodox Serbs use Cyrillic script.'

Recently, in 1999, Serbs, Bosnians and Croats most often declared that they spoke different languages where only a single language had been seen before, namely Serbo-Croat. So: one, two or three languages? No doubt, this question – 'is Serbo-Croat one language or two?', or rather 'do Serbs, Bosnians and Croats speak the same language?' – is badly formulated. It is of course possible to try and reply to it, on condition that we establish an unequivocal definition of language. When, indeed, does a language cease to be the same? Basically, when there is no longer mutual understanding – is the reply of functional linguistics. From this point of view, of course, since Serbs and Croats do understand one another, we would be led to conclude that 'Serbo-Croat' is one and the same language. But this is a rather hasty conclusion to draw since, apart from the 'objective view' of the 'object language', there is also the subjective view that speakers have of their objective situation. In other terms, alongside the question 'is Serbo-Croat one single language or two?' there appears another: 'Do Serbs and Croats think that they speak, or do they wish to speak, the same language?'

Let's begin with the facts. The 1988 Yugoslav encyclopedia gave its article on this language the title 'The Serbo-Croat/Croato-Serb/Croat or Serb language',[41] and this polynomial, four names for one language, covers a complex reality. A distinction is traditionally drawn, as by Verguin, between three dialects, depending on the way they say 'what': Kajkavian (the Zagreb region, where 'what' is *kaj*), Chakavian (Adriatic coast, where 'what' is *cha*) and Shtokavian, the central form spoken in the rest of Croatia, in Serbia, in Bosnia-Herzegovina and Montenegro, where 'what' is *shto*. In this set as a whole a further distinction is drawn based on the difference between *ije/e*, between the Iekavian dialect (spoken in a great part of Croatia, Bosnia, Montenegro and the west of Serbia) and Ekavian (spoken in Serbia, except in the west part).[42] This distinction is merely geographical and does not correspond to any national division. As Paul Garde writes, 'there is not a single feature that would oppose, for instance, the way all the Serbs speak, on the one hand, to the way all the Croatians speak, on the other. So it is impossible to define a "Serb accent" or a "Croat accent", in the way we have a "Belgian accent" or a "Canadian accent" in French.'[43] But a normalization of the written language became superimposed on this dialectal situation. The Croats, as Catholics, wrote Serbo-Croat in Latin characters from the eighteenth century onwards, while the Serbs and the Montenegrins, as Orthodox, used a form of the Cyrillic alphabet. Furthermore, the neologisms linked to scientific vocabulary are more often than not borrowings in Serbia and native creations in Croatia. All of this thus defined different usages but not different languages. Things became more tense with the birth of Yugoslavia (1918 for the kingdom, 1945 for the republic). The state, centralized in Belgrade, generally used the Latin alphabet and the Ekavian dialect in official texts, i.e., roughly speaking, the 'Serb language' and 'Croat writing'. And this amalgam was baptized Serbo-Croat, which was never going to satisfy the Croats. It was only in 1974 that the constitution gave the right to the different republics in the Federation to name their official languages. Croatia thereupon opted for Croat, and the three other republics concerned opted for Serbo-Croat.

Faced with these historico-ideologico-political tribulations, what is the linguist to say? The lexical differences between Serb and Croat are many, and they could be classified depending on whether there is a different evolution from the same etymon (as *gdje/gde*, 'where'), a borrowing from different languages (as *ulje/zejtin*, 'oil', the first term being of Latin origin and the second of Arabic origin) or of different neological creations (such as *brzojav/telegram*):

Croat	**Serb**	**Translation**
vlak	voz	train
kruh	hleb	bread
kava	kafa	coffee
gdje	gde	where
ulje	zejtin	oil
povijest	historija	history
zemljopis	geografija	geography
brzojav[44]	telegram	telegram
ratchunalo[45]	kompjuter	computer
limunika	grepfruit	grapefruit
gospodask	economia	economy
zrakoplov	avion	aeroplane

These lexical differences, which are acknowledged and catalogued, do not get in the way of communication but they make it possible to some extent to identify the speaker. A Serb academic will speak of the *univerzitet u beogradu*, the University of Belgrade, and a Croat academic will speak of the *sveutchilishte u zagrebu*, the University of Zagreb: the same construction, the same system of declension, but two different words. There are also syntactic differences. Where a Croat will say *trebam ici* or *moram ici* for 'I must go', a Serb will say *treba da idem* or *mora da idem*: in the first case we have a 'verb + infinitive' structure and in the second 'verb + conjunction + conjugated verb'. Roughly speaking, the French equivalent would be *je dois aller* ('I must go') versus *il faut que j'aille* ('it is necessary that I go').

This leaves, of course, the way these differences, which in the final analysis are minor, are actually used. Paul Garde writes of the lexicon:

> Words of this kind are extremely numerous in a dictionary, and certain Croat authors, in an attempt to demonstrate that we here have two different languages, draw up impressive lists of them. But these are technical words. In everyday life you can converse for a long time without using a single one of them.[46]

But we need to add straightaway that these minor differences can be used to mark one's own difference. In Bosnia, for example, the /h/ tends today to be considered as denoting that one is a Muslim, and they will say *lahko* rather than *lako* ('easy'), *mehko* rather than *meko* ('slow'), etc. Furthermore, certain borrowings from Turkish and Arabic add to the 'Muslim' aspect of the language: thus the expression *selam alaikum* is widespread in Bosnian greetings.[47] In 1990 Ranko Bugarski summed up this situation perfectly, even before the break-up of Yugoslavia: Serbo-Croat was generally held by linguists to be a single language; the problem lay in the sociolinguistic significance of the variants found in it. Differences in alphabet, phonology, grammar and lexicon did not usually affect communication; but linguistic distinctions could symbolize speakers' feelings – so that the identity of Serbo-Croat was largely a problem of attitude and depended on one's position in Yugoslav society.[48]

Thus, in his view, Serbo-Croat was linguistically a language and sociolinguistically the locus where ideological differences were made clear by the exploitation of variations: Serb, Croat or Serbo-Croat identity was a problem of attitudes. Seven years later Bugarski returned to the same question, writing that Serbo-Croat could still be considered linguistically as a single language, though from the political point of view it already comprised three languages.[49]

Can this future of this object – single or triple, depending on the point of view adopted – be predicted? Bugarski thinks that the three forms can only continue to diverge and become ever more different, which seems probable if the political situation continues to develop in the same way. And Dubravsko Skiljan concludes in the same way that 'we can imagine that the Serbo-Croat linguistic community will dissolve into many small communities, each of which will possess its own symbolic and communicative spaces'.[50]

However, the problem that I want to focus on here is not that of the transformation or the dissolution of a language, but first and foremost that of the conflict between names (and, behind it, that of the differences in analysis) between the linguists and the speakers. Throughout the world there are numerous situations in which speakers do not give their language the same name as linguists do, and we have just seen that the linguist does not necessarily produce the same reply as speakers to the question 'one language or two?' Now, this question in turn raises another: why do we wish to know whether there is one language or two? For typological, scientific reasons? Perhaps, but there is nothing scientific about the way this question is asked in Croatia. The Croats did not suddenly become fanatics of dialectology – rather, they were driven by an old ideology which deems that language is one of the criteria of national unity, and wished to bolster their recent political independence by a 'linguistic independence', rather in the same way that Noah Webster dreamed, at the start of the nineteenth century, of a republican American language different from the monarchical English language.

So Serbo-Croat can be considered as the linguistic result of a political project, that of Yugoslavia, and the embryonic situation that I have just described – in which three new languages are perhaps coming into being – is the result of political changes in ex-Yugoslavia, changes which are here highlighted by the linguistic attitudes of Serbs, Croats and Bosnians, or rather by the linguistic side of their political attitudes. The problem that appears here – one with a general value – is thus the following: what is the impact of linguistic representations on linguistic practices? This question is fundamental: if we do not speak the same language, it is because we are different, and if we want to affirm our difference, we need to speak different languages. We have a good example of this impact in the recent history of India: Hindi and Urdu – despite the efforts of Gandhi, who would like to have unified India linguistically around Hindustani – are today different languages that are spoken in two different states, India and Pakistan. Elsewhere, Kinyarwanda and Kirundi are the (different?) languages of two different states, Rwanda and Burundi, Czech and Slovak are (different?) languages of different states, etc. In other words, in Croatia as in Slovakia, in Rwanda as in Burundi, the above-mentioned paradigm has been established, based on a single root for the name of the country, that of the citizens and that of their language.

We can of course laugh at Slovaks or Croats, but we need rather to note that if they claim to speak different languages in spite of the linguists' opinion, they can end up speaking languages that linguists will recognize as different. And this last sentence, which describes the respective roles of speakers and linguists, at the same time raises another question, that of what is at stake in glossonymia.

Kraemer: the invention of French in the socio-professional context

Kraemer is a village situated 45 miles southwest of New Orleans (Louisiana), in the middle of swampland (the 'bayous'), where there is a professional community of a particular type. There is, for example, a restaurant situated on the edge of the Ox bayou, on which they have set up a small tourist concern organizing 'swamp visits' by boat, a souvenir shop selling local handmade products, and a trade in alligator heads and skins. The whole business involves both a family, who own it all, and neighbours who help out sporadically (in particular during the period of alligator hunting) – in all, some twenty or so people, from three different generations. All of them, including the youngest, are bilingual in creole/English. This social micro-community, in which I worked in September and October 1993,[51] has a certain number of characteristics that spring, as we shall be seeing, from the introduction of an exogenous norm into this ecolinguistic niche.

Evading creole

One of the languages used by the members of this community corresponds at every point to what Ingrid Neumann (for Bréaux-Bridge)[52] and Thomas Klingler (for La Pointe Coupée)[53] have described as Louisiana creole. Now, when asked about what they speak, the inhabitants of the village declare more often than not that they speak French, but they sometimes feel the need to add that this is a particular form of French (the term 'creole' is never used by them to describe their dialect): 'We all speak French here, but it's not . . . it's not French, it's Cajun.'[54]

In the same way, when asked about the relations between his dialect and that of La Vacherie (a village situated some miles away on the Mississippi, where they speak different varieties including creole and

Cajun), one speaker replied. 'The blacks, the blacks in La Vacherie even speak French the same way that we speak it, the white people speak differently from the rest of us.' By saying this, by situating his dialect with that of the blacks in La Vacherie, in the eyes of the linguist he is declaring clearly that he speaks creole, but he never says so. In other words, both of them classify their dialect in a category (French) which guarantees a certain prestige. But they both agree on the fact that it is different from standard French. In what ways? When asked about this point, they provide two types of reply:

- There are numerous lexical examples (*chaoui, crebisse, chevrette, poëlon, char, zozo*, etc., for 'racoon', 'crayfish', 'shrimp', 'oven', 'car', 'bird'). In addition, they are avid for information on this point. One old man, for instance, is highly astonished to learn that people speaking the French of metropolitian France say *avion* for aeroplane, and not *aéroplane* (which he pronounces with a dipthong /a/, in the English manner).
- There is a form borrowed from English, always the same: the postposition *back* (*vini bak, ale bak*, etc.) which is actually very frequent, but which also seems to be taken as a lexical example: I have the impression that my informants were more aware of the term *back* than of its postpositive usage.

They all seem reluctant to accept the word *creole*, or at least they give it a very individual sense, rather than a linguistic one: 'The name in creole is *manger* [eating]. Enne has Cajun *manger*, wit'. . . er . . . roux sauce, ev'ting that starts wit' a roux is Cajun, ev'ting wit' tomatoes is creole.' So, while in these representations the blacks of La Vacherie speak like the whites in Kraemer, the same is not true of the inhabitants of Chactaw (a village situated five miles away). One speaker says of them, 'It's a different French. If there's five Chactaws here, I shows you the difference [*mo se montre la difference*] . . . like I says you're on the boat [*comme mo dit toi su' le bateau*] . . . he'll say his one [*ye t'a dit ma sienne*].' He is here alluding to the forms *moken, token* and *saken* from the creole, for 'mine', 'yours', and 'his/hers'. And an old Chactaw gentleman who runs a bar explains that the people of Kraemer/parl drol/, i.e. *parlent drôlement*, 'speak funny', or that they speak 'patois', giving as an example /mole, tole/, i.e. 'I want', 'you want'. Now, if *ole* in the sense of 'to want' can, in Neumann's view, be replaced by /ve, vØ/, she points out that this is essentially in the negative form (vepa) and that

> the use of the morpheme ve/vØ as autonomous verb (without negative), or as an auxiliary verb in the negative form as well as the positive, does not seem to be basilectal. It is considered as 'French' by most of our black informers. . . . It is probable that in the shorter or longer term, the form *ve* will replace the form *ole* in the present.[55]

Klingler too points out that the use of *ve* is infrequent, and essentially in the negative.[56] The form *ole*, as is the case with other verbal forms (*wa* [cf. standard French *voir*], 'to see', *vini* [cf. standard French *venire*], 'to come', *pele* [cf. standard French *appeler*], 'to call', etc. is characteristic of the basilect and thus fits into a series of variations that can be represented thus:

Basilect	**Mesolect**	**Acrolect**
wa	wa	vwar
vini	vnir	vnir
pele	aple	aple
ole	vØ	vØ
gain	a	a

In other words, characterizing the dialect spoken in Kraemer by the forms *ole, tole*, our Chactaw speaker describes it as basilectal or creole. The speakers of Kraemer, for their part, are above all sensitive to lexical differences, contrasting for instance the forms they use as *goble dlo* ('a glass of water'), *mustik*, *mo gain li* ('I have it'), *trap mwa sa*, with the corresponding forms used at La Vacherie (*ver dlo, marangwî, jlé, empogne mwa sa*). In these four cases, what they do is select from La Vacherie forms that are close to Cajun so as better to bring out the difference from their own dialect. 'Down from La Vacherie it's Negro French [*français nèg*]', one female informer tells us, 'above it, proper French'.

In all of this we can see both the practice of creole (the speakers of Kraemer say *vini* for 'to come', *gain* for 'to have', *wa* for 'to see', etc.) and, on the level of representations, the fact that the term 'creole' is never used to name the language, though it *is* used to name local products that are deemed to be of good quality (creole tomatoes, a creole horse, etc.). It would be easy to see here the refusal of the white speakers to name their dialect in the same way they name that of the blacks, but this hypothesis is invalidated by the fact that the dialect of the blacks of La Vacherie, deemed to be similar to that spoken in Kraemer, is called both French (*français*) and Negro French (*français nèg*). The fact remains that, when confronted with the variety of dialects of La Vacherie, Chactaw and Kraemer, the linguist will be tempted to classify them under different headings (basilectal or mesolectal creole, Cajun, etc.) whereas the speakers of Kraemer insist first of all on the fact that they speak French before going on to introduce nuances: 'our French' is different. What we are again encountering here is, of course, the question that cropped up with regard to 'Serbo-Croat' (who is right, the linguist or the speaker?) and behind this rather rhetorical question rises the problem of representations in the evaluation of linguistic situations that I discussed at length in chapter 4. If the speakers from Kraemer declare that they speak French, this is, of course, for reasons that involve representations and a certain insecurity about their status. Another question is that of knowing whether these representations impact on their practices.

The invention of French

The ecolinguistic niche in which our micro-community lives has been drastically transformed by certain of its professional activities. The restaurant and the swamp visit have indeed drawn tourists, Americans (and English-speakers) but also Quebecois, Belgians or French, and the speakers of the local 'French' have been suddenly confronted by a standard, legitimate French, obviously different from their own. Thus, a guide relates that, showing some French people round the bayou, she pointed out a raccoon (in creole *chaoui*):

> *Je dis ga le chaoui et le français te fait: hein? Le chaoui? Le chaoui? Ga le chaoui, et là, quand ye té wa lo zanimal te dit oh, le raton laveur!* (I say, 'Look at the chaoui', and the Frenchman goes, 'what? The chaoui? The chaoui?' 'Look at the chaoui', and then, when he has seen the animal, he says, 'Oh, the raccoon'.)

This awareness of the difference has led to two types of reaction. First, a use of lexical variations identified as a capital, as a form of knowledge which is regularly displayed in front of tourists. When faced with

French-speaking visitors, everyone indulges in lexical mini-lectures whose function is to show that they *know* – they know that the French say *raton laveur* and not *chaoui*, *crevette* and not *chevrette*, *voiture* and not *char*, etc. But this knowledge soon reaches its limits, as is shown by the two following examples.

The speakers in our community have explained to me several times over that they were careful to use with French people the word *oiseau* ('bird') and not *zozo*, which is the form they habitually use, since they knew the meaning of this latter term in 'our' French. It took me a while to discover that they all thought that in standard French, *zozo* meant 'penis' (which is the case in certain creoles, that of Réunion for instance). I do not know the origin of this rumour (confusion with the French words for 'willy' or 'prick', *zozo* or *zob*?), but they all had a good laugh at this example and showed a certain pride in their ability to avoid this pitfall. Here is the second example: that of a guide who, while visiting the bayous, had explained at length to some French people present the difference between *marais* and *marécage*, and then, as they did not understand very well, had immediately translated these terms into English ('marsh' and 'swamp'), which was not any clearer. When questioned later by Thomas Klingler and myself, she embarked on a long, rather confused account, which I retranscribe here in its totality (our questions are in bold). [A translation follows the entire original version.]

'En dans le marais, le marégage, le si . . . le ba . . . , le *marsh*, le *swamp* . . .'

'Marais et marégage c'est même qui chose ou c'est différent?'

'Non, c'est différent. Le marais c'est . . . c'est terre vec d'l'eau d'sus.'

'Ça c'est marais?'

'C'est c'est marais, et le marégage c'est d'l'eau avec terre d'sus, et si vous allez en dans le marais et asseyez d'marcher vous va euh . . . ptête gain dl'eau achka vous g'nou ou vous cou.'

'Marégage c'est pas une prairie, c'est pas même qui chose, pas même z'affaire?'

'Non, le marécage c'est comme enne plairie mais ça peut flotter, c'est un flottant, c'est d'l'eau . . .'

'To peux marcher sur enne marégage?'

'Non, vous connaît marcher dans le marais . . .'

'Mais, vec d'l'eau . . .'

'Ouais . . . mais enne a d'l'eau en dans . . . mais vous connaît marcher d'l'eau enne va ête . . . enne va ête terre dure en bas . . . mais si vous asseyez marcher dessus le marégage vous va . . . caler.'

'Et marégage et marais ça c'est Cajun?'

'. . . non c'est pas ça, c'est pas ça . . . pelle ça . . . no va dit le flottant . . . et le marais.'

'In the *marais*, the *marégage*, the . . . the . . . the marsh, the swamp . . .'

'*Marais* and *marégage* – is that the same thing or are they different?'

'No, they're different. The *marais* is . . . it's land with water over it.'

'That's the *marais*?'

'That's the *marais*, and the *marégage* is water with land over it, and if you go off into the *marais* and try to walk on it, you'll, er . . . perhaps have water coming up to your knees or your neck.'

'*Marégage* isn't a meadow, it's not even anything?'

'No, the *marégage* is like a meadow but it can float, it's a floating thing, it's water . . .'

'Can you walk on a *marégage*?'

'No, you can walk in the *marais* . . .'

'But, with the water . . .'

'Yeah . . . but one of them has water in it . . . but you can walk in the water, the one will be . . . the one will be hard ground underneath . . . but if you try to walk on the *marégage* you will . . . sink.'

'And *marégage* and *marais* are Cajun terms?'

'. . . no, that's not right, that's not right . . . we call that . . . the floating thing . . . and the *marais*.'

Then our informer called for help from a man sitting at a nearby table, and the conversation hesitated between English and creole [here translated into English]:

'Brian, what do you call *marais* et *marécage*?'

'*What?*'

'What do you call *marais* and *marécage*? The *marais*?'

'*Marais* is a . . .'
'Swamp?'
'It's not a swamp. It's something like in front of your *peper*'s house, and all that is *marais*.'
'Then what's a *marécage* to you? Okay, what . . . How would you say . . . You know when you go walk in the swamp as the . . . as opposed to the marshland you know when the *flottant* is a floating thing?'
'Right.'
'That's *marécage*.'
'Okay.'
'You call that a *flottant*?'
'We call it a *flottant*. And what you call when you go walk in a swamp, when they got water but it's on ground? What do you call it?'
'*Cyprière*.' [In standard French, this means 'a cypress plantation' or 'a grove'.]
'*Cyprière*! The *cyprière* and the *marécage*, that's what I mean.'
'So here it's the *cyprière*.'
'The *cyprière* and the *flottant*, euh . . . When I do the tour, I know . . . I say the *flottant*, the *cyprière*, and he says, no! it's the *marais* and the *marécage*.'

So our informer had, in her creole, two words (*flottant* and *cyprière*) that she translated into English as 'swamp' and 'marsh' and for which the French tourists had proposed as equivalents *marais* and *marécage*, terms which she had adopted into her register of 'French for tourists'. And the chronology of this discussion

1 *marais/marécage*
2 marsh/swamp
3 *flottant/marais*
4 *cyprière/marécage*
5 *cyprière/flottant*

brings out in 1 and 2 a 'professional' register, used for French-speaking and English-speaking tourists, in 3 and 4 hesitations induced by our questions and in 5 the creole lexical pair. But the difference between *cyprière* and *flottant* is not really brought out by the words *marais* and *marécage*, and we thus have here an 'invention of French', of which we shall be finding more examples in certain phrases. The verb *avoir*, 'to have', is in Louisiana creole *gain* (whose origin is the French verb *gagner*, 'to gain, to win'), and in Kraemer you hear forms such as:

- *mo gain hont* (standard French: *j'ai honte*, 'I am ashamed');
- *mo té gain hont* (standard French: *j'avais honte*, 'I was ashamed');
- *mo gain peur* (standard French: *j'ai peur*, 'I am afraid'), *etc.*

Now, when they are addressing French-speaking tourists, our informers say *je suis honte, je suis peur*, etc., whereas the equivalence of *gain* and *avoir* ought to make it easier for them to move from creole to French. It is my hypothesis here that, in a conscious attempt to gallicize their creole, they have given themselves approximate rules that consist in fact of filtering creole through English:

mo gain hont > I am ashamed > je suis honte
mo gain peur > I am afraid > je suis peur

This invention of 'French' forms is thus mainly the product of two factors:

1 a modification of the ecolinguistic niche by the introduction of the standard French of tourists;
2 an insecurity as regards linguistic status which, granting to English a higher status than to creole, makes it a model enabling one to pass from creole to another language that also enjoys a higher status, namely French.

These two factors are summarized perfectly by Thomas Klingler when he writes: 'While it can be the source of a sense of linguistic unease, the ever-increasing presence of French-speaking tourists inevitably reinforces the value of creole, a value that is not simply symbolic, but also financial. Indeed, this language becomes a merchandise that can be sold to tourists.'[57]

We thus have, in this example, a summary of the different themes tackled in the previous chapters:

- the gravitational relations (here between creole and English);
- the notion of ecolinguistic niche;

- the role of linguistic representations and their impact on practices;
- self-regulation (leading to an 'invention of French') in reaction to an external stimulus (the introduction of an exogenous norm).

As for what I have called 'evading creole', the claim that local creole is French, this shows that what is at stake in naming linguistic practices is twofold. On the one hand, naming constitutes these practices as a language; it affirms the existence of something solid which, in certain situations, the norm will reinforce and legitimate. On the other hand, it plays a role in bestowing identity, establishing a link between a language and an ethnic group, a place or a State and, in the case of Kraemer, a micro-community.

An ecological niche: the island of Saint-Barthélemy

Saint-Barthélemy is a small island in the West Indies, an administrative dependency of Guadeloupe, in which there reside at present somewhat more than 5,000 inhabitants, a number swollen in the season by hordes of tourists.[58] Its population has certain particular features that have attracted the attention of biologists for a long time. This isolate is in fact divided into two endogamous parts, formed by the two parishes on the island: the one, Au Vent (Lorient), with a rate of endogamy of 96 per cent, the other, Sous le Vent (Gustavia), with a rate of 89.5 per cent. As Benoist writes, 'Saint-Barthélemy is in reality the juxtaposition of two isolates, themselves organized into relatively endogamous zones. The biological data should thus not be presented for the island as a whole, but we should consider each of the regions "Au Vent" and "Sous le Vent" separately.'[59]

Furthermore, blood groups in the population are overall different from what is found in France (more group O, less group A, etc.) and significantly different in the Au Vent and Sous le Vent parts of the island (see table 6.1).

We also see in the population of Saint-Barthélemy a pathological level of deafness, and subjects differ from one parish to the next in height, cephalic index, nasal index and transverse-zygomatic index.[60]

In other words, what we have here is a homogeneous whole versus a metropolitan whole, in which there appear secondary differences corresponding to the geographical division Au Vent/Sous le Vent.

Table 6.1

	O	A	B	AB
Sous le Vent	57.8%	42.2%	–	–
Gustavia	62.82%	33.33%	3.85%	–
Au Vent	56.13%	37.74%	4.52%	1.61%
France	42.70%	47.01%	7.24%	3.05%

Source: J. Benoist, 'Saint-Barthélemy'.

Now the island is also divided from the linguistic point of view. A regional French, 'patois', is spoken in the west part of the island, Sous le Vent, whereas the eastern part, Au Vent, speaks creole, and the population is to an overwhelming degree white.[61] What is the origin of this linguistic division? And should we compare these two sets of data (genetic on the one hand, linguistic on the other)? In May 1996 my colleague Robert Chaudenson and I worked for three weeks on the island studying the linguistic situation, the forms that exist, and carrying out a sociolinguistic survey, in an attempt to understand the origin of this unusual situation.

At this point, we should remember a fact that sheds a particular light on this situation. In the second half of the nineteenth century, a certain number of inhabitants on Saint-Barthélemy emigrated to the island of Saint Thomas (Virgin Islands) where they founded two communities: Carénage (or 'Frenchtown'), where 'patois' is spoken, and Northside where creole is spoken, in accordance with the same division between the professions as in Saint-Barthélemy: fishermen on the one hand, and farmers on the other.[62] This relation between Carénage and Northside tells us as much about Saint-Barthélemy as all the studies carried out in the island itself. In fact, as in cellular division which reproduces the original cell identically, the expatriated groups recreated the oppositional structure of Saint-Barthélemy, which would seem to prove that the relations between the Au Vent and Sous le Vent groups do not need a particular geography to survive, and that they can preserve themselves in another environment, in this case through the recreation of a geographical distance. This identical reproduction of the division on Saint-Barthélemy at the time of the migrations to Saint Thomas shows its strength: it was to some extent the niche of Saint-Barthélemy that was thus reconstituted and acclimatized.

But this in no way explains the reasons for this division. Was it social factors that produced linguistic effects or linguistic factors that produced social effects? Was it geography which produced social and linguistic differences, or did the latter constitute a way of managing geography? It is striking to note the similarities between our initial astonishment at the particular situation of this island and Darwin's astonishment at the Galapagos. Arriving on the archipelago in September 1835, he found that each of the islands had its own species (of turtles, mocking birds, sparrows, etc.), that the thickness and length of the beaks of chaffinches varied considerably from one island to another, that the turtles on Charles Island had a thicker and differently shaped shell from those on James Island, etc.[63] Only in 1859, in *The Origin of Species*, did he draw the lessons from these observations by formulating his theory of natural selection. It is not, of course, my intention to project that theory onto the situation in Saint-Barthélemy, but to bring out a striking parallel. Darwin emphasized that the difficulty

> arises in chief part from the deeply seated error of considering the physical conditions of a country as the most important for its inhabitants; whereas it cannot, I think, be disputed that the nature of the other inhabitants, with which each has to compete, is at least as important, and generally a far more important element of success.[64]

Now the first and simplest explanation, one which we have often thought of, is geographical. Communications on the island have always been difficult, roads were built only recently and in order to reach points that are close as the crow flies, one has to go up and down steep slopes. This entails the endogamy of the two groups and, as a corollary, the genetic idiosyncracies that I have pointed out (blood groups, hypoacousia, etc.). Geography also explains (and history confirms) how on the one side, Au Vent, the existence of a few rare 'plains' made it possible to try and develop medium-scale agriculture, while on the other side the absence of these 'plains' drove the inhabitants into fishing and a degree of subsistence culture. Thus, for these geographical reasons, there very rapidly arose a difference between the two parts of the island: two places, two parishes, two sectors of activity, but at the start, before the introduction of slaves in significant numbers, just one language. The initial factor of differentiation between the two groups, the absence of movement between families, seemed thus to be geo-professional. And the problem then arose of how to explain how a French-speaking community, arriving in successive waves from the seventeenth century onwards, was able to give rise to two linguistic groups: professional specialization does not, after all, imply linguistic separation, at least not to such a degree.

It was of course tempting to seek an external stimulus: the slaves. The few plantations situated on Au Vent needed a servile workforce; the blacks would seem to have creolized French, as they did elsewhere. The particularity of the island would then have resided in the fact that on the one side was the original form, patois, which of course followed its normal evolution, but without being influenced by a legitimate form (no official French, as the island had long been under Swedish domination); on the other, the result of approximation to this form by blacks from different regions of Africa. From the point of view of the genesis of creoles, this would have been a unique situation, since it would have enabled us to measure the effects of creolization on the initial language and to see the continuities and/or breaks.

But in fact there was no creolization on Saint-Barthélemy. The hypothesis that has just been formulated implies that black slaves were put ashore at Saint-Barthélemy by ships from Africa. Our investigations have shown that this was by no means the case: Saint-Barthélemy was a much too reduced market for slave ships to even dream of stopping off there, and the slaves came from the Lesser Antilles, essentially from Martinique. This historical fact raises the linguistic problem in a different form. Born – or having stayed for several years – on other islands where creoles had existed since the end of the seventeenth century, these slaves spoke the creoles of their islands. In other terms, there was no endogenous colonization, but the importing of a creole that came into contact with the local French. Geography thus enables us to understand, via the question of professional specialization (agriculture versus fishing) that there were more slaves in Au Vent, and thus more creole-speakers, and creole did not spread to Sous le Vent. So on the one hand, 'patois' was continuing to develop, like a ship gathering headway, while on the other it came into contact with exogenous forms of creole to create the form that is now spoken in Au Vent.

The initial idea that we have on the one hand, in Sous le Vent, the target language, and on the other, in Au Vent, the result of the appropriation of this target language, was thus false. What we have is, on the one hand, the language of migrants from France ('patois') and on the other the result of the action on this language of an imported creole which (and herein lies the unusual nature of the situation) came from the appropriation of this same language by blacks: there was in some degree the grafting of a branch (creole) onto a trunk (patois) from which it had already sprung. The differences between these two forms were preserved because the groups speaking them remained divided. And this enables us to understand better the tension between two contradictory facts: the opposition between the two groups (as it was reproduced identically, or indeed on a larger scale, in the migration to Saint Thomas) and the strong sense of identity which is evident on the island, in spite of this division, and which is revealed in our sociolinguistic survey.

We can thus give a general overview of the way events occurred. The economic development of the island remained very limited until the middle of the eighteenth century; the few slaves who were there were scattered through the settlements and played no linguistic role. In the third quarter of the eighteenth century attempts at agro-industrial development entailed a more significant immigration of slaves that was concentrated in the Au Vent zone, the only one whose geographical characteristics allowed plantations. It was at that time that there appeared a creole in Saint-Barthélemy, one which was basically imported from Martinique along with the slaves and came into contact with patois in the Au Vent part of the island. Thus the initial single language (a variety of French) evolved into the current duality (patois–creole): this evolution was the product of the convergence of the different social practices and geographical conditions that separated the inhabitants of the two parts of the island. The 'Saint-Barthélemy niche', defined by these geographical conditions and these social practices, produced linguistic results, just as it produced biological results (the blood groups I mentioned above, endogamy, etc.). From this point of view, the analysis of the linguistic situation of Saint-Barthélemy constitutes an exemplary illustration of what I mean by ecolinguistics or the ecology of languages. But it also permits us to illustrate linguistic *representations* as I defined them in chapter 4 and the *security/insecurity* they entail.

During our survey, we gave a questionnaire to the pupils in the Mireille-Choisy school, in Gustavia, which children from the three primary schools on the island (Colombiers, Lorient, Gustavia) enter when they are 11 years old, staying there for four years. The population surveyed (238 pupils) does not, properly speaking, constitute a sample but a group (almost an entire one) of the same age. (All the pupils in the school were questioned, but there may have been absentees and it is possible that some Saint-Barthélemy children of the same age go to school elsewhere, in Guadeloupe or in France.)

Using different formulations and approaches, five questions bore on the linguistic situation on the island: *What languages are spoken on the island?* (question 6); *What do people who live in Sous le Vent speak?* (question 8); *In what part of the island is patois spoken?* (question 15); *What do people who live in Au Vent speak?* (question 9); and *In what part of the island is creole spoken?* (question 16), and the replies show a good knowledge of the coexisting languages.[65] But the pupils are not linguistics researchers and it is improbable that at the age of 13 or 14 they have a direct, experimental knowledge of the situation; even if the school playground is a place where information is shared, a place where one becomes aware of the linguistic practices of others, it seems more likely that they are here reproducing a dominant discourse.

The linguistic division of Saint-Barthélemy is in fact an object of never-ending discussions. From the school teacher to the old retired fisherman via the museum curator or the Sunday footballers, everyone has an opinion on the question of languages, one that is expressed with considerable certainty in each case. We collected these discussions, these opinions, and the converging characteristics can be summarized as follows:

- the contrast Au Vent/Sous le Vent – all the islanders know and say that creole is spoken on the one side, patois on the other;
- the case of Gustavia, where English and French are thought to be spoken (in fact the traders, for obvious reasons, speak a *certain* English there, but the idea that the 'town' is an English-speaking area is deeply rooted);
- the case of Grande Salline and Lurin, where they believe that a third variety is spoken, one that the pupils often define as 'old French';
- among creole speakers, the affirmation of the difference between their dialect and that of Guadeloupe.

Now, we find these same characteristics, this same description, in the replies of the pupils, which suggests that they are reproducing a discourse they have inherited: the 'Saint Bartholomeans' are constantly producing a meta-discourse about their own situation, as if they were themselves fascinated by this rather unusual linguistic division.

As regards the linguistic practices of pupils and their representations, a rather ill-defined area – on the one hand, because the declared linguistic practices are always to be treated with caution; on the other, because linguistic representations are not easy to analyse – we asked various questions. *What languages do you speak?* (question 7); *What is the way of speaking characteristic of the island?* (question 12); *What is the best way of speaking on the island?* (question 13); *The preferred way?* (question 14); *Can you recognize someone who comes from Sous le Vent (or Au Vent)?* (question 10); and *Is the same French spoken in Saint-Barthélemy as in France?* (question 17).

The answers to these questions should obviously be taken for what they are: the impression that the pupils have or wish to give of their practices. When, for example, pupils declare that they speak English, this may be a magnified knowledge of a language they have learnt at school. But overall, if we tally these answers with the pupils' place of birth or residence, they appear trustworthy. Fewer than half of the pupils (43 per cent) declare that they speak only French. Patois is much more often cited alone (18 per cent) than is creole (2.5 per cent) and if we total up all the mentions of these languages, either together or with other languages, patois (38.2 per cent) is always ahead of creole (21.4 per cent). The pupils often specify, 'I speak patois in my family, and French in public', and, in one case, 'I speak creole with my grandmother', which is evidence of quite a precise sociolinguistic analysis of the usage of these languages. So overall, the people we surveyed who had been born on the island inherited languages that we would call 'identity-bestowing' as opposed to the 'legitimate' language, which is French: 38.2 per cent of them say they speak patois and 21.4 per cent that they speak creole, i.e. 59.6 per cent of them declare that they speak one identity-bestowing language, sometimes two. But, of course, it must be remembered that 71.5 per cent of pupils were born on the island: in fact, the rate of transmission of identity-bestowing languages (the relation between the number of self-proclaimed speakers and the number of pupils from the island) seems to be 83.3 per cent.

The two languages are treated differently in answers to the question, *What is the way of speaking characteristic of the island?*: 48 per cent of pupils consider that patois is the characteristic way of speaking in the island (52 per cent of boys, 43 per cent of girls), as opposed to 10 per cent for creole and 8.8 per cent for patois–creole. Among the other answers, we should note the mention not of languages but of ways of speaking: mixing, nasality, length, accent, etc. These answers as a whole (9.2 per cent) are almost equivalent to those which cite creole and more significant than those which mention bilingualism. The dominant image which pupils have of the situation is thus twofold: people speak patois and they speak a French marked by patois and/or creole. The comparison of the answers to questions 13 and 14 is interesting for, unlike what one might think and what the figures seem to show, there is no relation between what pupils consider as the best way of speaking and the language they declare that they themselves prefer. So it frequently happens that pupils consider French as the best way of speaking, but declare that they prefer patois or creole; or consider patois as the best way of speaking, but declare that they prefer creole. In other words, as the questionnaire in fact implied, question 13 was more often than not treated in a normative way and question 14 was seen as raising the question of identity. From this point of view, it is interesting to compare in a table the answers to question 13 (*best way of speaking on the island*) and 14 (*preferred way of speaking*).[66]

If we now compare the answers to questions 7 (*What language do you speak?*) and 14 (*What language do you prefer?*) we can see that the rate of preference for local languages is always less than the rate of those who actually speak them (see table).

The situation is thus extremely ambiguous. The language considered to be the best way of speaking on the island (French or patois, depending on the case) is not necessarily the one that is preferred (this is

Table 6.2

Best way of speaking on the island?		Preferred way?
French	41.5%	40.3%
Patois	23.4%	27.7%
Creole	11.7%	18.5%

Table 6.3

	Speak patois	Prefer patois	Speak creole	Prefer creole
Boys	41%	30.5%	22.3%	19.4%
Girls	34.6%	24%	20.1%	17.3%
Total	38.2%	27.7%	21%	18.4%

particularly striking in the case of creole: 11.7 per cent of those surveyed consider it as the 'best way of speaking', but 18.5 per cent make it their preferred language), which seems to reveal a clear choice in favour of a language that gives a sense of identity. But neither patois nor creole completely satisfy their speakers when it comes to expressed preference, which seems to reveal a latent linguistic insecurity.

A broad majority of pupils (73 per cent) declare in reply to question 10 that they can recognize the regional origin of the inhabitants of Saint-Barthélemy. The most interesting aspect is clearly how they replied to the question on the way they can recognize the origin of the speakers. The replies can be divided into three main groups.

Those who reply in a general way These pupils refer either to their language (their accent, their way of speaking, their pronunciation, their language – talking creole or patois – typical turns of phrase, words, etc.), or to broader semiological signs (the *calèche* or 'calash', the hairstyle of the women of Sous le Vent, the expression on their faces, etc.).

Those who define the way of speaking in Au Vent or Sous le Vent The answers are as follows:

1. 'In town they *speak slowly* while the districts like Colombier and Flamands have a *singsong accent.*'
2. 'The people who live in Au Vent *speak in a singsong way.*'
3. 'The people from Sous le Vent *speak though their noses*, and those from Au Vent *speak* with something of a *drawl.*'
4. 'The people from Au Vent *draw their words out.*'
5. 'In Sous le Vent people speak with more of a *drawl*, in Au Vent they *speak more quickly.*'
6. 'The people from Au Vent (creole) *draw their words out.*'
7. 'The people from Sous le Vent *draw their words out* a bit.'
8. 'The people from Sous le Vent *speak patois quickly.*'
9. 'The people from Sous le Vent *speak* patois much more *rapidly* and in a much more *high-pitched way* than the people from Au Vent.'
10. 'In Au Vent they have a *rising intonation* at the end of each sentence.'

Clearly, the themes are not very varied and, more often than not, they do not allow us to discriminate between speakers, since the same elements can be applied to the speakers of Au Vent or Sous le Vent: people speak slowly (in town), quickly (in Au Vent and Sous le Vent), with a singsong accent (in Au Vent and Sous le Vent), nasally (in Sous le Vent), drawing their words out (in Au Vent and Sous le Vent), in a high-pitched way (in Sous le Vent) and with a rising intonation (in Au Vent). These contradictions do not necessarily prevent pupils from recognizing people's origins and are above all evidence of their difficulties in describing in concrete form what they perceive. Furthermore, we need to underline the statistical importance of the usage of the verb *traîner*, to draw out or drawl, here probably referring to a characteristic lengthening of the vowels on both sides of the island: the pupils in Au Vent do not perceive it amongst themselves but they do perceive it in speakers from Sous le Vent and vice versa. Thus these descriptions show us in particular that, if it is the other that you are describing, as the question invited you to, the two sides of the island are a mirror image of one another: ultimately, everyone speaks drawlingly and in a singsong way.

Those who give concrete examples These are far and away the most numerous. Certain pupils, to mark the difference between Au Vent and Sous le Vent, give both ways of saying the same thing in the dialect of both zones. For instance:

> 'In Au Vent: *olà ou qu'à aller qu'en ça?* In Sous le Vent: *olà que té qui va?*' ('Hi, where you going?')
> 'In Sous le Vent people will say that he's in a coma, in Au Vent they'll say that he's immortalized (*immortalisé*).'
> 'In Sous le Vent: *o la t'ké ki va?* In Au Vent: *coté où calé?*
> 'Patois: *ou est-ce que ti va*, creole: *côté ou qu'a habité*.' (Patois: 'where you going?', creole: 'which side did he live?)'

Generally speaking, we should begin by emphasizing that the pupils find this question (regarding recognition) quite natural and normal (some of them reply, 'of course I recognize them,' etc.), but they rarely reply, 'I recognize the people from the other side because they speak another language.' If we were to ask Greek Cypriots how, linguistically, they recognize the Turks, they would probably reply, 'because they speak Turkish'. This is far from the case here: the pupils more often than not provide a small number of contrasting syntactic structures and a reduced vocabulary. Thus creole for them is practically reducd to the form *subject* + *ka* + *verb* (in phrases such as *ou l'a ou qua rester*, 'where do you live?', *olà ou qu'à aller*, 'where are you going?'), by the negative form *pa* + *ni*, always cited in the phrase *pa ni problem* ('there's no problem') and a few lexical elements (*moune* for 'people', *bitin* for 'furniture', etc.); whereas patois is characterized by the form *subject* + *être* + *ki* + *verb* (in phrases such as *j'suis qui va au travail*, 'I am going to work'), and, yet again, by a few lexical elements (*peinturer* for *peindre*, 'to paint', etc.), some of them being presented in contrasting forms (*veiller/garder, passé moué le stylo/bas moin pointe-là*, etc.).

So our survey brings out a limited number of stereotypes that concern either the totality of speakers on the island (they speak quickly, with a drawling or singsong accent) or, separately, the speakers of creole (*subject* + *ka* + *verb, pa ni problem, moune, bitin*), and patois (*subject* + *être* + *ki* + *aller, peinturer, veiller*). We come up against the same problem as in the analysis of questions on the linguistic situation on the island: the rate of error is low, but the knowledge thus demonstrated is reductive and stereotypical. Furthermore, we have the clear impression that the forms spoken in Au Vent and Sous le Vent are not really considered as different (patois versus creole), but as variants of a single variable, an impression that is confirmed by the answers to question 9, in which quite a significant number of pupils declare that, in Au Vent, a 'different patois' is spoken.

The answers to the question, *Is the same French spoken in Saint-Barthélemy as in France?* reveal for their part a certain linguistic insecurity ('Many of us make serious mistakes'; 'The people in Saint-Barthélemy make mistakes'; 'I think that the French spoken in France is rather more correct'), tempered by a sense of local specificity ('Our island'; 'We have a tendency to modify certain words in our own way and to use patois or creole in our French'; 'In Saint-Barthélemy we have always lived in different languages (patois, French, creole, etc.)').

What can we learn from this survey on the representations pupils hold of their island's situation?

The languages that characterize the island, patois and creole, are being transmitted relatively well if we judge from the declarations of those questioned: less than half the pupils (43 per cent) declare that they speak only French, 38.2 per cent that they speak patois and 21.4 per cent that they speak creole – i.e. 83.3 per cent of children born on the island claim to speak one of the two languages. While the island's geographical situation is fully recognized, we need to emphasize a tendency to privilege patois over creole: 48 per cent of pupils consider that patois is the characteristic way of speaking on the island, as against 10 per cent for creole and 8.8 per cent for patois–creole. When asked what they considered as the best way of speaking on the island, 41.5 per cent of pupils replied French, 23.4 per cent patois and 11.7 per cent creole: the legitimate form thus plays a dominant role in representations.

We should also note that girls seem generally more conformist than boys: 49 per cent of them declare that they speak only French, as against 38 per cent of boys; 43.2 per cent prefer French, as against 38 per cent of boys; 24 per cent of them declare that they prefer patois, and 17.3 per cent creole, as against 30.5 per cent and 19.4 per cent, respectively, of boys. Furthermore, if we compare the French of Saint-Barthélemy to that of metropolitan France, 53.8 per cent of girls reply that they are different, with 45.5 per cent of boys expressing the same opinion. But there is nothing very new in this: several surveys have brought out this tendency to linguistic conformism in women.

Representations concerning the linguistic situation (What is spoken? Where?) are sufficiently convergent for us to conclude that there is a diffusion of a conventional epilinguistic discourse, of stereotypes that are regularly repeated. The same is true as regards the differences between patois and creole. The examples provided refer to a few structures, a few words, always the same, and the pupils are doubtless reproducing a received discourse. But behind the answers we seem to glimpse the idea that patois and creole are merely variants ('different forms of patois') of a single form, the 'Saint-Barthélemy dialect'. Overall, patois thus seems to be hitched to French the way a carriage is to a locomotive. French and patois are perceived as the best ways of speaking on the island, are declared to be people's favourite languages, and creole, less well localized geographically, seems marginalized, reduced to one or two syntactic structures and to a few typical words. And this brings us back to the problem of linguistic representations.

The situation can be summed up in a few figures: 38.2 per cent of pupils say that they speak patois; 48 per cent consider it as a form that is characteristic of the island but only 23.4 per cent consider it as the best way of speaking; 18.4 per cent declare that it is their preferred linguistic form. In other words, their self-evaluation ('we speak patois') places them in the norm of the island ('patois is characteristic of the island') but their evaluation of the coexisting languages ('French is the best way of speaking') and the expression of their preferences ('we prefer French') devalue their practice. As for creole, we have a somewhat different situation: the self-evaluation of the pupils ('we speak creole': 21.4 per cent) excludes them from the norm of the island ('creole is characteristic of the island': 10 per cent). The self-declared speakers of patois thus find themselves using a form that in their view is characteristic of the island, which is not the case with the self-declared speakers of creole, whereas French imposes itself on everyone as the best way of speaking and as the preferred form.

These different data enable us to return to representations. Linguistic insecurity was, in the view of William Labov, based on nothing very much: a stylistic variation, the recognition of an external norm and the awareness of not conforming with this norm. And the *index of linguistic insecurity* that he calculated, a quantified value, was quite limited: the number of forms where the speaker sees a difference between his practice and the form he considers as correct. The notion of linguistic insecurity was thus a relation between a judgement of normativity (correct usage in the view of the speaker) and a self-evaluation (personal usage in the view of the speaker). Now we find in the replies to our questionnaire some much more diverse elements. What we have, in fact, is a general *representative insecurity* (we speak A but B is the best way of speaking), which is reinforced in the case of creole speakers by what ought to be called an *insecurity of identity*: unlike the patois speakers, they do not find that their linguistic practices place them in the dominant norm of the island. The same insecurity appears with regard to the French spoken on the island. Half the pupils consider that people there do not speak the same way as in France, but here, too, ambiguity reigns, since this difference is often equated with local specificities, which is one way of underscoring their aspect of bestowing identity. This problem of identity has been raised, in passing, by Didier de Robillard:

> If we think in more abstract categories, we could perhaps contrast, in a classical way, the semiotic function (conveying information in the most ordinary sense) and the identity-bestowing function of the language in order to distinguish two modes of linguistic insecurity [LI]. On the one hand, we would have speakers who are made insecure by the mere fact they find it difficult to communicate (a benign form of insecurity if we can accept the medical metaphor); on the other, speakers who are made

> insecure for reasons of identity (fear of rejection by a social, professional, ethnic category, etc.).[67]

But the question is here being examined only from an intralinguistic point of view, while my question is interlinguistic. We find ourselves, in fact, in the situation which Aude Bretegnier baptized as 'bi-linguistic insecurity': 'A sense of linguistic insecurity both in the so-called dominant language and in the so-called dominated language'.[68] But whereas Bretegnier, and her predecessors, are referring to the form of languages, it is their status that is here being investigated, and the example of Saint-Barthélemy leads to theoretical problems: the pairing security/insecurity needs to be combined with the pairing form/status of languages. Indeed, the self-declared speakers of patois (and, of course, French) present:

1 *a security of identity*: they consider what they speak as characteristic of the island;
2 *an insecurity of status*: they consider that French is the best way of speaking.

As for the self-declared speakers of creole (and French), they present:

1 *an insecurity of identity*: they do not consider creole as characteristic of the island;
2 *an insecurity of status*: they consider that French is the best way of speaking.

But while a binary presentation, in terms of security/insecurity, allows us to gain in elegance, it makes the situations seem too rigid: it is not in terms of security or insecurity that we need to discuss things, but rather in terms of more or less security or insecurity. So we need to calculate a rate of linguistic security (or insecurity), just as we calculate a rate at which languages are turned into vehicular languages or are transmitted. I propose for this purpose to establish a relation between representations and evaluation: the percentage of speakers (here, self-declared speakers) of a language who have a positive representation of that language: if 100 persons declare they speak language A and have a positive representation of A, we have a rate of linguistic security of 100 per cent; if only 50 per cent of them have a positive representation of A, we have a rate of 50 per cent; and if nobody has a

Table 6.4 Rate of security of status

	Language spoken	
Best way of speaking	Patois	Creole
Patois	**48**	13
Creole	7	**22**
French	24	10
English, French		1
No reply	12	5
Total	**91**	**51**
Rate of security	**52%**	**43%**

Table 6.5 Rate of security of identity

	Language spoken	
Language characteristic of the island	Patois	Creole
Patois	**56**	17
Creole	4	7
French	4	3
English	1	1
Patois and Creole	9	8
Patois and French		1
No reply	17	14
Total	**91**	**51**
Rate of security	**71.4%**	**29.4%**

positive representation of A, we have a rate of 0 per cent (or a rate of insecurity of 100 per cent). So, as far as we are concerned, we need to combine the replies to questions 7 (*What language do you speak?*) and 13 (*What is the best way of speaking on the island?*), leaving aside those pupils who speak neither patois nor creole. The rate of security/insecurity is thus here calculated as a continuous value.

The problem posed by the second question (security of identity) is hardly discussed in the literature concerning linguistic representations. If we combine the replies to questions 7 and 12, we can calculate in the same way a rate of security of identity, a relation between the number of self-declared speakers of a language and the number of times the language is cited (alone or with another) as characteristic of the island.

Nearly three-quarters of self-declared patois speakers feel that patois is a form characteristic of the island and are thus bolstered in their sense of identity, which is the case for fewer than one-third of self-declared creole speakers.

Confronted with three languages, French, patois and creole, pupils really seem to think of only two when asked to characterize the island or to express preferences: a large majority of them do not consider creole as characteristic of the island, and creole speakers thus show all the symptoms of uncertainty as to where they belong. To speak patois is to be from Saint-Barthélemy, but what about speaking creole? Finally, they all show an insecurity of status, considering that French is the best way of speaking: 41.5 per cent of pupils as against 23.4 per cent for patois and 11.7 per cent for creole.

We were asking what might be the relations between genetic differences and the linguistic differences that had been noted between the two groups on Saint-Barthélemy. It now appears that the conclusions of J.-L. Serre et al. in 1987, according to which Saint-Barthélemy originally consisted of one population that divided into two groups in which endogamy generated significant biological variations, are also applicable, *mutatis mutandis*, to the linguistic situation. The dialect of Saint-Barthélemy was originally a single language which, through the introduction of an exogenous creole, evolved into two forms within which history and the social situation generated significant linguistic variations. These forms were locally baptized as 'patois' and 'creole', but as we saw in our linguistic survey, for the teenagers on the island the differences between them do not amount to much. In other terms, they all consider themselves as 'Saint Bartholemeans'; they do not all speak exactly the same way, but these differences are, in the final analysis, constitutive of their collective identity. This changes nothing in the syntactic differences that we noted in the course of our fieldwork between creole and patois, but it does shows us that the young people we questioned do not have the same vision that we have of the linguistic situation.

This situation, which raises the problem of the contradictions between linguistic representations, or the *epilinguistic* discourse of speakers, and the descriptions of the linguist, or his *metalinguistic* discourse, raises in particular the question of the future of this ecolinguistic niche. Insofar as we view epilinguistic discourses as intervening in situations and the way they evolve, we need to take into account these differences of representation between patois speakers and creole speakers if we wish to have an idea of the linguistic future of Saint-Barthélemy. This, indeed, will not simply be the result of 'internal' factors (coexisting languages, their momentum, their interrelations) but also of different external factors, among which the representations I have been indicating will play a far from negligible role.

Our description has shown that on Saint-Barthélemy there are two dialects (three if we add standard French), while our sociolinguistic survey has revealed, in linguistic representations, a more schematic vision. Now if the generation which we have surveyed feels that the differences between patois and creole do not amount to much, we can imagine that their practices will end up by making their representations assume concrete form: the island will eventually evolve into a diglossia of standard French/local French, this latter being the product of a patois/creole convergence. But this is just a hypothesis that only further studies can confirm or invalidate.

CONCLUSION

Inventing Language, Giving it a Name

Let us remind ourselves, to begin with, of the principles we originally set out from.

I initially began, in a way that may have appeared rather provocative, by suggesting a hypothesis that, in my view, is fundamental: *languages do not exist*; the notion of a *language* is an abstraction that rests on the regularity of a certain number of facts, of features, in the products of speakers and in their *practices*. Coexisting with these practices there are *representations* – what people think about languages and the way they are spoken – representations that act on practices and are one of the factors of change. They produce in particular *security/insecurity* and this leads speakers to types of *behaviour* that transform practices.

I then indicated that this pairing – practices/representations – needed to be described, analysed, within a framework that would take into account the relations between different types of practices (different 'languages') and between these practices and their milieux – what I called their *ecolinguistic niche*. And, in order to carry out this analysis, I used a certain number of models:

- a *gravitational model* (chapter 2)
- a *homeostatic model* (chapter 3)
- a *model of representations* (chapter 4)
- a *model of transmissions* (chapter 5)

Linguistic ecology thus studies the relations between languages and their milieu, i.e. first of all between these languages and society, which leads us to the question of knowing whether the milieu has an influence on practices, on the form of languages. The many situations that I have analysed show that this question can be answered in the affirmative. We have seen, in the case of the varieties of French spoken in

Africa, an example of the language adapting to the milieu (African 'semantax' showing its presence in French); in the case of Saint-Barthélemy, an example of influence from the milieu (geography, the professional differences that result) on relations between languages; in the case of Kituba, an example of the influence of the milieu on the way a language is named, etc.

This last point leads us to a wider question. In a certain number of cases, we encountered the problem of knowing whether there was one language or two, in other words the problem of knowing at what point a language stops being itself. And we saw that the answer given by linguists was not necessarily the same as that of the speakers. This question is central. Whether we are talking, for instance, about varieties of Arabic (classical, Modern Standard, dialectal), Kituba, Serbo-Croat or Louisiana creole, the fact of naming a language constitutes an intervention in the milieu: the name given to languages is never neutral. When German linguistics, for instance, at the start of the colonial period, focused on the relatively homogeneous group of languages spoken from the east coast to the west coast in the south of Africa and baptized it *Bantu* from the root *ntu, 'man', and the prefix of the class ba-,[1] we can see in this name the hypothesis that, behind the homogeneity of languages and territory, there is a homogeneity of human groups, which we now know to be false. 'In fact, we encounter, among the peoples who speak the Bantu language, a very great diversity both of modes of social organization (of family, religion and economy) and of hereditary anatomical characteristics (height, cephalic and cornea indices, blood groups, etc.).'[2]

This brief example shows that there is a strong propensity to consider that languages, human beings and territories correspond, that political unity is accompanied by a linguistic unity and an ethnic unity. In old states, which present a tendency to superimpose political boundaries and the limits of a linguistic constellation, people have often constructed, on the basis of the same root, the name of the country, that of its citizens and that of the central language. Thus, according to the dominant representations, in France there live the French who speak French, in Italy (*Italia*) the Italians (*Italiani*) who speak Italian (*italiano*), in England the English who speak English, etc. This paradigm is of course undermined in the case of certain multilingual states (people do not speak Swiss in Switzerland, nor Belgian in Belgium), and there is also a distinction between the second term (the name of the inhabitants) and the third (the name of the language) in the states of more recent constitution: the inhabitants of Senegal are indeed Senegalese but they do not (yet?) speak Senegalese, the Malians do not speak Malian, the Gambians do not speak Gambian, the Congolese do not speak Congolese, etc. Between these two extreme poles, we come across intermediary cases in which there is an evident tendency to impose on the language a 'national' name, as is shown by the increasingly frequent use of expressions such as 'Anglo-American', or even 'American'; 'Spanish of Cuba', or 'of Chile', 'of Ecuador'; even 'Cuban', 'Chilean', 'Ecuadorean', etc. And political changes, particularly in the framework of decolonizations, have sometimes led to new labels, as when Malay for instance becomes, in Indonesia, *bahasa Indonesia*, 'the Indonesian language'.

These varied situations raise a certain number of questions: Who decides on the name of a language? What is the impact of linguistic theories on these names? What is at stake in the way languages are named? But the main question raised here is that of the definition of the language, that useful fiction spoken of by Einar Haugen: a *fiction* because languages are not things that can be shown, they do not exist like real, tangible objects; *useful* because the science of linguistics needed, before it could come into existence, to postulate the existence of structures that it baptized as languages. Now every time you baptize *a* language and give it a particular name, you also bolster the fiction of language: language exists because languages exist. This is why the problems I now wish to discuss are at the heart of a debate which the science of linguistics cannot evade.

When the Algerian Constitution declares that 'Arabic is the national and official language' or when the Chinese version of a Chinese–British text signed in 1984 declares that the official language of Hong Kong after 1 July 1997 will be *chung wen* (the English version of the text says 'Chinese', an equally ambiguous term), the name of the language is working as a mask, and we are confronted with a subtext of the greatest interest. In the first case, it is not specified (but it is obviously the case) that this Arabic is not spoken Arabic, the vernacular, but rather written Arabic. In the second case, by using a form that refers to written Chinese, the authors of the text avoid having to specify that this will be Mandarin and not Cantonese (the language spoken by the majority in Hong Kong). The fact that, according to the Spanish Constitition, the official language of the country is now Castilian and no longer Spanish also shows that the name of a language can be a political and ideological issue: if Spanish was officially baptized Castilian, this is partly to satisfy Basque, Galician or Catalan nationalists, to cut the radical link between the name of the state and that of the language, to bring this language down to its regional dimension – that of Castile.

On the other hand, creoles are only rarely named in reference to a territory or a state (which, more often than not, does not exist). In order to distinguish between them, linguists speak of 'Réunion creole' or of 'the creole dialect of Réunion', of 'Guadeloupean creole', more rarely of 'Reunionese' or of 'Haitian'.[3] This name creates meaning: the speaker who declares he speaks French and creole is not saying the same thing as if he declared he were speaking French and Guadeloupean, just as a Poitevin, i.e. someone from the region of Poitou in France, by declaring that he speaks patois or Poitevin, is classifying his vernacular in a different way and telling us something about his linguistic representations. To say 'I speak patois' or 'I speak creole' is to situate one's vernacular in a relation of diglossia with a high variety of the language, whereas to say 'I speak Poitevin' or 'I speak Guadeloupean' is to grant to that vernacular the status of a language and to situate it in a more egalitarian relationship to the others. From this point of view, the question 'one language or two?' could become 'French and/or creole versus French and/or Guadeloupean, Haitian, Reunionese, etc.' And even if this problem of naming can seem marginal, it lies at the centre of the linguistic representations that, on my hypothesis, play a fundamental role in the dynamics of different situations.

But the most interesting thing about these situations is the fact that, as in the case of 'Serbo-Croat', the speakers and the linguist are not in agreement. Salikoko Mufwene told me that when he was researching into Gullah, a creole spoken in the coastal zones of South Carolina and Georgia, his informers most often declared that they spoke English and did not even know the word *Gullah*. In chapter 6 I described the same situation in the white community in Louisiana, in Kraemer, whose members spoke creole[4] but declared that they spoke French. In these situations, who is right – the linguist who labels as 'Gullah' or 'creole' what he hears and describes, or the speaker who thinks that he speaks (or wants or decides to speak) English or French? It would be pointless here to advance an argument based on authority (the linguist knows what he is talking about, so from the scientific point of view he is right):

the existence of one language or two is not just a technical problem but a problem of representations, and the whole challenge I have been faced with is precisely that of studying the effect of these representations on practices. In addition, this polynomia is not just the result of a disagreement between the linguist and the speakers – often, the speakers themselves have different names for the same language. Situations of this type are far from rare, but what can we learn from them? In the first case, differences between languages are not just linguistic but also social: by denying that the Serbs speak the same language as they do, Croats classify them as different, and thus exclude them from their own community. But the fact that they do not want to speak the same language as the other has effects on the languages themselves. Thus we have seen that in the above-mentioned case the speakers of coexisting linguistic forms borrow from different languages in order to differentiate themselves from their neighbours, and this desire to mark a difference or an identity has an effect on the form of the language and its evolution, whether we are considering its vocabulary, the way it is written, or its name.

One language or two? This question which, as we have seen, does not have an immediate answer nor a general answer, needs to be examined from the point of view both of practices and of representations – in the practices of speakers. In any 'naming' of a language there are two types of actor: the one who names the language and the one who names the language of the other. The speaker generally represents the first type, when he declares 'I speak this or that language', or 'my language is called X'. The linguist, for his part, represents the second type, declaring 'this is an example of X'. Then there is another difference: the speaker easily accepts that their language may not have a name, or may have several names, while the linguist thinks that languages have to be named, and named in an unequivocal way. And this difference symbolizes another, fundamental difference: for some people, 'language' is a practice, while for others it is an item in a taxonomy. In a language's name there are connotations that are not the same for the linguist and for the speaker. When linguists speak of a *creole* they are signalling to their alert readers that the language in question developed in specific sociolinguistic conditions, that its mode of emergence brings it close to other languages that have also been baptized as creoles. When speakers declare that they speak *creole*, on the other hand, they accept the linguist's label and situate their language in a relation with another co-present language. To say, of any sentence, 'that is creole', thus does not always have the same meaning. For the linguist, this affirmation means: this sentence is constructed in accordance with the rules of such-and-such a grammar, its vocabulary has sprung from such-and-such a lexicon. But the speaker who hears this affirmation can interpret it differently: you do not speak French (or English, etc.), you speak creole. In the first case, once more, there is a reference to a taxonomy; in the other a reference to a power relation of a diglossic type. And above all, in the two cases, we have different universes of representations. For the fact that linguists continue to baptize as a 'creole' whatever functions in the same way as all other languages is, in their view, part and parcel of a system of representations that sees history as of more importance than synchrony – but only in certain situations: we do not speak of French or Italian as dialects (of Latin) but as languages. Conversely, to name one's language 'creole' (and not Haitian, Martiniquais, etc.) means that one is drawing on another system of representations which draws nourishment from the previous one and, by projecting diachrony onto synchrony, by a hypertrophy of history, grants one's language a different status, a *difference* that social relations soon transform into an *inferiority*.

Hence, the question 'one language or two?' is no longer merely a scientific question and cannot be given a merely scientific answer. Just as the Croats will perhaps speak Croat one day, a different form from the Serb spoken by Serbs, it is possible that the inhabitants of Réunion will one day speak only French and the Haitians will speak Haitian. In other words, we may witness a de-creolization in the first case and, conversely, a radicalization of the independence of creole in the second. And this different evolution would not be linked to any intrinsic characteristics in what are conventionally called creoles, but rather to different political and social evolutions in which linguistic representations play a central role.

Certain of the colleagues whom I asked to read the manuscript of this book asked me with a hint of malice what difference there was between what I have called linguistic ecology and sociolinguistics. Behind their question there lurked the insinuation that I was perhaps just using one more metaphor to analyse things when I could equally well have analysed them from the standpoint of sociolinguistics. Now sociolinguistics has generally been considered as a part – a marginal part, in the view of some people – of linguistics, and in spite of the positions adopted by William Labov, in whose view it comprises *the whole of linguistics*, this vision persists: on the one side, they claim, there is hard linguistics, which is central, and on the other the various more peripheral types of linguistics (socio-, psycho-, ethnolinguistics, etc.), which are 'soft' and less 'scientific'. This situation has generated a tendency among 'sociolinguists' to abandon certain domains – those of the syntactic or phonological *description* of languages – and to devote themselves to the study of the relations between language and society, to the study of multilingualism, to linguistic politics, thereby bolstering the way the proponents of 'hard' linguistics circumscribe their discipline. In 1978, for example, Pierre Achard, presenting the objectives of the review *Langage et Société*, defined 'the proper object of linguistics' as 'the regular mechanisms of language',[5] thereby apparently excluding the possibility that these 'regular mechanisms' might be the object of study of sociolinguistics or the sociology of language. Abandoning the description of these mechanisms to the proponents of 'hard' types of linguistics, sociolinguistics thus to some extent connived in its own marginalization. This allowed Joshua Fishman to write, in his preface to a work by Glyn Williams, 'After three decades, sociolinguistics has remained just as it was: a province of linguistics and anthropology, and a rather provincial province at that'.[6]

On the contrary, what I have sought in the present work is to argue for an *ecological* approach to the world's languages, to *languages*, i.e. to their form (the 'regular mechanisms') and to their relations, to *practices* and *representations*, to their *gravitational* organization, to *self-regulation*, to the *transmission* of practices and situations, etc. It is in this respect that the notion of ecolinguistic niche seems to me of a nature to enrich our point of view; in this respect that an ecolinguistics is much more than a new metaphor, a descriptive and explanatory principle. This is why I have insisted at length on the importance of *representations*, which, if they do not of course create the history of languages all by themselves, are one of its driving forces. Indeed, 'hard' linguistics hardly looks at the effects of representations on the objects that it invents by describing them, namely 'languages'. I thus went on to insist on the fact that social situations construct these representations, but that they can at the same time be modified by them, and that linguistic *practices* are thus determined by the whole set of relations that are made manifest in their *ecolinguistic niche*. We have seen that within these niches, shifting populations could entail the *acclimatization* or *acclimatation* of languages, which could be transmitted or vanish, leaving traces of their existence behind them, so that linguistic situations were subject to a constant *evolution* that was sometimes drastically affected by *revolutions*. There is here a descriptive and explanatory principle that can only lead us to show a certain modesty in our desire to predict the future: we are bringing out tendencies and not laws. But above all, all of this shows that *the invention of a language* and consequently the *way it is named* constitute an intervention in and modify the ecolinguistic niche.

In this sense, while I have frequently underlined the fact that linguistic ecology is not to my mind synonymous with the protection of endangered languages, it is difficult to end without a reference to the responsibility of the linguist in the development of ecolinguistic niches. This, of course, is a problem of ethics and this book was devoted to something quite different. But, in conclusion, it is useful to remind ourselves that our task as linguists does not consist simply in describing 'languages' or linguistic situations. Working as we do on social facts, we cannot forget their nature. And, if we accept my analysis, we cannot ignore the fact that our descriptive and analytical practice also constitutes an intervention in ecolinguistic niches and can modify them considerably.

Notes

Introduction   Practices and Representation

1 Translator's note: I thus translate the French '*langue véhiculaire*' throughout, as both of the usual English translations, 'lingua franca' and 'contact language', have slightly different meanings from that intended by Calvet: a *langue véhiculaire* is any language which is used as a means of communication between communities with different mother tongues.
2 I myself have introduced, in previous works, two metaphors, that of 'the war of languages' and that of 'glottophagia'. But it is clear that languages do not actually make war on each other and do not really devour each other: it is the practices of their speakers that confront one another or make other practices disappear.
3 Einar Haugen, *The Ecology of Language* (Stanford: Stanford University Press, 1972). This work draws its title from a paper given by Haugen in 1970.
4 Ibid., p. 325.
5 Ibid., p. 335.
6 Peter Mühlhäusler, *Linguistic Ecology* (London and New York: Routledge, 1996).
7 Ibid., p. 5.
8 Ibid., p. 281.
9 Ibid., p. 28.
10 S. Mufwene, 'Language ecology and creole genesis', paper presented to the Society for Pidgin and Creole Linguistics, San Diego, January 1996.
11 In *Plurilinguismes*, 8 (1994).
12 In Pauline Christie (ed.), *Caribbean Language Issues, Old and New* (Kingston, Jamaica: University of the West Indies Press, 1996).
13 In *Diachronica*, 13 (1996), 83–134.
14 Salikoko Mufwene, 'Métissage des peuples et métissage des langues', in M.-C. Hazaël-Massieux and D. de Robillard (eds), *Contacts de langues, contacts de culture, créolisation* (Paris: L'Harmattan, 1997).
15 Ibid., p. 52.
16 Ibid., p. 53.

17 Albert Bastardas i Boada, *Ecologia de les llenguës: medi, contactes i dinamica sociolinguistica* (Barcelona: Proa, 1996), p. 19.
18 Ibid., p. 42.
19 Ibid., p. 167.
20 I use the term 'variable' to mean 'what is prone to vary', and 'variant' in the sense of 'the result of a variation'.
21 Only secret societies, such as Freemasonry, function on the basis of an internal consensus alone.
22 During a presentation on Chomsky's theories in 1970 or 1971 at André Martinet's seminar at the École Pratique des Hautes Études, I had suggested that his analysis in terms of deep/surface structures, if reread in the light of his book on Cartesian linguistics, would inevitably lead him to the idea that all the languages in the world were merely surface grammars resting on a single deep grammar. The text of my paper, some twenty pages or so, had circulated quite widely in Paris at the time, but I myself have since mislaid it. If any reader happens to have a copy, I'd be very glad to reread my thoughts.
23 Steven Pinker, *The Language Instinct* (London: Penguin, 1995), p. 232.
24 Ibid., pp. 240–1.
25 Ibid., p. 27.
26 Ibid., p. 111.
27 Ibid., p. 112.
28 Ibid., p. 278.
29 There is of course one exception to this universal characteristic: the group of sign languages used by the deaf, which do not operate in a purely linear way, but also spatially.

Chapter 1 The Ecology of Languages

1 Celso Alvarez Caccamo, 'Da biolingüistica a ecolingüistica: um câmbio de paradigma necessario', *A Trabe de Ouro*, 18 (1994).
2 Salamatou Alhassoumi Sow, 'Grands et petits peuls: représentation et hiérarchisation des différents parlers peuls par les locuteurs de l'ouest du Niger', in Cécile Canut (ed.), *Imaginaires linguistiques en Afrique* (Paris: L'Harmattan, 1998), p. 65.
3 Ibid., p. 67.
4 Ndiassé Thiam, 'Catégorisations de locuteurs et représentations sur le mélange wolof-français à Dakar', in Canut, *Imaginaires linguistiques*.
5 We could devise an equivalent expression of the type 'Dupont English' to designate a Frenchman who prides himself on speaking English but in fact speaks it badly. ['Dupont' is here the 'typical' French surname.]
6 Thiam, 'Catégorisations', pp. 95–6.

7 For the meaning of these two terms, see the following chapter.
8 A journalist from *Libération* in July 1997 followed a group of young people from the Paris region who had gone down to a beach in the Roussillon area, at Argelès, for their holiday, and noted their way of speaking. This example is taken from one of his articles.
9 Louis-Jean Calvet, *Les Voix de la ville: introduction à la sociolinguistique urbaine* (Paris: Payot, 1994).
10 'Beur' is 'Arabe' ['Arab'] in *verlan*, French backwards slang.
11 This example was given me by Denis Vanou, one of my students at the Senghor University in Alexandria.
12 Pieter Muysken, 'Halfway between Quechua and Spanish: the case for relexification', in A. Highfield and A. Valdman (eds), *Historicity and Variation in Creole Studies* (Ann Arbor: Karoma, 1981).
13 See Louis-Jean Calvet, *Linguistique et colonialisme: petit traité de glottophagie* (Paris: Payot, 1974, reprinted 1988).
14 Bernard Spolsky and Robert Cooper, *The Languages of Jerusalem* (Oxford: Oxford University Press, 1991).
15 J. C. Gonzalez Faraco and M. D. Murphy, 'Street names and political regimes in an Andalusian town', *Ethnology*, 36, 2 (Spring 1997).
16 Rabah Kahlouche, 'Les enseignes à Tizi-Ouzou: un lieu de conflit linguistique', in N. Labrie (ed.), *Études récentes en linguistique de contact* (Bonn: Dümmler, 1997).
17 Ibid., p. 177.
18 Ibid., p. 178.
19 Ibid., pp. 181–3.
20 Charles Darwin, *The Origin of Species*, ed. Gillian Beer (Oxford: Oxford University Press, World's Classics, 1996), pp. 77–8.
21 See Louis-Jean Calvet, 'Des mots sur les murs: une comparaison entre Paris et Dakar', in Calvet et al., *Des langues et des villes* (Paris: Didier érudition, 1993); Myriam Dumont, *Les Enseignes de Dakar: un essai de sociolinguistique africaine* (Paris: L'Harmattan, 1998).
22 Stephen Wurm, Peter Mühlhäusler and Darrell Tryon (eds), *Atlas of Languages of International Communication in the Pacific, Asia and the Americas* (Berlin: Mouton de Gruyter, 1996).
23 P. Mühlhäusler, 'Post contact languages in mainland Australia after 1788', in Wurm et al., *Atlas*, pp. 11–16.
24 See Calvet, *Linguistique et colonialisme*.
25 Ibid., p. 11.
26 Rob Amery and Peter Mühlhäusler, 'Pidgin English in New South Wales', in Wurm et al., *Atlas*, pp. 32–52.
27 Peter Mühlhäusler, 'Pidgins and Creoles of Queensland', in Wurm et al., *Atlas*, pp. 69–82.

28 A. Dineen and P. Mühlhäusler, '19th-century language contact in South Australia', in Wurm et al., *Atlas*, pp. 83–99.
29 Peter Mühlhäusler and William McGregor, 'Post contact languages of Western Australia', in Wurm et al., *Atlas*, pp. 101–21.
30 Diana Eades, 'Aboriginal English', in Wurm et al., *Atlas*, pp. 133–41.
31 Mercado Común del Sur, an economic agreement signed in 1994 by Argentina, Brazil, Paraguay and Uruguay, whose official languages are Spanish and Portuguese, with the case of Guarani being left in suspense.
32 Graciela Barrios, 'Minorias lingüisticas e integracion regional: la region fronteriza uruguayo-brasileña', paper given at the Congresso International Politicas Linguisticas para America Latina, Buenos Aires, 26–30 November 1997.
33 Ibid., p. 4.
34 See for example Adolfo Elizaincin, 'Contacto entre lenguas geneticamente emparentadas: el caso del español y del portugués', *Signo & Seña*, 6 (June 1996).
35 For example, L. E. Behares, 'Diglossia escolar en la frontera uruguaya con Brazil: matriz social del bilingüismo', in *Cuadernos de Estudos Linguisticos* (Montevideo: 1984).
36 Graciela Barrios, 'Planificacion lingüistica e integracion regional: el Uruguay y la zona de frontera', in A. M. Trindade and L. E. Behares (eds), *Fronteiras, educação, integração* (Santa Maria: 1996), p. 97.
37 Roland Barthes, *Sade, Fourier, Loyola*, tr. Richard Miller (London: Jonathan Cape, 1977), p. 49.
38 Calvet, *Linguistique et colonialisme*, p. 65.
39 André Martinet, *Des Steppes aux océans: l'indo-européen et les 'indo-européens'* (Paris: Payot, 1986).
40 Eugenio Ramon Lujan Martinez, 'Pragmatics and Indo-European linguistics', *Journal of Pragmatics*, 28, 2 (August 1997).
41 Marija Gimbutas, 'Prehistory of Eastern Europe: Neolithic and Copper Age culture in Russia and the Baltic area', *American School of Prehistoric Research Bulletin no. 20* (Cambridge, Mass.: Harvard University, Peabody Museum, 1956).
42 See Martin Huld, 'Early Indo-European weapons terminology', *Word*, 44, 2 (August 1993), pp. 223–33.
43 Ibid., p. 231.
44 In *Le Langage* (Paris: Gallimard, Encyclopédie de la Pléiade, 1968), p. 1268.
45 See Adrian Parvulescu, 'The Indo-European horse: a linguistic reconstruction', *Word*, 44, 1 (April 1993), 69–75.
46 Marija Gimbutas, 'The Indo-Europeanization of Europe: the intrusion of steppe pastoralists from south Russia and the transformation of Old Europe', *Word*, 44, 2 (August 1993), 219.

47 Didier de Robillard, 'Langues, îles, simplicité, déterminisme, chaos: quelques réflexions fragmentaires sur l'utilisation de l'insularité', in *Plurilinguismes*, 15 (June 1998), 63.
48 This is a typewritten text of 34 pages, 'Experimental creation of a natural language', which, as far as I know, has never been published but was sent to a certain number of linguists in the western world.
49 I will not be discussing these statements here, as they belong to a different set of issues.
50 'Experimental creation of a natural language', p. 5.
51 In July 1998, at a conference at Chuo University, Tokyo, as I was making a presentation on the theme of linguistic ecology, my colleague Florian Coulmas pointed out to me that languages were not living organisms. True: they are variables, sets of practices, in a word, populations.

Chapter 2 The Galaxy of Languages

1 Abraam de Swaan has set out his positions in a certain number of publications, including 'The evolving European language system: a theory of communication potential and language competition', *Revue internationale de science politique*, 14, 3 (July 1993); *Unequal Relationships between Language Groups*, (Amsterdam: Amsterdamse School vor Sociaalwetenschappelijk Ondserzoek, 1995); 'La francophonie en Afrique: une vision de la sociologie et de l'économie politique de la langue', in C. Juillard and L.-J. Calvet, *Les Politiques linguistiques, mythes et réalités* (Beirut: FMA-AUPELF-UREF, 1996).
2 Marianne Gehnen, 'Die Arbeitssprachen in der Kommission der Europäischen Gemeinschaften unter besonderer Berücksichtigung des Französischen', *Sociolinguistica*, 5 (Tübingen: Niemeyer Verlag, 1991).
3 In any case, these figures vary with the age of those questioned, and there is a notable increase in English the younger they are.
4 Louis-Jean Calvet, 'Le bambara: planification linguistique par défaut', in I. Fodor and C. Hagège (eds), *La Réforme des langues*, vol. 1 (Hamburg: Buske Verlag, 1983).
5 See Grant McConnell, 'Analyses et comparaisons des situations de contact en Inde', in Normand Labrie (ed.), *Études récentes en linguistique de contact* (Bonn: Dümmler 1997).
6 See ibid., p. 301.
7 See ibid., p. 315.
8 Gérard Dumestre (ed.), *Stratégies communicatives au Mali: langues régionales, bambara, français* (Paris: Didier érudition, 1994).
9 I am here drawing on a survey carried out among schoolchildren by

Klaudia Dombrosky, and presented in 'La situation socio-linguistique du sud du Mali', in Dumestre, *Stratégies communicatives*.

10 Valentin Vydrine, 'Étude sociolinguistique en pays Khassonké', in Dumestre, *Stratégies communicatives*.

11 I am here drawing on an article by Abdoulaye Barry, 'Étude du plurilinguisme au Mali: le cas de Djenné', in *Boucle du Niger*, vol. 2 (Tokyo: 1990). The calculation of the rate of vehicular language is based on the same principle as in the previous examples.

12 See L.-J. Calvet, 'Les langues des marchés au Mali', in Calvet et al., *Les Langues des marchés en Afrique* (Paris: Didier, 1992).

13 Dumestre, *Stratégies communicatives*, p. 7.

14 See L.-J. Calvet, *Histoire de l'écriture* (Paris: Plon, 1996).

15 Ibid.

Chapter 3 Regulation and Change

1 L.-J. Calvet, *L'Europe et ses langues* (Paris: Plon, 1993).

2 N. Wiener, *Cybernetics or Control and Communication in the Animal and the Machine*, 2nd edition (Cambridge, Mass.: MIT Press, 1961).

3 Henri Frei, *La Grammaire des fautes* (Paris/Geneva: Slatkine, 1929), p. 292.

4 Emanuel Drechsel, *Mobilian Jargon* (Oxford: Clarendon Press, 1997), pp. 334–6.

5 Ibid., p. 339.

6 This is the reason why *solutionner*, for 'to solve', a regular verb but one condemned by certain purists, is replacing *résoudre* ('to solve, resolve'), whose irregular conjugation is difficult to master.

7 See for example François Grin, 'Aménagement linguistique: du bon usage des concepts d'offre et de demande', in Labrie, *Études récentes*.

8 Philippe Martinon, *Comment on parle en français* (Paris: Larousse, 1927), p. 258.

9 Frei, *La Grammaire des fautes*, p. 147.

10 Françoise Gadet, *Le Français populaire* (Paris: PUF, 'Que sais-je?', 1992), p. 70.

11 Robert Chaudenson, Raymond Mougeon and Édouard Beniak, *Vers une approche panlectale de la variation du français* (Paris: Didier érudition, 1993), p. 85.

12 Ibid., pp. 90–1.

13 These details were given to me by Patrice Brasseur.

14 'In languages with conjugated verbs, it is the verbal forms of the third person singular that the child learns first and that he then, in his ignorance, sometimes over-generalizes to other contexts' (Raymond

Mougeon and Édouard Beniak, 'Le français en situation de contact et la variation linguistique: le français parlé en Ontario (Canada)', in *Actes du XVIIe congrès international de linguistique et philologie romanes*, vol. 6 (Aix-en-Provence, Publications de l'Université de Provence, 1986), p. 298).

15 Henri Bauche, *Le Langage populaire* (Paris: Payot, 1920).

16 Auguste Brun, *Le Français de Marseille* (Marseille: Bibliothèque de l'institut historique de Provence, 1931).

17 Frédéric Mistral, *Lou tresor dou Felibrige, ou Dictionnaire provençal-français* (1877) (Aix-en-Provence: Edicioun Ramoun Berenguié, 1968).

18 These details were given me by Lise Pedri.

19 Brun, *Le Français de Marseille*, p. 66.

20 Ibid., pp. 144–5.

21 Patrice Brasseur, 'Créoles à base lexicale française et français marginaux d'Amérique du Nord: quelques points de comparaison', in Marie-Christine Hazaël-Massieux and Didier de Robillard (eds), *Contacts de langues, contacts de cultures, créolisation* (Paris: L'Harmattan, 1997), p. 144.

22 Daniel Defoe, *General History of the Robberies and Murders of the most Notorious Pirates*, first published in London under the pseudonym Captain Charles Johnson (1724); text reproduced in Charles Ellms, *The Pirates Own Book* (New York: Dover, 1993), p. 306.

23 Defoe, *General History*, p. 145.

24 *The Pirates Own Book*, p. 302 (first published 1837).

25 Gilles Lapouge, *Les Pirates* (Paris: Payot, 1991), p. 75.

26 Ibid., p. 80.

27 Ibid., p. 81.

28 José Lenzini, *Barberousse, chemin de proies en Méditerranée* (Arles: Actes Sud, 1995).

29 Edward John Trelawny, *Adventures of a Younger Son*, ed. William St Clair (Oxford: Oxford University Press, 1974), p. 51.

30 Ibid., p. 369.

31 Ibid., p. 99.

32 De las Casas, while respecting the texts, points out that Columbus 'no penetra la significacion de los vocablos de la lengua castellana' – 'does not understand the sense of the words in the Castilian tongue'.

33 Cristóbal Colón, *Textos y documentos completos*, ed. Consuelo Varela and Juan Gil (Madrid: Alianza Universidad, 1982); I have used the 1995 reprint.

34 Claire Blanche-Benveniste and André Valli, 'Les langues de Christophe Colomb', in *L'Intercompréhension: le cas des langues romanes* (Paris: CLE, 1997), pp. 54–8.

35 Menéndez Pidal, in *Bulletin hispanique*, LXII, 1940; reprinted in *La lengua de Cristóbal Colón, el estilo de santa Teresa y otros estudios* (Madrid: Espasa-Calpe, 1942).
36 Ibid., p. 13.
37 Cristóbal Colón, *Textos*, p. 31.
38 Ibid., p. 14.
39 Marianne Mahn-Lot, 'Colomb (Christophe)' in *Encyclopedia universalis* (Paris), vol. 6, p. 105.
40 Pidal, *Lengua de Cristóbal Colón*, p. 15.
41 Gil, in Cristóbal Colón, *Textos*, p. 431.
42 Pidal, *Lengua de Cristóbal Colón*, p. 12.
43 Ibid., p. 56.
44 Language of the Franks, i.e. 'the French', an expression that may have been calqued on the Arabic *lisan al-faranq*.
45 Much earlier, in the opinion of some scholars: 'The lingua franca in this wider sense stems from as early as the ninth century, but became established firmly in the eleventh century when the Crusaders roamed far and wide in the Levant' (Max Adler, *Pidgins, Creoles and Lingua Francas: A Sociolinguistic Study* (Hamburg: Helmut Buske Verlag, 1977), p. 105).
46 Keith Whinnom, 'The context and origins of lingua franca', in Jürgen Meisel (ed.), *Langues en contact: Pidgins-Créoles* (Tübingen: TBL Verlag Gunter Narr, 1977), p. 17.
47 Hugo Schuchardt, 'On lingua franca', in *The Ethnography of Variation: Selected Writings on Pidgins and Creoles* (Ann Arbor: Karoma, 1979), p. 26; originally published as 'Die Lingua Franca' in 1909.
48 Ibid., p. 35.
49 F. Diego de Haedo, *Topografia e historia general de Argel* (Valladolid: 1612), quoted by Schuchardt in *Ethnography*.
50 Cf. Laurent d'Arvieux, *Mémoires du chevalier d'Arvieux* (Paris: 1735).
51 Salvatore Santoro, 'Lingua franca in Goldoni's *Impresario delle Smirne'*, *Journal of Pidgin and Creole Languages*, 11, 1 (1996), 89.
52 Louis-Léon-César Faidherbe, 'L'Alliance française pour la propagation de la langue française dans les colonies et les pays étrangers', *Revue scientifique*, 3rd series, 7 (1884).
53 Paul Siblot, 'Mise en texte de la pluriglossie dans la littérature coloniale', *Cahiers de praxématique*, 5 (1985), 106.
54 Robert Hall Jr, *Pidgin and Creole Languages* (New York: Cornell University Press, 1966).
55 Whinnom, 'Lingua franca'.
56 Santoro, 'Lingua franca', p. 89.
57 Ibid., p. 93.

58 Pierre Dan, *Histoire de la barbarie et de ses corsaires* (Paris: Racolet, 1637), quoted by Schuchardt in *Ethnography*, p. 38.
59 Olfert Dapper, *Umbständliche und eigentliche Beschreibung von Africa, und denen darzu gehörigen Königreichen und Landschaften* (Amsterdam: J. Van Meurs, 1670), quoted by Schuchardt in *Ethnography*, p. 39.
60 In addition there are, on the symbolic level, the formulas of greeting, but all of this does not add up to a language.
61 R. Arveiller, *Contribution à l'étude des termes de voyage en français (1505–1722)* (Paris: d'Artrey, 1963), p. 52.
62 Robert Chaudenson, *Le Lexique du parler créole de la Réunion* (Paris: Honoré Champion, 1974), vol. I, pp. 591–2.
63 J.-B. Labat, *Nouvelle Relation de l'Afrique occidentale* (Paris: 1728), quoted by Chaudenson in *Le Lexique du parler créole*.
64 Quoted by Whinnom, 'Lingua franca', p. 13.
65 J. Blondé, P. Dumont and D. Gontier, *Lexique du français du Sénégal* (Dakar: NEA-Edicef, 1979) [i.e. *Lexicon of the French of Senegal*].
66 Équipe IFA, *Inventaire des particularités du français en Afrique noire* (Paris: AUPELF, 1983).
67 Marie-Louise Moreau, Ndiassé Thiam and Cécile Bauvois, 'Le marquage identitaire dans le français d'Afrique: étude exploratoire au Sénégal', in L.-J. Calvet and M.-L. Moreau (eds), *Une ou des normes? Insécurité linguistique et normes endogènes en Afrique* (Paris: CIRELFA, Agence de la Francophonie, Didier érudition, 1998).
68 See for example L.-J. Calvet, *Les Voix de la ville*.
69 G. Manessy, 'Créolisation et français régionaux', in P. Wald and G. Manessy, *Plurilinguismes, normes, situations, stratégies* (Paris: L'Harmattan, 1979), pp. 16, 21.
70 Ibid., p. 22.
71 G. Manessy, 'L'évolution du français d'Afrique et la formation des créoles français', in *Présence francophone*, 27 (1985).
72 G. Manessy, 'Pratique du français en Afrique noire francophone', in *Langue française*, 104 (December 1994), 15.
73 G. Manessy, 'Créolisation et créolité', *Études créoles*, 10, 2 (1987); reprinted in *Créoles, pidgins, variétés véhiculaires* (Paris: CNRS, 1995), p. 212.
74 I will merely cite, for the specialist reader, the contrast between aspects, serial verbs, etc.
75 G. Manessy, 'De la subversion des langues importées: le français en Afrique noire', in R. Chaudenson and D. de Robillard (eds), *Langues et développement* (Paris: Didier érudition, 1989), pp. 133–45.
76 Auguste Moussirou-Mouyama, 'Norme officielle du français et normes endogènes au Gabon', in Calvet and Moreau, *Une ou des normes?*

77 Didier Goyvaerts, 'Indoubil: a Swahili hybrid in Bukavu (with comments on Indoubil by K. Kabongo-Mianda)', *Language in Society*, 17, 2 (1988), p. 238.
78 Ibid., p. 232.
79 Didier Goyvaerts, 'Kibalele: form and function of a secret language in Bukavu (Zaire)', *Journal of Pragmatics*, 25, 1 (1996), p. 140.
80 Gisèle Prignitz, 'Rôle de l'argot dans la variation et l'appropriation: le cas du français au Burkina-Faso', *Langue française*, 104 (1994).
81 In Foued Laroussi (ed.), *Plurilinguisme et identités au Maghreb* (Rouen: Publications de l'Université de Rouen, 1997), p. 31.
82 G. Manessy, 'Modalités d'appropriation d'une langue seconde (français d'Afrique et créoles français)', in Daniel Véronique (ed.), *Créolisation et acquisition des langues* (Aix-en-Provence: Publications de l'Université de Provence, 1994), p. 222.
83 Salikoko Mufwene, 'New Englishes and criteria for naming them', *World Englishes*, 13, 1 (1994).

Chapter 4 Lingustic Representations and Change

1 See W. Lambert et al., 'Evaluational reactions to spoken language', *Journal of Abnormal and Social Psychology*, 60 (1960); W. Lambert et al., 'Judging personality through speech: a French-Canadian example', *The Journal of Communication*, 16 (1966).
2 W. Cheyne, 'Stereotyped reactions to speakers with Scottish and English regional accents', *British Journal of Social and Clinical Psychology*, 9 (1970).
3 Ivan Kalman, Zhong Yong and Xiao Hong, 'Language attitudes in Guangzhou, China', *Language in Society*, 16, 4 (1987).
4 Vivian de Klerk and Barbara Bosch, 'Linguistic stereotypes: nice accent – nice person?', *International Journal of the Sociology of Language*, 116 (1995), 17–37.
5 131 spoke English, 69 Afrikaans, 73 Xhosa and 26 two or more of these languages.
6 Klerk and Bosch, 'Linguistic stereotypes', p. 35.
7 Einar Haugen, 'Schizoglossia and the linguistic norm', *Georgetown University Monographic Series on Language and Linguistics*, 15 (1962).
8 Labov, *Sociolinguistic Patterns* (Oxford: Blackwell, 1978), p. 117.
9 Ibid., p. 133.
10 Alain Rey, 'Usages, jugements et prescriptions linguistiques', *Langue française*, 16 (December 1972).
11 Ibid., p. 5.

12 Essentially 'The social motivation of a sound change', *Word*, 19 (1963), 273–309 (his first work on Martha's Vineyard) and *The Social Stratification of English in New York City* (Washington: Centre for Applied Linguistics, 1966); his work on the 'inner city' (*Language in the Inner City: Studies in the Black English Vernacular*) was published in 1972 (Philadelphia: University of Philadelphia Press).
13 Rey, 'Usages', p. 14.
14 Ibid., p. 16.
15 J.-B. Marcellesi and B. Gardin, *Introduction à la sociolinguistique* (Paris: Larousse, 1974), pp. 137–8.
16 Pierre Bourdieu, *Language and Symbolic Power*, ed. and intro. John B. Thompson, tr. Gino Raymond and Matthew Adamson (Cambridge: Polity, 1991), p. 52.
17 Anne-Marie Houdebine, 'Pour une linguistique synchronique dynamique', *La Linguistique*, 21 (1985).
18 Ibid., p. 7.
19 Ibid., p. 17.
20 Cécile Canut, 'Dynamique et imaginaire linguistiques dans les sociétés à tradition orale: le cas du Mali', unpublished dissertation supervised by Anne-Marie Houdebine, Université de Paris III, 1995, pp. 708, 41–2.
21 Anne-Marie Houdebine, 'L'imaginaire linguistique et son analyse', *Travaux de linguistique*, 7 (May 1996), 17.
22 Anne-Marie Houdebine, 'Imaginaire linguistique', in Marie-Louise Moreau (ed.), *Sociolinguistique, concepts de base* (Sprimont: Mardaga, 1997), p. 65.
23 Cécile Canut, 'Acquisition, production et imaginaire linguistiques des familles plurilingues à Bamako (Mali)', *Travaux de linguistique*, 7 (May 1996), 43.
24 Houdebine, 'L'imaginaire linguistique et son analyse', p. 15.
25 Houdebine, 'Imaginaire linguistique', pp. 165–6.
26 Dominique Lafontaine, 'Attitudes linguistiques', in Moreau, *Sociolinguistique*, pp. 56–7.
27 Nicole Gueunier, 'Représentations linguistiques', in Moreau, *Sociolinguistique*, pp. 247–8.
28 M.-L. Moreau, 'Norme', in *Sociolinguistique*, p. 222.
29 Rosaleen Howard-Malverde, 'Pachamama is a Spanish word: linguistic tension between Aymara, Quechua and Spanish Northern Potosi (Bolivia)', *Anthropological Linguistics*, 37, 2 (1995), 141–68.
30 Michel Francard, 'L'insécurité en communauté française de Belgique', *Français et Société*, 6 (April 1993), 13.
31 Ibid., p. 19.
32 Labov, *Sociolinguistic Patterns*, p. 132.

33 Louis-Jean Calvet, 'Les "Edwiniens" et leurs langues: sentiments et attitudes linguistiques dans une communauté créolophone blanche de Louisiane', *Revue québécoise de linguistique théorique et appliqué*, 13, 1 (1996).
34 Cécile Canut and Boniface Keita, 'Dynamique linguistique en zone mandingue: attitudes et comportements', in Dumestre, *Stratégies communicatives*.
35 This is all summarized in tabular form in Canut, 'Dynamique et imaginaire linguistiques', p. 59.
36 L.-J. Calvet, 'Une ou deux langues? Ou le rôle des représentations dans l'évaluation des situations linguistiques', *Études créoles*, XIX, 2 (1996).
37 This problem does not arise for Serb alone, of course; we can also mention, at random, Czech and Slovak, Hindi and Urdu, Moldavian and Romanian, etc.
38 Cf. Calvet, *Linguistique et colonialisme*.
39 Antoine Meillet, *Les Langues dans l'Europe nouvelle* (Paris: Payot, 1928).
40 See Louis-Jean Calvet, 'Antoine Meillet, la politique linguistique et l'Europe: les mains sales', in *Plurilinguismes*, 5 (1993).
41 I have described this situation at length in *Les Voix de la ville*.
42 Amidou Maïga, 'Pratiques et représentations linguistiques des locuteurs du songhay au Mali', unpublished dissertation, Université de Paris V, 1998.
43 Cf. Maurice Delafosse, *Haut-Sénégal Niger* (Paris: 1912), vol. 1, p. 117.
44 Tullio de Mauro, *Une introduction à la sémantique* (Paris: Payot, 1969), p. 48.
45 In fact, I was focusing on practices concerning the order in which languages are acquired, as described by speakers themselves – but this is another problem, of a methodological nature.
46 Canut and Keita, 'Dynamique linguistique'.
47 Ibid., p. 90.
48 We can postulate that this length is in fact due to the omission of an intervocalic consonant. It is not my purpose to develop this hypothesis here, but several examples support it: thus *baa*, a term of respect for men, seems to come from *baba*, 'father'; *dooni*, 'a little' from *dogoni*, a diminutive of *dogo*, 'little'; *kale*, 'distaff' from *kala*, 'rod', while *lahiya*, 'a sheep sacrificed for a feast' alternates with *laaya* (same meaning), and *kaafiri* with *kafiri* ('pagan'), etc.
49 Maurice Delafosse, *La Langue mandingue et ses dialectes* (Paris: P. Geuthner, 1929).
50 Canut and Keita, 'Dynamique linguistique', p. 132.
51 Ibid., p. 137.
52 Bourdieu, *Language and Symbolic Power*, p. 226.

53 Fabrice Hauchecorne and Rodney Ball, 'L'accent du Havre: un exemple de mythe linguistique', *Langage et Société*, 82 (December 1997), p. 23.
54 Ibid., p. 24.

Chapter 5 Transmission and Change

1 Notes taken by Riedlingerdu from the first course given by Saussure, *Ferdinand de Saussure: cours de linguistique générale*, ed. Eisuke Komatsu (Tokyo: Gakushuin University, 1993), p. 13.
2 It was probably A. Schleicher who, in his *Compendium der vergleichenden Grammatik der indogermanischen Sprachen* (1861–62), was the first to utilize the image of the genealogical tree of languages, echoing that of the genealogical tree of species.
3 Here, and in the following lines, I am following the data published and discussed at greater length in Louis-Jean Calvet, *Language Wars and Linguistic Politics*, tr. Michel Petheram (Oxford: Oxford University Press, 1998), ch. 6.
4 Klaudia Dombrowsky, 'La situation socio-linguistique', p. 26.
5 The following data come from a preliminary survey carried out in February/March 1998 in Libreville with students and researchers from the École normale supérieure de Libreville.
6 See François Héran, 'L'unification linguistique de la France', *Population et Société*, 285 (December 1993).
7 Fabienne Leconte, *La Famille et les langues* (Paris: L'Harmattan, 1997).
8 Ningsheng Xia, 'Maintenance of the Chinese language in the United States', *Bilingual Review/Revista Bilingüe* (Arizona State University), 17, 3 (1992).
9 Ibid., p. 202.
10 On this point, see for instance Dan Munteaunu, *El Papiamento: lengua criolla hispanica* (Madrid: Gredos, 1996).
11 Cf. Lia Varela, 'Interventions sur la langue et construction de l'État argentin (1830–1880)', DEA dissertation, Université de Provence, 1999.
12 Angel Rosenblat, 'Bases des Español en America: nivel social y cultural de los conquistadores y pobladores', in *Actas de la primera reunion latinoamericana de linguistica y filologia* (Bogota: 1973), p. 371.
13 Varela, 'Interventions'.
14 In other words, an Italian dialect.
15 Maria Beatriz Fontanella de Weinberg, 'Contacto lingüistico: lenguas inmigratorias' *Signo & Seña*, 6 (June 1996), 442–3.
16 Similar situations are found in Africa; see L.-J. Calvet and M. Dreyfus, 'La famille dans l'espace urbain: trois modèles de plurilinguisme', *Plurilinguismes*, 3 (January 1992).

17 Carmen Bertrand, *Histoire de Buenos Aires* (Paris: Fayard, 1997), pp. 218–19.
18 Beatriz R. Lavandera, *Variacion y significado* (Buenos Aires: Hachette, 1984), p. 61.
19 Giovanni Meo Zilio, 'Influenze dello spagnolo sull'italiano parlato nel Rio de la Plata', *Lingua Nostra*, 16, 1 (1955), 16.
20 Giovanni Meo Zilio, 'Contaminazioni morfologiche nel cocoliche rioplatense', *Lingua Nostra*, 16, 3 (1955), 112.
21 L. Segovia, *Diccionario de argentinismos* (Buenos Aires: Coni, 1911). I am grateful to Lia Varela for this reference.
22 Ibid., p. 64.
23 Ibid., p. 70.
24 Ibid., pp. 74–5.
25 Maria Beatriz Fontanella de Weinberg, *El español bonaerense* (Buenos Aires: Hachette, 1987), p. 138.
26 Meo Zilio points out for example that in the La Boca district in Buenos Aires, people speak a Cocoliche 'of a Genoan kind'.
27 Fontanella de Weinberg, *El español bonaerense*, p. 141.
28 Christine Deprez, *Les Enfants bilingues: langues et familles* (Paris: Didier, 1994), p. 81.
29 Giovanni Meo Zilio, 'El Cocoliche rioplatense', in *Boletin de filologia* (1963), 14, quoted by Fontanella de Weinberg.
30 Fontanella de Weinberg, 'Contacto linguistico', p. 449.
31 Rosalba Campra, *Como con bronca y junando . . . La retorica del tango* (Buenos Aires: Edicial, 1996), pp. 9–10.
32 'Woman who has abandoned me/in the bloom of my life/leaving my soul wounded/and thorns in my heart.'
33 Robert Chaudenson, *Les Créoles* (Paris: PUF, 'Que sais-je?', 1995), p. 17.
34 Kees Versteegh, 'Levelling in the Sudan: from Arabic creole to Arabic dialect', *International Journal of the Sociology of Language*, 99 (1993); Catherine Miller, 'Restructuration morpho-syntaxique en juba-arabic et ki-nubi: à propos du débat universaux/substrat et superstrat dans les études créoles', in *Matériaux arabes et sudarabiques* (Paris: Paul Geuthner, 1993).
35 Versteegh, 'Levelling in the Sudan', p. 72.
36 Miller, 'Restructuration', p. 141.
37 Mauro Tosco, 'A pidgin verbal system: the case of Juba Arabic', *Anthropological Linguistics*, 37, 4 (Winter 1995), p. 423.
38 Jonathan Owens, 'Nubi genetic linguistics and language classification', *Anthropological Linguistics*, 33, 1 (Spring 1991); 'Arabic-based pidgins and creoles', in Sarah Thompson (ed.), *Contact Languages: A Wider Perspective* (Amsterdam/Philadelphia: Benjamins, 1996).

39 See, for example, William Samarin, 'The origins of Kituba and Lingala', *Journal of African Languages and Linguistics*, 12 (1990–91); 'Official language: the case of Lingala', in Ulrich Ammon (ed.), *Status and Function of Languages and Language Varieties* (Berlin and New York: Walter de Gruyter, 1989); 'Colonization and pidginization on the Ubangi River', *Journal of African Languages and Linguistics*, 4 (1982).
40 See Chaudenson, *Les Créoles*, pp. 68–71.
41 César de Rochefort, *Histoire naturelle et morale des îles Antilles de l'Amérique* (Rotterdam: 1658), p. 392. In the examples he gives, the most striking is *mouche*, 'much', from the Spanish *mucho*: *Moy mouche lunes*, 'I am old'.
42 Miller, 'Restructuration'.
43 At this point I would like to recount a personal anecdote – though one which may have a more general value, being endlessly reproducible. In September 1998, during a conference in Rabat (Morocco), I was present at the attempt at communication (which I had encouraged) between a Lebanese woman and an Algerian man, each of then speaking his or her native language, Lebanese Arabic and Algerian Arabic. The result outstripped my expectations: they did not understand each other.
44 See, for example, Alain Kihm, 'Qu'est-ce qu'une théorie rationnelle de la formation des langues créoles?' and Claire Lefebvre and John Lumsden, 'Le rôle central de la relexification dans la genèse des langues créoles', *Plurilinguismes*, 8 (1994). This last article includes an appendix of some ten pages, 'Liste des travaux publiés dans le cadre du projet *La Genèse du créole haïtien*'.
45 Derek Bickerton, *Roots of Language* (Ann Arbor: Karoma, 1981).
46 I have taken this expression from Claude Hagège.
47 See, for example, Daniel Véronique (ed.), *Créolisation et acquisition des langues* (Aix-en-Provence: Publications de l'Université de Provence, 1994).
48 From the Greek *alleles*, marking reciprocity, and *morphos*, form.
49 Robert Chaudenson, 'Créolisation et appropriation linguistique: de la théorie aux exemples', in Véronique, *Créolisation*.
50 Ibid., pp. 186–7.
51 See the *Inventaire des particularités lexicales du français en Afrique noire*, (Paris: AUPELF/ACCT, 1983).
52 Salikoko Mufwene, 'La fonction et les formes réfléchies dans le mauricien et le haïtien', *Langages*, 138 (2000).
53 Chaudenson, *Les Créoles*, p. 72.
54 John McWhorter, 'The scarcity of Spanish-based creoles explained', *Language in Society*, 24, 2 (1995).
55 See for example Mena Lafkioui, 'Les berbères et leur langue: les cas des

immigrés berbères en Belgique', in Cécile Canut (ed.), *Imaginaires linguistiques en Afrique* (Paris: L'Harmattan, 1998).

56 Gisela Bruche-Shulz, ' "Fuzzy" Chinese: the status of Cantonese in Hong Kong', *Journal of Pragmatics*, 2, 2 (1997), p. 296.

57 Peter Nelde, 'Identity among bilinguals: an ecolinguistic approach', paper presented at I Simposio Internacional sobre o Bilingüismo, Vigo, 21–5 October 1997.

58 On this point, see Louis-Jean Calvet, *Les Politiques linguistiques* (Paris: PUF, 1996).

Chapter 6 Five Case Studies

1 Haugen, 'Schizoglossia', pp. 65 and 69.

2 Dalila Morsly, 'Attitudes et représentations linguistiques', *La Linguistique*, 6, 3 (1990), p. 82.

3 Catherine Miller, 'Contacts de langues: à propos des dialectes arabes', *Paroles*, 7 (Cairo: 1995), p. 77.

4 See for example Djamel-Eddine Kouloughli, 'Sur quelques approches de la réalité sociolinguistique arabe', *Égypte/monde arabe*, 27–8 (Cairo: CEDEJ, 1996).

5 See Alan Kayes, 'Formal vs informal in Arabic: diglossia, triglossia, tetraglossia, etc.: polyglossia-multiglossia viewed as a continuum', *Zeitschrift für arabische Linguistik*, 27 (1994).

6 Here is an anecdote. A few years ago, during a seminar I gave in Algeria, I was developing the idea that all languages were destined to disappear by transformation: I'd mentioned English and French and as I started to mention Arabic, a furious student stood up and told me, 'Monsieur, the language of God cannot die'. My answer – 'unless God so wills' – left him greatly perplexed.

7 This attempted typology owes a great deal to my discussions with Pierre Larcher and his seminar on Arabic sociolinguistics that I followed in autumn 1998. I am of course solely responsible for any errors that may be found here.

8 For some people (Charles Ferguson, 'The Arabic Koinè', *Language*, 35, 4 (1959)) this was a military-urban koine, for others (Kees Versteegh, *Pidginization and Creolization* (Amsterdan: Benjamins, 1984)) a pidgin/creole, but this debate is of little relevance here.

9 Kayes, 'Formal vs informal in Arabic'.

10 The majority of Muslims would reject this classification: 'classical' Arabic is not dead since it is sometimes used. Let's say, to stay within the same metaphor, that it is a language being kept alive 'on a drip'.

11 Mohamed Benrabah, 'L'arabe algérien véhicule de la modernité', *Cahiers de linguistique sociale*, 22 (Rouen: 1993), p. 37.
12 Mohamed Benrabah, 'La langue perdue', *Esprit* (Paris: January 1995), p. 45.
13 Benrabah, 'L'arabe algérien'.
14 The title of the original paper was indeed 'Ce que parler veut dire' – 'What talking means'. This paper was first given in October 1977 at the Congress of the Association française des enseignants de français (AFEF), published in March 1978 in the review *Le Français aujourd'hui* and reprinted in 1984 in Pierre Bourdieu, *Questions de sociologie* (Paris: Minuit) (English version: *Sociology in Question*, tr. Richard Nice (London: Sage, 1993)). Meanwhile, Bourdieu had used the title of his paper for his book *Ce que parler veut dire* (Paris: Fayard, 1982): most of its contents were published in English as *Language and Symbolic Power* (Cambridge: Polity, 1991).
15 Bourdieu, *Sociology in Question*, p. 66.
16 Ibid., p. 70.
17 Bourdieu, *Language and Symbolic Power*, p. 45.
18 This is the title of one of the chapters in Bourdieu's *Language and Symbolic Power*.
19 Niloofar Haeri, 'The reproduction of symbolic capital: language and class in Egypt', *Current Anthropology*, 38, 5 (December 1997), 799.
20 This is increasingly true, in fact, especially in Morocco, where we are starting to see a conflict between French-speaking and English-speaking elites.
21 Haeri, 'The reproduction of symbolic capital', p. 802.
22 Gilbert Grandguillaume, 'Le multilinguisme dans le cadre national au Maghreb', in Foued Laroussi (ed.), *Plurilinguisme et identités au Maghreb* (Rouen: Publications de l'Université de Rouen, 1997), p. 17.
23 *Mutatis mutandis*, this practice is similar to that of Saddam Hussein in the Gulf War when he added to the Iraqi flag the formula *allahu akbar*, 'God is great'.
24 My Arabist colleague Pierre Larcher has pointed out to me that he already has several examples of this situation, especially from the press.
25 L.-J. Calvet, 'Le bambara'.
26 *Les Langues dans le monde ancient et moderne: Afrique subsaharienne, pidgins et créoles*, ed. Jean Parrot (Paris: CNRS, 1981).
27 Ibid., p. 407.
28 Ibid., p. 413.
29 Ibid., p. 413.
30 Ibid., p. 364.
31 Ibid., p. 641.

32 Salikoko Mufwene, 'Kituba', in Thompson, *Contact Languages*, pp. 173–208.
33 However, he leaves some of them out, such as Fiot (see above), or Kimbulu Mbulu, 'language of the militia' (François Lumwamu, personal communication, 1980).
34 Mufwene, 'Kituba', p. 176.
35 Harold Fehderau, 'The origin and development of Kituba', Ph.D. dissert., Cornell University, Ithaca, NY, 1966.
36 Samarin, 'The origins of Kituba and Lingala', p. 53.
37 Ibid., p. 56.
38 See Louis-Jean Calvet, *Les Langues véhiculaires* (Paris: PUF, 1981).
39 Mufwene, 'Métissage', p. 183.
40 Joseph Verguin, 'La situation linguistique du monde contemporain', in A. Martinet (ed.), *Le Langage* (Paris: Gallimard, 1968), p. 1138.
41 Quoted by Paul Garde in *Vie et mort de la Yougoslavie* (Paris: Fayard, 1992), p. 127.
42 More recently, Paul Garde – 'Langue et nation: le cas serbe, croate, bosniaque', *Cahiers de l'ILSL*, 8 (1996) – proposes a more subtle division into four dialects (he adds Torlak) and three sub-dialects of Shtokavian. But this does not change my views here.
43 Garde, *Vie et mort*, p. 129.
44 Meaning 'to inform quickly'.
45 Meaning 'an object that calculates', 'a calculator'.
46 Garde, *Vie et mort*, p. 133.
47 Jasna Levinger, 'Language war – war language', *Language Sciences*, 16, 2 (1994), pp. 229–36.
48 R. Bugarski, 'The social basis of language conflict and language attitudes', in P.-H. Nelde (ed.), *Language Attitudes and Language Conflict* (Bonn: Dümmler, 1990), pp. 44–5.
49 R. Bugarski, 'Language: internal conflict and language dissolution', in W. Wölck and A. de Houver (eds), *Recent Studies in Contact Linguistics* (Bonn: Dümmler, 1997), p. 32. [In this and the previous quotation, being unable to access the original English-language articles, I have summarized Calvet's quotation.]
50 D. Skiljan, 'La langue entre symboles et signes: le cas serbo-croate', *Cahiers de l'ILSL*, 8 (1996), p. 327.
51 I was an invited professor at Tulane University (New Orleans) and I would do fieldwork here every Sunday with two students (Julia Brehm, Claire Lebas) and a colleague (Thomas Klingler). A more detailed presentation of this community can be found in Calvet, 'Les "Edwiniens"', pp. 9–50.
52 Ingrid Neumann, *Le Créole de Bréaux-Bridge, Louisiane* (Hamburg: Helmut Buske Verlag, 1985).

53 Thomas Klingler, 'A descriptive study of the creole speech of Pointe Coupée Parish, Louisiana, with focus on the lexicon', unpublished Ph.D. dissertation (Ann Arbor: University Microfilm International, 1992).

54 [The author's original French here transcribed the responses of his informers into more standard French: a phonetic transcription of this corpus can be found in Calvet, 'Les "Edwiniens"'.]

55 Neumann, *La Créole de Bréaux-Bridge*, p. 232.

56 Klingler, 'A descriptive study', p. 171.

57 T. Klingler, 'Norme, tourisme et étiolement linguistique chez les créolophones en Louisiane', *Cahiers de l'Institut de linguistique de Louvain*, 20, 1–2 (1994), 127.

58 The data presented below were gathered during fieldwork carried out with Robert Chaudenson in April–May 1996 (see Calvet and Chaudenson, *Saint-Barthélemy: une énigme linguistique?* (Paris: Agence de la Francophonie–ACCT, 1998)).

59 Jean Benoist, 'Du social au biologique: étude de quelques interactions', *L'homme*, VI (1966).

60 Jean Benoist, 'Saint-Barthélemy: physical anthropology of an isolate', *American Journal of Physical Anthropology*, XXII, 4 (1964).

61 We of course need to add to these two languages ('patois' and 'creole') the standard French that is the language of administration, education, etc.

62 A. R. Highfield, *The French Dialect of St Thomas, US Virgin Islands* (Ann Arbor: Karoma, 1979).

63 Charles Darwin, *The Voyage of the 'Beagle'*, (London: Penguin, 1989), pp. 268–90.

64 Darwin, *Origin of Species*, p. 324.

65 Details of the answers to the questionnaire as a whole and their statistical treatment can be found in Calvet and Chaudenson, *Saint-Barthélemy*.

66 In this table I am reporting only the three main reponses (French, creole and patois), leaving out the various minority responses (creole and French, French and patois, etc.). The total of percentages is thus less than 100.

67 Didier de Robillard, 'Le concept d'insécurité linguistique: à la recherche d'un mode d'emploi', in C. Bavoux (ed.), *Français régionaux et insécurité linguistique* (Paris: L'Harmattan, 1996), pp. 69–70.

68 Aude Bretegnier, 'L'insécurité linguistique: objet insécurisé? Essai de synthèse et de perspectives', in Didier de Robillard and M. Beniamino (eds), *Le Français dans l'espace francophone*, vol. 2 (Paris: Champion, 1996).

Conclusion Inventing Language, Giving it a Name

1 W. Bleek, *A Comparative Grammar of South African Languages* (London and Cape Town: Trübner, 1862).
2 F. Lacroix, 'Les langues bantu', in *Les Langues dans le monde ancien et moderne, Afrique subsaharienne, pidgins et créoles* (Paris: CNRS, 1981), p. 353.
3 One exception should however be noted: Chaudenson, *Les Créoles*, pp. 30–1.
4 I mean they spoke what I. Neumann and T. Klingler described respectively in Bréaux-Bridge and Pointe Coupée.
5 Pierre Achard, 'Quelques propositions naïves sur le langage et la linguistique', *Langage et Société*, supplement to no. 1 (Paris: 1978).
6 G. Williams, *Sociolinguistics: A Sociological Critique* (London: Routledge, 1992), p. viii.

Bibliography

Achard, Pierre, 'Quelques propositions naïves sur le langage et la linguistique', *Langage et société*, supplement to no. 1 (1978).

Adler, Max, *Pidgins, Creoles and Lingua Francas: A Sociolinguistic Study* (Hamburg: Helmut Buske Verlag, 1977).

Alvarez Caccamo, Celso, 'Da biolingüistica a ecolingüistica: um câmbio da paradigma necessario', *A Trabe de Ouro*, 18 (1994).

Amery, Rob, and Peter Mühlhäusler, 'Pidgin English in New South Wales', in Stephen Wurm, Peter Mühlhäusler and Darrell Tryon (eds), *Atlas of International Communication in the Pacific, Asia and the Americas* (Berlin: Mouton de Gruyter, 1996).

Arveiller, Raymond, *Contribution à l'étude des terms de voyage en français (1505–1722)* (Paris: d'Artrey, 1963).

Arvieux, Laurent d', *Mémoires du chevalier d'Arvieux* (Paris: 1735).

Auzanneau, Michelle, 'Paroles de marché', *La Linguistique*, 31, 2 (1995).

Baggioni, Daniel, 'La notion d'insécurité linguistique chez Labov et la sociolinguistique co-variationniste et ses précurseurs littéraires', in Claude Bavoux (ed.), *Français régionaux et insécurité linguistique* (Paris: L'Harmattan, 1996).

Barrios, Graciela, 'Planificacion lingüistica e integracion regional: el Uruguay y la zona de frontera', in Aldema Menine Trindade and Luis Ernesto Behares (eds), *Fronteiras, educação, integração* (Santa Maria: 1996).

—— 'Minorias lingüisticas e integracion regional: la region fronteriza uruguayo-brasileña', paper given at the Congresso International Politicas Linguisticas para America Latina, Buenos Aires, 26–30 November 1997.

Barry, Abdoulaye, 'Étude du plurilinguisme au Mali: le cas de Djenné', in *Boucle du Niger*, vol. 2 (Tokyo: 1990).

Barthes, Roland, *Sade, Fourier, Loyola*, tr. Richard Miller (London: Jonathan Cape, 1977).

Bastardas i Boada, Albert, *Ecologia de les llenguës: medi, contactes i dinamica sociolinguistica* (Barcelona: Proa, 1996).

Bauche, Henri, *Le Langage populaire* (Paris: Payot, 1920).

Behares, L. E., 'Diglossia escolar en la frontera uruguaya con Brazil: matriz social del bilingüismo', in *Cuadernos de Estudos Linguisticos* (Montevideo: 1984).

Benoist, Jean, 'Saint-Barthélemy: physical anthropology of an isolate', *American Journal of Physical Anthropology*, XXII, 4 (1964).

—— 'Du social au biologique: étude de quelques interactions', *L'homme*, VI (1966).

Benrabah, Mohamed, 'L'arabe algérien véhicule de la modernité', *Cahiers de linguistique sociale*, 22 (1993).

—— 'La langue perdue', *Esprit* (January 1995).

Bertrand, Carmen, *Histoire de Buenos Aires* (Paris: Fayard, 1997).

Bickerton, Derek, *Roots of Language* (Ann Arbor: Karoma, 1981).

—— 'Experimental creation of a natural language', MS.

Blanche-Benveniste, Claire, and André Valli, 'Les langues de Christophe Colomb', in *L'Intercompréhension: le cas des langues romanes* (Paris: CLE, 1997).

Bleek, W., *A Comparative Grammar of South African Languages* (London/ Cape Town: Trübner, 1862).

Blondé, J., P. Dumont and D. Gontier, *Lexique du français du Sénégal* (Dakar: NEA-Edicef, 1979).

Bourdieu, Pierre, *Ce que parler veut dire* (Paris: Fayard, 1982).

—— *Language and Symbolic Power*, ed. and intro. John B. Thompson, tr. Gino Raymond and Matthew Adamson (Cambridge: Polity, 1991).

—— *Sociology in Question*, tr. Richard Nice (London: Sage, 1993).

Brann, Conrad, 'Réflexions sur la langue franque (lingua franca): origine et actualité', in *La Linguistique*, 30, 1 (1994).

Brasseur, Patrice, 'Créoles à base lexicale française et français marginaux d'Amérique du Nord: quelques points de comparaison', in Marie-Christine Hazaël-Massieux and Didier de Robillard (eds), *Contacts de langues, contacts de cultures, créolisation* (Paris: L'Harmattan, 1997).

Bretegnier, Aude, 'Le français régional de la Réunion: variété linguistique de rencontre ou d'exclusion?' paper given at the Congrès international d'études créoles, Pointe-à-Pitre, May 1996.

—— 'L'insécurité linguistique: objet insécurisé? Essai de synthèse et de perspectives', in Didier de Robillard and Michel Beniamino (eds), *Le Français dans l'espace francophone*, vol. 2 (Paris: Champion, 1996).

Bruche-Shulz, Gisela, ' "Fuzzy" Chinese: the status of Cantonese in Hong Kong', *Journal of Pragmatics*, 2, 2 (1997).

Brun, Auguste, *Le Français de Marseille* (Marseille: Bibliothèque de l'institut historique de Provence, 1931).

Bugarski, R., 'The social basis of language conflict and language attitudes', in P.-H. Nelde (ed.), *Language Attitudes and Language Conflict* (Bonn: Dümmler, 1990), pp. 41–7.

—— 'Language: internal conflict and language dissolution', in W. Wölck and

A. de Houver (eds), *Recent Studies in Contact Linguistics* (Bonn: Dümmler, 1997).

Caitucoli, Claude, and Bernard Zongo, 'Éléments pour une description de l'argot des jeunes au Burkina Faso', in Claude Caitucoli (ed.), *Le Français au Burkina-Faso* (Rouen: CNRS, 1993).

Calvet, Louis-Jean, *Linguistique et colonialisme: petit traité de glottophagie* (Paris: Payot, 1974, reissued 1988).

—— *Les Langues véhiculaires* (Paris: PUF, 1981).

—— 'Le bambara: planification linguistique par défaut', in I. Fodor and C. Hagège (eds), *La Réforme des langues*, vol. 1 (Hamburg: Buske Verlag, 1983).

—— *Language Wars and Linguistic Politics*, tr. Michel Petheram (1987; Oxford: Oxford University Press, 1998).

—— 'Les langues des marchés au Mali', in Louis-Jean Calvet et al., *Les Langues des marchés en Afrique* (Paris: Didier, 1992).

—— *L'Europe et ses langues* (Paris: Plon, 1993).

—— 'Antoine Meillet, la politique linguistique et l'Europe: les mains sales', *Plurilinguismes*, 5 (1993).

—— 'Des mots sur les murs: une comparaison entre Paris et Dakar', in Louis-Jean Calvet et al., *Des langues et des villes* (Paris: Didier, 1993).

—— *L'Argot* (Paris: PUF, 'Que sais-je?', 1994).

—— *Les Voix de la ville: introduction à la sociolinguistique urbaine* (Paris: Payot, 1994).

—— *Histoire de l'écriture* (Paris: Plon, 1996).

—— *Les Politiques linguistiques* (Paris: PUF, 'Que sais-je?', 1996).

—— 'Les "Edwiniens" et leurs langues: sentiments et attitudes linguistiques dans une communauté créolophone blanche de Louisiane', *Revue québécoise de linguistique théorique et appliqué*, 13, 1 (1996).

—— 'Une ou deux langues? Ou le rôle des représentations dans l'évaluation des situations linguistiques', *Études créoles*, XIX, 2 (1996).

Calvet, Louis-Jean, and Robert Chaudenson, *Saint-Barthélemy: une énigme linguistique* (Paris: ACCT-CIRELFA, distributed by Didier érudition, 1998).

Calvet, Louis-Jean, and M. Dreyfus, 'La famille dans l'espace urbain: trois modèles de plurilinguisme', *Plurilinguismes*, 3 (January 1992).

Campra, Rosalba, *Como con bronca y junando . . . La retorica del tango* (Buenos Aires: Edicial, 1996).

Canut, Cécile, 'Dynamique et imaginaire linguistiques dans les sociétés à tradition orale', unpublished doctoral dissertation supervised by Anne-Marie Houdebine, University of Paris III, 1995.

—— 'Acquisition, production et imaginaire linguistiques des familles plurilingues à Bamako (Mali)', *Travaux de linguistique*, 7 (May 1996).

Canut, Cécile, and Gérard Dumestre, 'Français, Bambara et langues nationales au Mali', in D. de Robillard and M. Beniamino (eds), *Le Français dans l'espace francophone*, vol. 1 (Paris: Champion, 1993), pp. 219–28.

Canut, Cécile, and Boniface Keita, 'Dynamique linguistique en zone mandingue: attitudes et comportements', in G. Dumestre (ed.), *Stratégies communicatives au Mali: langues régionales, bambara, français* (Paris/Aix-en-Provence: Didier érudition, 1994).

Chaudenson, Robert, *Le Lexique du parler créole de la Réunion*, 2 vols (Paris: Honoré Champion, 1974).

—— 'Créolisation et appropriation linguistique; de la théorie aux exemples', in Daniel Véronique (ed.), *Créolisation et acquisition des langues* (Aix-en-Provence: Publications de l'Université de Provence, 1994).

—— *Les Créoles* (Paris: PUF, 'Que sais-je?', 1995).

Chaudenson, Robert, Raymond Mougeon and Édouard Beniak, *Vers une approche panlectale de la variation du français* (Paris: Didier érudition, 1993).

Cheyne, W., 'Stereotyped reactions to speakers with Scottish and English regional accents', *British Journal of Social and Clinical Psychology*, 9 (1970).

Clements, N., 'African linguistics and its contributions to linguistic theory', *Studies in the Linguistic Sciences*, 19, 2 (1989).

Colón, Cristóbal, *Textos y documentos completos*, ed. Consuelo Varela and Juan Gil (Madrid: Alianza Universidad, 1995; first published 1982).

Dan, Pierre, *Histoire de la barbarie et de ses corsaires* (Paris: Racolet, 1637).

Dapper, Olfert, *Umbständliche und eigentliche Beschreibung von Africa, und denen darzu gehörigen Königreichen und Landschaften* (Amsterdam: J. Van Meurs, 1670).

Darwin, Charles, *The Voyage of the 'Beagle'*, ed. Janet Browne and Michael Neve (London: Penguin, 1989).

—— *The Origin of Species*, ed. Gillian Beer (Oxford: Oxford University Press, World's Classics, 1996).

Defoe, Daniel, *General History of the Robberies and Murders of the most Notorious Pirates* (London, 1724: published under the name Captain Charles Johnson, usually taken to be a pseudonym of Defoe).

De Klerk, Vivian, and Barbara Bosch, 'Linguistic stereotypes: nice accent – nice person?', *International Journal of the Sociology of Language*, 116 (1995), 17–37.

Delafosse, Maurice, *Haut-Sénégal Niger* (Paris: 1912).

—— *La Langue mandingue et ses dialectes* (Paris: P. Geuthner, 1929).

De Mauro, Tullio, *Une introduction à la sémantique* (Paris: Payot, 1969).

Deprez, Christine, *Les Enfants bilingues: langues et familles* (Paris: Didier, 1994).

Dineen, A., and P. Mühlhäusler, 'Nineteenth-century language contact in South Australia', in Stephen Wurm, Peter Mühlhäusler and Darrell Tryon (eds), *Atlas of Languages of International Communication in the Pacific, Asia and the Americas* (Berlin: Mouton de Gruyter, 1996).

Dombrowsky, Klaudia, 'La situation socio-linguistique du sud du Mali', in Gérard Dumestre (ed.), *Stratégies communicatives au Mali: langues régionales, bambara, français* (Paris: Didier érudition, 1994).

Drechsel, Emanuel, 'Native American contact languages of the contiguous United States', in Stephen Wurm, Peter Mühlhäusler and Darrell Tryon (eds), *Atlas of Languages of International Communication in the Pacific, Asia and the Americas* (Berlin: Mouton de Gruyter, 1996).

—— *Mobilian Jargon* (Oxford: Clarendon Press, 1997).

Dumestre, Gérard (ed.), *Stratégies communicatives au Mali: langues régionales, bambara, français* (Paris: Didier érudition, 1994).

Dumont, Myriam, *Les Enseignes de Dakar: un essai de sociolinguistique africaine* (Paris: L'Harmattan, 1998).

Eades, Diana, 'Aboriginal English', in Stephen Wurm, Peter Mühlhäusler and Darrell Tryon (eds), *Atlas of Languages of International Communication in the Pacific, Asia and the Americas* (Berlin: Mouton de Gruyter, 1996).

Elizaincin, Adolfo, 'Contacto entre lenguas geneticamente emparentadas: el caso del español y del portugués', *Signo & Seña*, 6 (June 1996).

Ellms, Charles, *The Pirates Own Book* (New York: Dover, 1993; first published in this format 1837).

Équipe IFA, *Inventaire des particularités du français en Afrique noire* (Paris: AUPELF, 1983).

Faidherbe, Louis-Léon-César, 'L'Alliance française pour la propagation de la langue française dans les colonies et les pays étrangers', *Revue scientifique*, 3rd series, 7 (1884).

Fehderau, Harold, 'The origin and development of Kituba', Ph.D. dissert., Cornell University, Ithaca, NY, 1966.

Féral, Carole de, 'Le français au Cameroun: approximatisation, vernacularisation et camfranglais', in Didier de Robillard and Michel Beniamino (eds), *Le Français dans l'espace francophone*, vol. 1 (Paris: Champion, 1993).

Ferguson, Charles, 'The Arabic Koinè', *Language*, 35, 4 (1959).

Fontanella de Weinberg, Maria Beatriz, *El español bonaerense* (Buenos Aires: Hachette, 1987).

—— 'Contacto lingüistico: lenguas inmigratorias', *Signo & Seña*, 6 (June 1996).

Francard, Michel, 'L'insécurité en communauté française de Belgique', *Français et Société*, 6 (April 1993), 13.

—— 'L'insécurité linguistique dans les communautés francophones périphériques', *Cahiers de l'institut de linguistique de Louvain*, 19, 1 (1993).

Francard, Michel, 'L'insécurité linguistique dans les communautés francophones périphériques', *Cahiers de l'institut de linguistique de Louvain*, 20, 2 (1994).

Frei, Henri, *La Grammaire des fautes* (Paris/Geneva: Slatkine, 1929).

Gadet, Françoise, *Le Français populaire* (Paris: PUF, 'Que sais-je?', 1992).

Garde, Paul, *Vie et mort de la Yougoslavie* (Paris: Fayard, 1992).

—— 'Langue et nation: le cas serbe, croate, bosniaque', *Cahiers de l'ILSL*, 8 (1996).

Gehnen, Marianne, 'Die Arbeitssprachen in der Kommission der Europäischen Gemeinschaften unter besonderer Berücksichtigung des Französischen', in *Sociolinguistica*, 5 (Tübingen: Niemeyer Verlag, 1991).

Gimbutas, Marija, 'Prehistory of Eastern Europe: Neolithic and Copper Age culture in Russia and the Baltic area', *American School of Prehistoric Research Bulletin 20* (Cambridge, Mass.: Harvard University, Peabody Museum, 1956).

—— 'The Indo-Europeanization of Europe: the intrusion of steppe pastoralists from south Russia and the transformation of Old Europe', *Word*, 44, 2 (August 1993), 219.

Gonzalez Faraco, J. Carlos and Michael Dean Murphy, 'Street names and political regimes in an Andalusian town', *Ethnology*, 36, 2 (Spring 1997).

Goyvaerts, Didier, 'Indoubil: a Swahili hybrid in Bukavu (with comments on Indoubil by K. Kabongo-Mianda)', *Language in Society*, 17, 2 (1988).

—— 'Secret languages and cultural niches in Bukavu', in *Des langues et des villes* (Paris: Didier érudition, 1993).

—— 'Kibalele: form and function of a secret language in Bukavu (Zaire)', *Journal of Pragmatics*, 25, 1 (1996).

Grandguillaume, Gilbert, 'Le multilingualisme dans le cadre national au Maghreb', in Foued Laroussi (ed.), *Plurilinguisme et identités au Maghreb* (Rouen: Publications de l'Université de Rouen, 1997).

Grin, François, 'Aménagement linguistique: du bon usage des concepts d'offre et de demande', in Normand Labrie (ed.), *Études récentes en linguistique de contact* (Bonn: Dümmler, 1997).

Gueunier, Nicole, *Le Français du Liban: cent portraits linguistiques* (Paris: Didier érudition, 1993).

Gueunier, Nicole, E. Genouvrier and A. Khomsi, *Les Français devant la norme: contributions à une étude de la norme du français parlé* (Paris: Champion, 1978).

Haedo, F. Diego de, *Topografia e historia general de Argel* (Valladolid: 1612), reprinted in 2 vols (Madrid: Sociedad de Bibliófilos Españoles, 1927).

Haeri, Niloofar, 'The reproduction of symbolic capital: language, state and class in Egypt', *Current Anthropology*, 38, 5 (December 1997).

Hall, Robert, *Pidgin and Creole Languages* (New York: Cornell University Press, 1966).

Hauchecorne, Fabrice, and Rodney Ball, 'L'accent du Havre: un exemple de mythe linguistique', *Langage et Société*, 82 (December 1997), 23.

Haugen, Einar, 'Schizoglossia and the linguistic norm', *Georgetown University Monographic Series on Language and Linguistics*, 15 (1962).

—— *The Ecology of Language* (Stanford: Stanford University Press, 1972).

Héran, François, 'L'unification linguistique de la France', *Population et Société*, 285 (December 1993).

Highfield, A. R., *The French Dialect of St Thomas, US Virgin Islands* (Ann Arbor: Karoma, 1979).

Houdebine, Anne-Marie, 'Norme, imaginaire linguistique et phonologie du français contemporain', *Le Français moderne*, vol. 1 (Paris: Cilf, 1982).

—— 'Pour une linguistique synchronique dynamique', *La Linguistique*, 21 (1985).

—— 'De l'imaginaire des locuteurs et de la dynamique linguistique', *Cahiers de l'institut de linguistique de Louvain*, 19, 1 (1993).

—— 'L'imaginaire linguistique et son analyse', *Travaux de linguistique*, 7 (May 1996).

Howard-Malverde, Rosaleen, 'Pachamama is a Spanish word: linguistic tension between Aymara, Quechua and Spanish Northern Potosi (Bolivia)', *Anthropological Linguistics*, 37, 2 (1995), 141–68.

Huld, Martin, 'Early Indo-European weapons terminology', *Word*, 44, 2 (August 1993).

Kahlouche, Rabah, 'Les enseignes à Tizi-Ouzou: un lieu de conflit linguistique', in N. Labrie (ed.), *Études récentes en linguistique de contact* (Bonn: Dümmler, 1997).

Kalman, Ivan, Zhong Yong and Xiao Hong, 'Language attitudes in Guangzhou, China', *Language in Society*, 16, 4 (1987).

Kayes, Alan, 'Formal vs informal in Arabic: diglossia, triglossia, tetraglossia, etc.: polyglossia-multiglossia viewed as a continuum', *Zeitschrift für arabische Linguistik*, 27 (1994).

Kihm, Alain, 'Qu'est-ce qu'une théorie rationnelle de la formation des langues créoles?', *Plurilinguismes*, 8 (1994).

Klingler, Thomas, 'A descriptive study of the creole speech of Pointe Coupée Parish, Louisiana, with focus on the lexicon', unpublished Ph.D. dissertation (Ann Arbor: University Microfilm International, 1992).

—— 'Norme, tourisme et étiolement linguistique chez les créolophones en Louisiane', *Cahiers de l'institut de linguistique de Louvain*, 20, 1–2 (1994).

Komatsu, Eisuke (ed.), *Ferdinand de Saussure: cours de linguistique générale* (Tokyo: Gakushuin University, 1993), p. 13.

Kouloughli, Djamel-Eddine, 'Sur quelques approches de la réalité sociolinguistique arabe', *Égypte/monde arabe*, 27–8 (Cairo: CEDEJ, 1996).

Labat, J.-B., *Nouvelle Relation de l'Afrique occidentale* (Paris: 1728).
Labov, William, 'The social motivation of a sound change', *Word*, 19 (1963), 273–309.
—— *The Social Stratification of English in New York City* (Washington: Centre for Applied Linguistics, 1966).
—— 'Hypercorrection by the lower middle class as a factor in linguistic change', in W. Bright (ed.), *Sociolinguistics* (The Hague: Mouton, 1966).
—— *Language in the Inner City: Studies in the Black English Vernacular* (Philadelphia: University of Philadelphia Press, 1972).
—— *Sociolinguistic Patterns* (Oxford: Blackwell, 1978).
Lacroix, F., 'Les langues bantu', in *Les Langues dans le monde ancien et moderne, Afrique subsaharienne, pidgins et créoles* (Paris: Centre National de la Recherche Scientifique, 1981), p. 353.
Lafkioui, Mena, 'Les berbères et leur langue: les cas des immigrés berbères en Belgique', in Cécile Canut (ed.), *Imaginaires linguistiques en Afrique* (Paris: L'Harmattan, 1998).
Lafontaine, Dominique, 'Attitudes linguistiques', in Marie-Louise Moreau (ed.), *Sociolinguistique, concepts de base* (Sprimont, Belgium: Mardaga, 1997).
Lambert, Wallace et al., 'Evaluational reactions to spoken language', *Journal of Abnormal and Social Psychology*, 60 (1960).
—— 'Judging personality through speech: a French-Canadian example', *The Journal of Communication*, 16 (1966).
Lapouge, Gilles, *Les Pirates* (Paris: Payot, 1991).
Larcher, Pierre, 'La linguistique arabe d'hier à demain: tendances nouvelles de la recherche', *Arabica*, 4 (1998).
Laroussi, Foued, 'Langue, peuple et nation arabes, l'imaginaire linguistique du locuteur tunisien', *Travaux de linguistique*, 7 (May 1996).
—— 'Plurilinguisme et identités au Maghreb', in Foued Laroussi (ed.), *Plurilinguisme et identités au Maghreb* (Rouen: Publications de l'Université de Rouen, 1997).
Lavandera, Beatriz R., *Variacion y significado* (Buenos Aires: Hachette, 1984).
Leconte, Fabienne, *La Famille et les langues* (Paris: L'Harmattan, 1997).
Lefebvre, Claire, and John Lumsden, 'Le rôle central de la relexification dans la genèse des langues créoles', *Plurilinguismes*, 8 (1994).
Lenzini, José, *Barberousse, chemin de proies en Méditerranée* (Arles: Actes Sud, 1995).
Levinger, Jasna, 'Language war – war language', *Language Sciences*, 16, 2 (1994).
Lujan Martinez, Eugenio Ramon, 'Pragmatics and Indo-European linguistics', *Journal of Pragmatics*, 28, 2 (August 1997).

McConnell, Grant, 'Analyses et comparaisons des situations de contact en Inde', in Normand Labrie (ed.), *Études récentes en linguistique de contact* (Bonn: Dümmler, 1997).

McGregor, William, 'Post contact languages of Western Australia', in Stephen Wurm, Peter Mühlhäusler and Darrell Tryon (eds), *Atlas of Languages of International Communication in the Pacific, Asia and the Americas* (Berlin: Mouton de Gruyter, 1996).

McWhorter, John, 'The scarcity of Spanish-based creoles explained', *Language in Society*, 24, 2 (1995).

Maïga, Amidou, 'Pratiques et représentations linguistiques des locuteurs du songhay au Mali', dissertation, Université de Paris V, 1998.

Mahn-Lot, Marianne, 'Colomb (Christophe)', in *Encyclopedia universalis* (Paris), vol. 6, p. 105.

Makonda, Antoine, *Quatre-vingts et un congolismes* (Brazzaville: INKRAP, 1987).

Manessy, Gabriel, 'Créolisation et français régionaux', in P. Wald and G. Manessy, *Plurilinguismes, normes, situations, stratégies* (Paris: L'Harmattan, 1979).

—— 'Expansion fonctionnelle et évolution', in A. Highfield and A. Valdman (eds), *Historicity and Variation in Creole Studies* (Ann Arbor: Karoma, 1981); reprinted in *Créoles, pidgins, variétés véhiculaires* (Paris: CNRS, 1995).

—— 'Créolisation sans pidgin: variants approximatives et variétés créolisées', *Études créoles*, 4, 1 (1982); reprinted in *Créoles, pidgins, variétés véhiculaires* (Paris: CNRS, 1995).

—— 'L'évolution du français d'Afrique et la formation des créoles français', in *Présence francophone* (University of Sherbrooke), 27 (1985).

—— 'Créolisation et créolité', *Études créoles*, 10, 2 (1987); reprinted in *Créoles, pidgins, variétés véhiculaires* (Paris: CNRS, 1995).

—— 'De la subversion des langues importées: le français en Afrique noire', in R. Chaudenson and D. de Robillard (eds), *Langues et développement* (Paris: Didier érudition, 1989),

—— 'Pratique du français en Afrique noire francophone', *Langue française*, 104 (December 1994).

—— 'Modalités d'appropriation d'une langue seconde (français d'Afrique et créoles français)', in Daniel Véronique (ed.), *Créolisation et acquisition des langues* (Aix-en-Provence: Publications de l'Université de Provence, 1994).

Manessy-Guitton, Jacqueline, 'L'indo-européen', in *Le Langage* (Paris: Gallimard, Encyclopédie de la Pléiade, 1968).

Martinet, André, *Des Steppes aux océans: l'indo-européen et les 'indo-européens'*, (Paris: Payot, 1986).

Martinon, Philippe, *Comment on parle en français* (Paris: Larousse, 1927).

Meillet, Antoine, *Les Langues dans l'Europe nouvelle* (Paris: Payot, 1928).

Meo Zilio, Giovanni , 'Influenze dello spagnolo sull'italiano parlato nel Rio de la Plata', *Lingua Nostra*, 16, 1 (1955).

—— 'Contaminazioni morfologiche nel cocoliche rioplatense', *Lingua Nostra*, 16, 3 (1955).

—— 'El Cocoliche rioplatense', *Boletin de filologia* (1963).

Miller, Catherine, 'Restructuration morpho-syntaxique en juba-arabic et ki-nubi: à propos du débat universaux/substrat et superstrat dans les etudes créoles', in *Matériaux arabes et sudarabiques* (Paris: Paul Geuthner, 1993).

—— 'Contacts de langues: à propos des dialectes arabes', *Paroles*, 7 (Cairo: 1995).

Mistral, Frédéric, *Lou tresor dou Felibrige, ou Dictionnaire provençal–français*, 1877; republished 1968 by Edicioun Ramoun Berenguié.

Moreau, Marie-Louise, ' "Nous avons la langue trop épaisse", ou comment être un francophone sénégalais', *Cahiers de l'institut de linguistique de Louvain*, 20 (1994).

—— (ed.) *Sociolinguistique, concepts de base* (Sprimont, Belgium: Mardaga, 1997).

Moreau, Marie-Louise, Ndiassé Thiam and Cécile Bauvois, 'Le marquage identitaire dans le français d'Afrique: étude exploratoire au Sénégal', in L.-J. Calvet and M.-L. Moreau (eds), *Une ou des normes? Insécurité linguistique et normes endogènes en Afrique* (Paris: CIRELFA, Agence de la Francophonie, Didier érudition, 1998).

Morsly, Dalila, 'Attitudes et représentations linguistiques', *La Linguistique*, 6, 3 (1990).

Mougeon, Raymond, and Édouard Beniak, 'Le français en situation de contact et la variation linguistique: le français parlé en Ontario (Canada)', in *Actes du XVIIe congrès international de linguistique et philologie romanes*, vol. 6 (Aix-en-Provence: Publications de l'Université de Provence), 1986, p. 298.

Moussirou-Mouyama, Auguste, 'Norme officielle du français et normes endogènes au Gabon', in L.-J. Calvet and M.-L. Moreau, *Une ou des normes? Insécurité linguistique et normes endogènes en Afrique* (Paris: CIRELFA, Agence de la Francophonie, Didier érudition, 1998).

Mufwene, Salikoko, 'Genèse des populations et genèse des langues', *Plurilinguismes*, 8 (1994).

—— 'New Englishes and criteria for naming them', *World Englishes*, 13, 1 (1994).

—— 'Creole genesis, a population genetics perspective', in Pauline Christie (ed.), *Caribbean Language Issues, Old and New* (Kingston, Jamaica: University of the West Indies Press, 1996).

—— 'The founder principle in creole genesis', *Diachronica*, 13 (1996), 83–134.

—— 'Language ecology and creole genesis', paper presented to the Society for Pidgin and Creole Linguistics, San Diego, January 1996.

—— 'Kituba', in Sarah Thompson (ed.), *Contact Languages* (Amsterdam/Philadelphia: Benjamins, 1997).

—— 'Métissage des peuples et métissage des langues', in M.-C. Hazaël-Massieux and D. de Robillard (eds), *Contacts de langues, contacts de culture, créolisation* (Paris: L'Harmattan, 1997).

—— 'La fonction et les formes réfléchies dans le mauricien et le haïtien', *Langages*, 138 (2000).

—— 'The legitimate and illegitimate offspring of English', in *The Ecology of Language Evolution* (Cambridge: Cambridge University Press, 2001).

Mühlhäusler, Peter, *Linguistic Ecology* (London/New York: Routledge, 1996).

—— 'Pidgins and creoles of Queensland', in Stephen Wurm, Peter Mühlhäusler and Darrell Tryon (eds), *Atlas of Languages of International Communication in the Pacific, Asia and the Americas* (Berlin: Mouton de Gruyter, 1996).

Munteanu, Dan, *El Papiamento: lengua criolla hispanica* (Madrid: Gredos, 1996).

Muysken, Pieter, 'Halfway between Quechua and Spanish: the case for relexification', in A. Highfield and A. Valdman (eds), *Historicity and Variation in Creole Studies* (Ann Arbor: Karoma, 1981).

Nelde, Peter, 'Identity among bilinguals: an ecolinguistic approach', paper given at I Simposio Internacional sobre o Bilingüismo, Vigo, 21–5 October 1997.

Neumann, Ingrid, *Le Créole de Bréaux-Bridge, Louisiane* (Hamburg: Helmut Buske Verlag, 1985).

Owens, Jonathan, 'Nubi genetic linguistics and language classification', *Anthropological Linguistics*, 33, 1 (Spring 1991).

—— 'Arabic-based pidgins and creoles', in Sarah Thompson (ed.), *Contact Languages: A Wider Perspective* (Amsterdam/Philadelphia: Benjamins, 1997).

Parvulescu, Adrian, 'The Indo-European horse: a linguistic reconstruction', *Word*, 44, 1 (April 1993).

Perrot, Jean (ed.), *Les Langues dans le monde ancient et moderne: Afrique subsaharienne, pidgins et créoles* (Paris: Centre National de la Recherche Scientifique, 1981).

Pinker, Steven, *The Language Instinct* (New York: Harper Perennial/London: Penguin, 1995).

Prignitz, Gisèle, 'Le français parlé en Haute-Volta: orientations et recherches en cours', in *Annales de l'Université* (Ouagadougou, Burkina Faso: 1984).

—— 'Rôle de l'argot dans la variation et l'appropriation: le cas du français au Burkina Faso', *Langue française*, 104 (1994).

Queffelec, Ambroise, and Augustin Niangouna, *Le Français au Congo* (Aix-en-Provence: Publications de l'Université de Provence, 1990).

Rey, Alain, 'Usages, jugements et prescriptions linguistiques', *Langue française*, 16 (December 1972).

Robillard, Didier de, 'L'insécurité linguistique à l'île Maurice: quand le chat n'est pas là les souris dansent', *Cahiers de l'institut de linguistique de Louvain*, 20, 2 (1994).

—— 'Le concept d'insécurité linguistique: à la recherche d'un mode d'emploi', in Claude Bavoux (ed.), *Français régionaux et insécurité linguistique* (Paris: L'Harmattan, 1996).

—— 'Langues, îles, simplicité, déterminisme, chaos: quelques réflexions fragmentaires sur l'utilisation de l'insularité', *Plurilinguismes*, 15 (June 1998).

Rochefort, César de, *Histoire naturelle et morale des îles Antilles de l'Amérique* (Rotterdam: 1658).

Rosenblat, Angel, 'Bases des Español en America: nivel social y cultural de los conquistadores y pobladores', in *Actas de la primera reunion latinoamericana de linguistica y filologia* (Bogota: 1973).

Samarin, William, 'Colonization and pidginization on the Ubangi River', *Journal of African Languages and Linguistics*, 4 (1982).

—— 'Official language: the case of Lingala', in Ulrich Ammon (ed.), *Status and Function of Languages and Language Varieties* (Berlin and New York: Walter de Gruyter, 1989).

—— 'The origins of Kituba and Lingala', *Journal of African Languages and Linguistics*, 12 (1990/91).

Santoro, Salvatore, 'Lingua Franca in Goldoni's *Impresario delle Smirne*', *Journal of Pidgin and Creole Languages*, 11, 1 (1996).

Schleicher, A., *Compendium der vergleichenden Grammatik der indogermanischen Sprachen* (Weimar: H. Böhlau, 1861–2).

Schuchardt, Hugo, 'On lingua franca', in *The Ethnography of Variation: Selected Writings on Pidgins and Creoles* (Ann Arbor: Karoma, 1979).

Segovia, L. *Diccionario de argentismos* (Buenos Aires: Coni, 1911).

Siblot, Paul, 'Mise en texte de la pluriglossie dans la littérature coloniale', *Cahiers de Praxématique*, 5 (1985).

Skiljan, D., 'La langue entre symboles et signes: le cas serbo-croate', *Cahiers de l'ILSL*, 8 (1996), 305–8.

Sow, Salamatou Alhassoumi, 'Grands et petits peuls: representation et hiérarchisation des différents parlers peuls par les locuteurs de l'ouest du Niger', in Cécile Canut (ed.), *Imaginaires linguistiques en Afrique* (Paris: L'Harmattan, 1998).

Swaan, Abraam de, 'The evolving European language system: a theory of communication potential and language competition', *Revue internationale de science politique*, 14, 3 (July 1993).

—— *Unequal Relationships between Language Groups* (Amsterdam: Amsterdamse School vor Sociaalwetenschappelijk Ondserzoek, 1995).

—— 'La francophonie en Afrique: une vision de la sociologie et de l'économie politique de la langue', in C. Juillard and L.-J. Calvet, *Les Politiques linguistiques, mythes et réalités* (Beirut: FMA-AUPELF-UREF, 1996).

—— 'Leçon inaugurale faite le vendredi 24 octobre 1997', Collège de France, Paris, 1997.

Thiam, Ndiassé, 'Catégorisations de locuteurs et représentations sur le mélange wolof-français à Dakar', in Cécile Canut, *Imaginaires linguistiques en Afrique* (Paris: L'Harmattan, 1998).

Tosco, Mauro, 'A pidgin verbal system: the case of Juba Arabic', *Anthropological Linguistics*, 37, 4 (Winter 1995).

Trelawny, Edward John, *Adventures of a Younger Son*, ed. William St. Clair (Oxford: Oxford University Press, 1974).

Varela, Lia, 'Interventions sur la langue et construction de l'État argentin (1830–80)', DEA dissertation, Université de Provence, 1999.

Verguin, Joseph, 'La situation linguistique du monde contemporain', in André Martinet (ed.), *Le Langage* (Paris: Gallimard, 1968).

Véronique, Daniel (ed.), *Créolisation et acquisition des langues* (Aix-en-Provence: Publications de l'Université de Provence, 1994).

Versteegh, Kees, *Pidginization and Creolization: The Case of Arabic* (Amsterdam: Benjamins, 1984).

—— 'Levelling in the Sudan: from Arabic creole to Arabic dialect', *International Journal of the Sociology of Language*, 99 (1993).

Vydrine, Valentin, 'Étude sociolinguistique en pays Khassonké', in Gérard Dumestre (ed.), *Stratégies communicatives au Mali: langues régionales, bambara, français* (Paris: Didier érudition, 1994).

Wenezoui-Déchamps, Martine, 'Entre langue coloniale et langue nationale: le franc-sango des étudiants de Bangui', *Lengas*, 23 (1988).

Whinnom, Kenneth, 'The context and origins of lingua franca', in Jürgen Meisel (ed.), *Langues en contact: Pidgins-Créoles* (Tübingen: TBL Verlag Gunter Nar, 1977).

Whiteley, W., *Swahili, the Rise of a National Language* (London: Methuen, 1969).

Wiener, N., *Cybernetics or Control and Communication in the Animal and the Machine*, 2nd edition (Cambridge, Mass: MIT Press, 1961).

Williams, G. *Sociolinguistics: A Sociological Critique* (London: Routledge, 1992).

Wittmann, Henri, and Robert Fournier, 'Le créole haïtien, langue kwa relexifiée: vérification d'une hypothèse "P&P" ou élaboration d'astuces computationnelles', *Plurilinguismes*, 8 (1994).

Wurm, Stephen, Peter Mühlhäusler and Darrell Tryon (eds), *Atlas of Languages of International Communication in the Pacific, Asia and the Americas* (Berlin: Mouton de Gruyter, 1996).

Xia, Ningsheng, 'Maintenance of the Chinese language in the United States', *Bilingual Review/Revista Bilingue*, 17, 3 (1992).

Index